"The story of the lost lens will take a top place in lighthouse lore and history. It's the sort of find for which an archeologist waits his entire life."

Bruce and Cheryl Roberts
Lighthouse News

"Duffus' eventual discovery of the whereabouts of the original 'lost' Hatteras light Fresnel lens is an astonishing surprise that makes the book an even more amazing read. Educational, fascinating, and one of the great stories of Outer Banks history, The Lost Light will brighten and reader's day."

Alan Hodge
Our State Magazine

"Kevin Duffus unravels one of the greatest enigmas of American maritime history...and along the way documents the science of lenses and the history of the Cape Hatteras Lighthouse in an engaging style and with interesting details that entwine the sentinel's own history with that of the Outer Banks, other North Carolina lighthouses, and the nation as a whole... Thanks to [Duffus'] tenacious scrutiny of government records and impeccable scholarship, we now know the truth about [Cape Hatteras'] long-missing lens."

Elinor De Wire
The Beachcomber

"It's a tremendous find—like a lost shipwreck."

Jim Woodward
Fresnel lens expert

The Lost Light

A CIVIL WAR MYSTERY

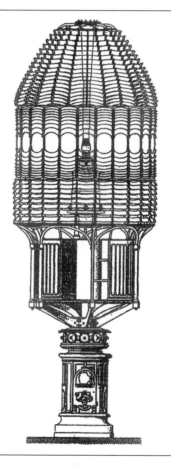

THE TRUE STORY OF THE EXTRAORDINARY ODYSSEY OF
THE CAPE HATTERAS LIGHTHOUSE 1854 FRESNEL LENS

Kevin P. Duffus

For Sue
My light.

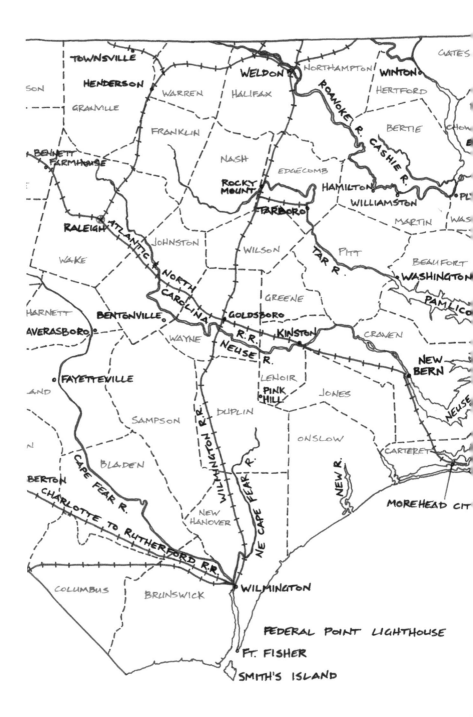

CAMDEN

TH
TY

ALBEMARLE
SOUND

TYRRELL

ALLIGATOR R.

HYDE

VAN
UARTER

PAMLICO
SOUND

HATTERAS INLET
FT. HATTERAS

OCRACOKE

FT.
CLARK

OCRACOKE LIGHTHOUSE

PORTSMOUTH

ROANOKE ISLAND

OREGON INLET

1859 BODIE ISLAND
LIGHTHOUSE

CHICAMACOMICO

CAPE HATTERAS
LIGHTHOUSE

DIAMOND SHOALS

AUFORT

PE LOOKOUT LIGHTHOUSE

MACON

E LOOKOUT SHOALS

EASTERN NORTH CAROLINA IN 1860

"Even to this day, the whereabouts of the first-order Fresnel lens taken from Cape Hatteras remains one of the great-unsolved mysteries of American lighthouse history."

Timothy Harrison
Lighthouse Digest
2001

"Faithfulness to the truth of history involves far more than a research, however patient and scrupulous, into special facts. The narrator... must study events in their bearings near and remote; in the character, habits, and manners of those who took part in them. He must be, as it were, a sharer or a spectator of the action he describes."

Francis Parkman
Pioneers of France in the New World [1865]
American Historian 1823-1893

"When you have eliminated the impossible, whatever remains, however improbable, must be the truth."

Sir Arthur Conan Doyle
The Sign Of Four [1890]

Contents

A note from the author

My quest for the lost Cape Hatteras Lighthouse Fresnel lens began with an innate curiosity about the past and an unwillingness to accept established history that does not make sense. When this book was first published in 2002, I was unaware that the story was yet evolving, the history yet finished. The remarkable odyssey of the historic Henry-Lepaute lens and pedestal, since called "a national treasure," is now complete. Herein is the complete story.

Prologue

A GREAT UNSOLVED MYSTERY

I was submerged in what seemed like a river of tea below the tawny surface of Chicod Creek, a wide, deep and slow-moving tributary of the Tar River in Eastern North Carolina. Refracted dimly above me was a wavering, nickel-sized image of the sun. Along the banks of the creek, Spanish moss draped the limbs of cypress trees, and occasionally, a water moccasin slithered its way across the water. My friends and I had just conducted an inconclusive debate about the innately curious and poisonous vipers' ability to bite underwater —no facts were presented, just guesses. It was then that I had slipped below the surface—the moccasins would have to find me first. Diving in a snake infested, blackwater creek, may be difficult to imagine, and hardly sensible. However, I was 17 years old, a recently certified scuba diver, and I was about to enter the hold of a mysterious sunken ship. It was the spring of 1971.

We had no clue to the ship's identity or why it was there, although there was no shortage of fantastic, urban legends. Some said it belonged to Black Beard the pirate. All the better reason to explore the interior to see if he had left his calling card, or maybe his treasure.

We had already examined the wreck's exterior, including its massive rudderpost, but only recovered a half dozen broken outboard motor skegs. Someone had to do it, so I entered the vessel through an open hatch on its still sturdy deck, just 18 inches below the surface of the creek. Within seconds, the clarity of the water turned from tea into black coffee. We thought if anything could be retrieved from within the dark, silt-filled interior of the hull, the identity of the ship might be determined. So, I felt my way downward, into the darkness, careful to avoid invisible sharp objects that might simulate the fangs of a snake. In the bottom of the hold I began to comb my fingers through the muck. Clouds of thick silt erupted before my eyes, making my six-volt Dacor diver light shine like a headlight in a thick fog. I felt a strange and unfamiliar sensation, that maybe I had passed into another dimension of time and space. I could faintly hear an odd, rhythmic thumping sound—thump...thump...thump—like an old steam engine, far in the distance, as if a 19th century launch was churning its way up the creek. I held my breath and listened intently. It was my own heartbeat that I was hearing. It was then that I decided that it might be better to continue the search for the ship's identity in a library, free of silt and snakes.

This story started as a search for the identity of a sunken ship, and maybe a pirate's treasure, and it led to a mystery and a quest for something altogether different. After playing a boy's game in Chicod Creek, my older brother and I retreated to the East Carolina University library for a more scholarly, less dangerous pursuit. We somehow found among the 100 or more volumes of the *Official Records of the Union and Confederate Navies in the War of the Rebellion*, the answer to the mysterious ship's identity—a Confederate gunboat, unfinished and scuttled to avoid capture by the enemy. But within the same letter written by a Union Navy lieutenant in 1862, was a curious reference. "The most valuable part of the Hatteras light property, the lenses, have been taken to Tarboro [N.C.]." I wanted to learn more about the Hatteras light property but I had other things to do—for 30 years. Those words eventually became a vague and distant image, settled in the back of my mind.

I later learned about Fresnel lenses in 1979, when I produced a documentary film for WRAL-TV in Raleigh about North Carolina's lighthouses and how erosion threatened the Cape Hatteras and Cape Lookout lights. Once, while traveling along the coast I discovered an antique store on a busy thoroughfare in Wilmington. On the lawn in front of the weathered old shop, stood a large Fresnel lens. The proprietor explained he had bought it from the Coast Guard and the lens had once been at the top of the Cape Fear light that had since been torn down. Fresnel lenses seemed to have no value, at least not to the government. The old-timer had been selling crown-crystal prisms from the lens, one at a time, for $35. Hundreds of its prisms had been torn out of the frame giving the once magnificent artifact a decrepit, toothless appearance. It made no sense that the incredible optical invention of Frenchman Augustine Fresnel would not be worth more intact. My thoughts drifted back to the Cape Hatteras lens and what might have happened to it.

While I was researching a future documentary, the spectre of the lens reappeared; this time as a footnote in John Barrett's groundbreaking book, *The Civil War in North Carolina*: "One object of the expedition was to recover the lenses taken from the lighthouse at Hatteras, but they had been moved previously to Tarboro." A visit to Tarboro provided no new answers to my old questions. Later, after reading, *America's Lighthouses—An Illustrated History* by Francis Ross Holland, Jr., I learned that during the Civil War, most, if not all, Southern lighthouses had their Fresnel lenses removed and hidden, supposedly by Confederate troops. Some lenses had been found after the war, but I could find no reference to what happened to the Hatteras lens taken to Tarboro. I searched for Confederate records in Virginia, but almost everything had been burned during the fall of Richmond. Fortunately, another piece of the puzzle appeared when the Virginia Historical Society discovered a letter, written by Thomas Martin, then with the Confederate Lighthouse Bureau. In 1861, Martin requested information regarding lighthouses that had been extinguished, the lenses of which were removed and in the possession of the letter's recipient.

A significant clue emerged in a magazine article about Cape Hatteras in the Summer, 1998, issue of *The Keeper's Log*. A series of letters written by a Confederate quartermaster to Thomas Martin revealed how the Hatteras lens had been taken by train to Townsville in Granville County by a doctor and then hidden. The lens appeared to have traveled no farther. The train tracks were removed before the end of the Civil War. Storage buildings and houses had long since been torn down. No one had ever heard the Hatteras lens was hidden in the area. In the 1950s, the Corps of Engineers had constructed Kerr Lake over the Roanoke River and its tributaries, flooding much of the land where the lens could have been hidden. The hope of finding the "the lost light" was growing dimmer.

I drove up from Raleigh to have a look around. With a number of Geologic Survey quadrangles on the passenger seat, I followed a road out of Townsville. "Mine Road," as it was coincidentally called, paralleled what was marked on a map as an abandoned railroad bed. The road led into a rugged, sparsely populated area—a wilderness of sorts—and it seemed a perfect place to hide something large and valuable. I discovered the old railroad grade and it passed through a deep gorge in the woods, walls of granite lining the sides. I decided to enlist some help. Doug Ellington, a native of Washington, North Carolina (where the Hatteras lens was stored for a time and where the Chicod Creek gunboat had been built) is a geologist living in Chapel Hill, and he too has a passion for historical mysteries. Doug and I went back to Townsville many times, and tirelessly searched for caves, mines, old barns and other potential hiding places. Deep in the woods, we found two pairs of magnificent granite piers that were once part of railroad trestles crossing deep creeks that flowed into the now submerged Roanoke. We found a mysterious, large, and decades-old hole in the ground near the plantation house where the doctor hid his family during the war. Could the lens have been buried there and since exhumed? We later learned the hole was once a subterranean icehouse for the plantation. Doug and I also found snakes on the ground and got hundreds of chigger bites on our bodies. I suffered for about a week. Doug had to seek medical help. I decided to continue the search in a library, once again.

Joined by my wife, Susan, we started examining the fragile, 140-year-old letters written by the quartermaster from Tarboro. The letters were kept in a dusty, old pasteboard file box in the very modern National Archives building in Maryland. There were dozens more, written by various people affiliated with lighthouses in 1861 and 1862. Numerous letters yielded hundreds of clues. The vast, mysterious puzzle of extinguished Southern lighthouses and missing lenses began to take shape. There were no immediate solutions to what happened to the Hatteras lens, but I began to see and understand the much larger story of what happened to the lighthouses of the Confederacy. Previous accounts of Confederate troops tearing lenses from Southern lighthouses without regard for their preservation were mostly incorrect.

At the Washington, D.C., headquarters of the National Archives, we delved into Record Group 26, the holdings of the U.S. Coast Guard and the consolidated organizations that preceded it, including the Lifesaving Service, the Lighthouse Service and the Revenue Cutter Service. The records comprise 10,194 cubic feet of material, a veritable Everest-sized "haystack" in which to search for the proverbial "needle." It took many trips to Washington and even more hours of searching through original, handwritten documents, letterbooks and maps; rolls and rolls of microfilm of War Department letters; and the published memoirs of Civil War generals. The task would have been impossible without the help of the people who knew where to look—dedicated research advisors and archivists.

I compiled a collection of hundreds of photocopied papers and the puzzle became more complete. Still, the solution to the mystery of the Cape Hatteras lens was elusive. When I thought I was close to determining the whereabouts of the lens, I was surprised by yet another sharp turn in the story. One archival letter indicated that the lens had been found, another that it was again missing. Among another box of index listings, of more than 1,000 slips of paper, were two, suspiciously marked with paper clips—and those two were the only listings that referred to the lost Hatteras lens. The revelation was like digging for a buried treasure and finding a greeting from someone who had been there before me. An archivist vaguely recalled a researcher who had also been looking for the lost Hatteras lens and who had recently made significant progress. Weak at the knees, I felt discouraged, defeated, and worried that months of work and sacrifice would soon be wasted. Then, I heard my name being called in the typically quiet Archives reading room and my self-pity evaporated. An emergency phone call was waiting, my father critically ill back home. Days later, my search for the lost light of Hatteras was shelved indefinitely while I grieved over the death of my father.

Two months passed and I renewed my resolve to solve the mystery of the lost Henry-Lepaute lens and returned to the Library of Congress and the National Archives. The collection of research and its analysis had become my full-time job, the search for the Hatteras lens my quest for the "holy grail of lighthouses." But after years of what I thought was fruitless searching, my quest was seeming more like a fool's errand.

As it happened, the ultimate destination in the incredible odyssey of the Cape Hatteras Fresnel lens was revealed to me when I was nearly ready to give up my search. I was on what I considered my final visit to the National Archives in Washington. (I had made a promise to my wife that it would soon be time to pursue more lucrative work.) So began three more days in the costly city with no guarantees of success, and no underwriting support. I had high hopes that I would finally find the answer to the ultimate question, "What happened to the Cape Hatteras lens?" I thought I knew where to look. I even thought I knew what had happened to the lens. I was wrong.

There was only one possibility left—a group of records from a district far from Cape Hatteras and its lighthouse. With my retrieval request submitted, I sat back and wondered what I would do next with my life, should I come up empty handed. Eventually, beside my table was a cart-full of ornately bound, handwritten letter books through which I had to search. Each volume contained more than 500 pages of correspondence. Indexes were of no use—I was looking for something that theoretically did not exist. I speed scanned page after page, once for a six-hour stretch without leaving my chair. The days had passed and my time in Washington was nearly over; just one hour remained and still no answer. It was a Thursday evening. The Archives closed at 9 P.M., and I was one of only a few researchers remaining in the stone and oak vaulted room, the green shades of reading lights casting the only light. Across Pennsylvania Avenue, a military band and choir had been playing patriotic songs: "Battle Hymn of the Republic," "My Country 'Tis of Thee," "Stars and Stripes Forever." At 8:45 P.M., the security officer announced the Archives would close in 15 minutes. There was still no answer to the mystery of the "lost light." The choir began to sing "America the Beautiful," as the guard hovered impatiently behind me. I thought of giving up, but just before I did, a faint voice in my head said, *Turn one more page.* So I did, turn one more page. Unbelievably, there it was, the evidence I needed, the answer for which I had searched for so long. Thirty years after exploring a mysterious shipwreck in a black-water estuary, I had solved the mystery of the "lost lens." I was stunned when I realized what became of the crown-glass, first-order Fresnel lens from the Cape Hatteras Lighthouse. I knew just where it was located—the lens was not lost, only carelessly destroyed. It was the one potential outcome I had fervently wished had not happened.

What I did not know, nor could have imagined, was where this odyssey would yet lead; how one of my own ancestors may have played a role in the lens's story 141 years earlier; and how an unlikely turn of fate for the historic artifact would restore its purpose, and significance, for a third time.

As the naturalist Loren Eisley once wrote, "The door to the past is a strange door."

One

With Murderous Indifference

Benjamin Fulcher was a conflicted man, but no Yankee could accuse him of acting with murderous indifference.

Fulcher could hear his name distantly being called over the whistling wind and the cackles of seagulls. "Cap'n Ben!" Fulcher continued polishing the glass. It was his favorite part of the morning, when sunlight cast a spectrum of colors throughout the lantern. He hoped the calling would go away. But the voice from far below did not go away. It interrupted the old mariner's work on a day when the rising sun had lit the tops of dark, spring rain clouds approaching from the west—"Red sky at morning, sailors take warning." The islanders naturally viewed such an occasion as an ominous sign. "Cap'n Ben!" His assistant, Andrew Williams, was on the ground standing next to a stranger on horseback and was shouting and frantically waving a paper. "Cap'n Ben," Williams yelled over the din of the surf, "you'd best come down and read this." Annoyed that he would be making an unnecessary descent down the hundreds of steps of the rickety wooden staircase, Fulcher set down his implements to attend to all the excitement. Fulcher liked his routine and he was not happy when it was altered, especially by a stranger. But Williams had not been impetuous. When he finally stood on the wind eroded sand hill at the place simply known as "The Cape," Fulcher could scarcely believe the words in the message he held in his weather-beaten, 51-year-old hands. Through piercing blue eyes, he read the message a second time. It was unbelievable what they wanted him to do. Sailors take warning, indeed.

Fulcher lived on an island 35 miles from the mainland of the United States where news and correspondence arrived by unconventional routes. Steam packets and brigantines, schooners and revenue cutters, hailing from ports in the West Indies to Boston and beyond, stood in at the entrance of the harbor and waited for a local pilot. The pilot's knowledge of day-to-day changes in the perplexing and dangerous inlet was invaluable. With a pilot aboard, the anchor was hoisted, a small amount of canvas was set and the inbound vessel got underway for the moorings on the soundside of the island. Close by on both port and starboard beams, confused waves raced from every point on the compass and crashed headlong into each other and over hidden shoals. It was unsettling for the ships' masters, who preferred the sounds and hues of the deep ocean, so the pilots engaged them in conversation. On the way in, the talk was inevitably about what was going on in the world. The recent news was unsettling. There was a new president who, it seemed, no one much liked. Seven Southern states had seceded from the Union, and thus far, North Carolina's loyalties were divided, but the momentum was tugging her heart South.

The most important news always came from the harbor pilots and from the sea. However, on the day when Ben Fulcher had been called to read the urgent message, the news had come from the mainland. It originated as a telegram from the state Capitol at Raleigh. It was received and endorsed by Mr. H. F. Hancock at the Customs Collector's office in Washington, North Carolina and then rushed across Pamlico Sound to Hatteras village by steamer. At Hatteras, Postmaster Robert Styron, dispatched the message by mounted courier 10 miles up the beach to its destination. Hastily scribbled, the note was addressed to Benjamin Fulcher, Esquire, from no less than the Honorable John W. Ellis, governor of the state of North Carolina.

Fulcher knew the country was treading in dangerous waters, and there was no doubt but that Mr. Lincoln, the country lawyer from Illinois, was the root of the evil. Never in his imagination did Fulcher think the troubles would involve him way out on Hatteras Island. "The mainland could keep her politics," the old Outer Banker might have thought. Yet there in his hands was the Governor's message asking him to do the unthinkable. It is not difficult to appreciate the emotions Fulcher must have felt that day—anger, disappointment, frustration, certainly bewilderment. He would lose his job over this, no doubt, Fulcher realized. For 15 years, Fulcher toiled on the job as an assistant before he was promoted. It was one of his proudest achievements, an esteemed government appointment on an impoverished island that offered few such career opportunities for men and their families. Now, just six months after his promotion, he was ordered to put himself out of business, to render his place of work inoperable. It was just bad luck.

Ben Fulcher looked up during his moment of revelation at the stone building he cared for, considered the most important in North America—the lighthouse at Cape Hatteras.

By decree of the governor of North Carolina, Principal Keeper Benjamin T. Fulcher of the United States Lighthouse Service was duly ordered to contradict his keeper's solemn oath to protect lives and property by extinguishing the lighthouse without delay so that its guiding light would not offer comfort to the warships of the Union Navy. That night, and for an indefinite period, the flashing light would no longer guide vessels at sea and navigators who desperately attempted to avoid the deadly banks and their attendant shoals that tore the bottoms out of countless hapless ships. It was an act that was later denounced in the North as committed with "murderous indifference." With "murderous indifference," maybe, but it was an act committed in a merciless age. The darkness on the Cape that night, unnatural as it must have seemed, was soon consumed by a greater gloom that enshrouded the nation. The date was sometime in late April, 1861 and during the next few months along the seacoast and in the estuarine sounds and rivers from Cape Henry in Virginia to Point Isabel near the Mexican border, more than 100 lighthouses were extinguished.

Keeper Fulcher may have been ambivalent about Ellis' decree. Although he was putting himself out of a job, he likely agreed with the secessionist governor's politics. Fulcher was a rarity among year-round residents on Hatteras Island, not because he was listed as a mariner in the 1850 census and supplemented his modest assistant keeper income as a harbor pilot and lighter captain, but rather for the fact that he, like Keeper Joseph Jennett before him, was a slave owner. Born in the Trent community between the Cape and Hatteras village in 1810, Fulcher inherited "a few" slaves from his father, Joseph, as well as 500 acres of land.[1] Most other permanent residents of the Outer Banks were too poor to be slaveholders, although many wealthy tidewater and mainland planters owned property there and from time to time used slave labor for fishing, boat construction, piloting, housekeeping, and in one documented instance, for lighthouse keeping.

The 1850 census indicated that out of 661 people living in the vicinity of Cape Hatteras, 104 were slaves.[2] The 1860 census, while incomplete, lists more than 250 men working in Hatteras village as fishermen, mariners and pilots.[3] Portsmouth Island, which for 150 years provided pilots, a chandlery and later medical services for the principal port at Ocracoke Inlet, listed one fourth of its population as slaves. Ocracoke village on the northeast side of the inlet had a slave population of 103 out of a total of 603 people.[4] Nevertheless, for the most part, Outer Bankers were anxious about the direction in which the South was headed. For almost two centuries, the Banks were populated with people who liked living there precisely because of its distance from government of any kind—British, Spanish, French, or Federal rule. If pressed for a stance on the issues of States' rights and slavery, as they were when they voted in a referendum calling for a convention to determine the question of secession, most Bankers in 1861 leaned toward the Unionists. Yet, even as the political landscape shifted, Fulcher must have been confused about whether the North Carolina governor outranked Federal Lighthouse Service supervisors.[5] One may be sure Governor Ellis expressed his wishes in language forceful enough to persuade Fulcher and dozens of his fellow keepers that the Federal Government in Washington, D.C., no longer had authority over its property in the state of North Carolina.[6]

In addition to the lighthouse at Cape Hatteras, Keeper Fulcher was also responsible for the diminutive Cape Hatteras beacon light, built in 1856 near the tip of the Cape.[7] The square, one-story wood-framed structure, topped with a sixth-order lens, was built to guide shoal draft fishing boats and coasting vessels through the exciting, whitecap and white-knuckle Slue Channel between the middle "Diamond" shoal and the inner shoal. This provided the impatient but daring mariner with an alternative to the longer and deeper course eight miles further out in the Atlantic. The second assistant keeper was assigned to tend the little light, either Andrew Williams or Bateman Williams, both of whom served under Fulcher, and one of the two would have been instructed by Fulcher to discontinue lighting the beacon.

For Governor Ellis and his Council of State, the decision to prepare the North Carolina coast for the worst came two days after the fall of Fort Sumter. On that day, April 15, 1861, a telegram was received at the Raleigh Capitol from President Lincoln's Secretary of War requesting Ellis to dispatch two regiments of militia to help put down the Southern "insurrection." The governor's reply, sent almost immediately, did not equivocate: "I regard the levy of troops...in violation of the Constitution, and a gross usurpation of power. I can be no party to this wicked violation of the laws of the country and to this war upon the liberties of a free people. You can get no troops from North Carolina."[8]

Not one to sit on his hands, Ellis sent out a flurry of orders to military commanders and superintendents of the state's lighthouse districts at Wilmington, Beaufort, Washington and Elizabeth City, ordering the lighthouses along the ocean extinguished. But it was not the radical move it may seem. Ellis' fellow governor in neighboring South Carolina had long since ordered his state's lighthouses darkened as did other Southern governors. Without considering the practical or strategic value, Ellis simply repeated the actions of states already seceded. On April 17, one telegram read, "You will take the most active measures for the defense of the post under your command. Extinguish all harbor and other lights."[9] Then, overcome with optimism despite his failing health, Ellis sent a telegram to President Jefferson Davis in Montgomery, exclaiming that, "We are ready to join you to a man. Strike the blow quickly and Washington will be ours." On the same day, President Lincoln issued a proclamation declaring a Federal blockade of Southern ports from South Carolina to Texas. The "Anaconda Plan," as it was called by General Winfield Scott, was a strategy conceived to squeeze and starve the South into submission.

One week later, Ellis assigned Major William H. C. Whiting, an engineer sent to North Carolina by Jefferson Davis, to serve as inspector general in charge of the defenses of North Carolina. "Your attention will be particularly directed to the Forts Caswell and Johnson on the Cape Fear, and Fort Macon and Fort Ocracock [sic] and the Coast generally. Exercise the powers necessary to the public defense. Extinguish lights. Seize vessels belonging to the enemy and do whatever may seem necessary," Ellis ordered Whiting.[10] In addition to the State's existing coastal fortifications, the strategic inlets at Hatteras, and to a lesser extent, Oregon Inlet, were the remaining navigable points of entry into the state without adequate defenses, and the Raleigh government dispatched men to those places to begin building fortifications.[11] As Governor Ellis anticipated, Lincoln extended the blockade to include the states of North Carolina and Virginia on April 27. There was no turning back.

Amid the blossoming of azaleas, dogwoods and wisteria in Raleigh and dozens of other eastern North Carolina towns, citizens anticipated their fate in high style. "The people here are very excited," read one account. In every community, spirited townspeople lined the streets and cheered their young men as they volunteered for hometown units. Bands played "Dixie" on mainstreets across the state. Along the railroads leading into the capital city, "ladies showered the men with 'flowers and Godspeed.'"[12] In Beaufort County on the Pamlico River, a unit formed under the name, "Washington Grays," and the young and naïve troops were feted by practically the entire town's population of 2,500 people who came to witness the pageant with unprecedented interest.[13] Flags were waved and women in white dresses made speeches and presented bouquets to their brave soldiers as they boarded the dispatch and tow steamer, *Post Boy*, bound for Ocracoke Inlet and Portsmouth Island.

Most likely watching with curiosity among those in the crowd at Washington were, D. T. Tayloe, the town physician; John Myers, a prominent merchant; and the Customs Collector and town apothecary, H. F. Hancock, who had conveyed the order to extinguish the

Hatteras light. None of the three would be present almost ten months later when a strangely similar but quite different town celebration occurred on the streets of Washington.

The telegram that was sent to Keeper Fulcher was one of many dispatched from Raleigh in April of 1861. In fact, keepers at all of North Carolina's principal lighthouses that could provide navigational assistance to the warships of the Union blockade received the same orders from Governor Ellis. The blacked-out lights included the big Outer Banks coastal towers at Bodie Island and Cape Lookout and the smaller inlet and harbor lighthouses, including Ocracoke and Beacon Island lights at Ocracoke Inlet, Bogue Banks Harbor lighthouse marking Beaufort Inlet, and Confederate Point, Bald Head and the twin Oak Island range lights marking the two entrances to the Cape Fear River.[14]

The governor planned to block Ocracoke Inlet with sunken vessels so the inland waterways would be safe from enemy intrusion. With the inlet blocked, the other two dozen inshore beacons, sound and river screwpile lights and light vessels could remain operating as the state's maritime traffic increased exponentially between mainland towns and fortifications on the barrier islands.[15] North Carolina had yet to secede from the Union, but Governor Ellis, feeling it was just a matter of time, wrote to Confederate President Jefferson Davis on April 27 informing him of his recent accomplishments:

> The State is to all intents and purposes practically out of the Old Union, and we are deciding on the speediest mode of giving legal sanction to this state of facts... All lights have been extinguished on the coast. Vessels have been sunk in the Ocrachoche [sic] Inlet and a fleet of armed vessels (small) is now being fitted out to protect our grain crops lying on the inland waters of the [northeastern] part of the State.... We have on these waters some bold and skillful seamen.... The enemy's commerce between N. York and all the West Indies and South American ports could be cut off by privateers on the coast of No. Carolina.[16]

Word quickly spread within the maritime community that the coast of North Carolina, after years of Federal investment and painstaking labor, was once again the dark, foreboding and dangerous place it was just a half century earlier. One especially vituperative observer of current events later wrote: "Soon after the bombardment of Fort Sumter the Confederate Government, with that murderous indifference to human life which has distinguished them from the first, extinguished all the lights they could reach, and among others the lighthouse erected at Cape Hatteras."[17]

Almost all of North Carolina's lighthouses and beacons had been installed only after years of pleading, political persuasion and many publicized deaths. For the Southerners who campaigned for, and cared for the lights and those who made their living on the water, the dousing of the lamps was a distasteful business. Fulcher, like his fellow keepers at other darkened lighthouses, would have been all too aware of the consequences for seafarers all along the southern coast, but especially those attempting to make the passage around Cape Hatteras and its dreaded Diamond Shoals. As the Civil War unfolded, men were to learn just how unpleasant war could be. "War is at best barbarism," said William Tecumseh Sherman at his address to the graduating class at Michigan Military Academy in 1879. "It is only those who have neither fired a shot or heard the shrieks and groans of the wounded who cry aloud for blood, more vengeance, more desolation. War is hell."

Whether the failure to light the lamps in a lighthouse was the equivalent of murder was a moral question that hung as heavily in the air as the winter fog that often blanketed the Gulf Stream. It was certainly a precedent that was later considered by Northern lawyers with an eye on retribution. Some years after the war the Light House Board re-emphasized the symbolic purpose of lighthouse keeping by stating that "Nothing indicates the liberality, prosperity or intelligence of a nation more clearly than the facilities which it affords for the safe approach of the mariner to its shores." And so for Governor Ellis and his fellow governors along the southern coast, who also ordered the darkening of the lights, their actions reflected, at the least, a lack of intelligence. As the coming months were to prove, the Union Navy would find the Southern coast and its harbors just fine, with or without the lights.

Such were the considerations that led to Ben Fulcher's decision to carry out one of his last chores as keeper of the Cape Hatteras Lighthouse. Ben Fulcher was a conflicted man. But he did not act with murderous indifference. He was just following orders from Raleigh.

Over the next year, the Southern lighthouses and lightships were not just extinguished. Their expensive and delicate crown-crystal lenses, brass oil-lamps and bronze rotating machinery were removed and hidden in warehouses and barns or dumped in streams. Some lighthouse structures were damaged or destroyed by fire or explosives. Other towers were shelled by rifled cannon, and lightships were torched and sunk—depredations inflicted by Confederate and Union forces alike. Most lighthouse keepers and their superiors in the Southern lighthouse establishment participated in the removal of lenses and other desperate acts of vandalism, and all lost their careers and their family's livelihoods as a result. Some keepers and superintendents moved their families to the interior of their respective states to avoid prosecution. At least one keeper was kidnapped and imprisoned in retribution for his collusion with the enemy.

Twenty years before the Civil War, a sailor upon sighting a lighthouse wrote: "There are no words to express the feelings that induce a sailor to offer fervent prayers when he sees this mark of sympathy expressed by his fellow man…he is no longer alone in the midst of the ocean waves; he sees that people are caring for him with paternal solicitude."[18] In 1861, south of Cape Henry, Virginia, there were no marks of sympathy to induce fervent prayers, only the darkened abyss; no keepers caring for friendless mariners at sea with paternal solicitude, only men with hatred in their hearts. It was indeed a dark period in the divided nation's history. But out of the conflict's darkness were found the better instincts of humankind. Throughout the war and after, the government of the United States endeavored to re-establish the lights, to locate and repair lost lenses, lamps and lanterns, to rebuild the bombed-out towers and to recruit and appoint new, trustworthy keepers and their assistants. The decade following the commencement of hostilities at Fort Sumter was, at times, the most distressing and disappointing, the most earnest and courageous, and in the end, the most triumphant period in nearly three centuries of American lighthouse history.

Of all the Southern lighthouses and of all the innumerable dramatic, intriguing and mysterious stories of stolen and missing lenses, none are more astonishing than that of the Cape Hatteras Lighthouse on North Carolina's Outer Banks. Throughout its history, Cape Hatteras has been universally recognized as America's most important lighthouse, situated at one of the world's most heavily traveled and most deadly ocean passages. Eventually, the second tower constructed at Cape Hatteras in 1870, became known as the standard-bearer of all American lighthouses, a monument to the maritime heritage of the nation.

Throughout the Civil War, the United States government desperately wanted to re-establish the Hatteras light, not only for humanitarian reasons, but more importantly, as a symbolic pronouncement proving that the Union, like the lighthouse, would prevail. The Cape Hatteras Lighthouse lens was extinguished, removed and hidden from Federal forces far into the interior of North Carolina. Later, parts of the lens were held captive by a desperate Southern-loyalist with hopes for a much-needed reward. At the Cape, the tower itself was nearly destroyed by Confederate troops, and its keeper vanished and was later investigated by Federal prosecutors. Records of the lens's odyssey survived in bits and pieces while other official documents detailing its story were lost in a Washington, D.C., fire. Fantastic urban legends were created, further concealing the truth. The story of what happened to the Hatteras lens, and its whereabouts, has been described as "one of the great-unsolved mysteries of American lighthouse history."

Its fate is a mystery no more. This is the story of "the lost light" and where the Cape Hatteras Lighthouse Fresnel lens is today.

TWO

THE OLD LIGHTHOUSE ON THE CAPE

In April, 1861, Hatteras light keeper Benjamin Fulcher was not just conflicted, he was dismayed. Fulcher was almost as old as the octagonal, federal-style lighthouse that he cared for, and he knew its history as well as anyone. The keeper was also a lifelong mariner and pilot and to him, extinguishing the light made no sense at all. The politicians in Raleigh knew little of lighthouses, and Hatteras in particular.

Seven years earlier, the Federal government transformed the Hatteras lighthouse from a travesty into a triumph and Fulcher was there when it happened. For the first five decades of its service, the light at the top of the lighthouse had been a fitful, flickering, and often non-existent beacon for mariners who were attempting to avoid the Cape, not run into it in search of the lighthouse. The lighthouse was too short, too dim, and poorly operated.

In 1794, the fledgling U.S. Treasury Department, led by Alexander Hamilton, was authorized by an act of Congress to construct a lighthouse on the headland of Cape Hatteras, "affording the most eligible site for a light-house." The proposed lighthouse was among the first commissioned by the nation warning mariners to avoid a specific navagational hazard. Previously, colonial lights had been established to guide vessels into port. Urgency was paramount. By the late eighteenth century, Diamond Shoals off Cape Hatteras had already earned the title, "the graveyard of the Atlantic." As the young nation's growth was being fueled by the cargoes of merchant vessels, an increasing and disproportionate number of hulls were disgorging their wares on the dark and low-lying beaches along the Outer Banks. However, because of delays in finding a qualified and willing builder, the 1794 cession of land by the state of North Carolina to the federal government expired and the entire process had to be repeated.[19-1] Not until August of 1798 did construction actually begin.[19-2]

The selection of a "most eligible" site for the lighthouse was the first, and worst misstep in the stormy 68-year tenure of the original Cape Hatteras light. It was, in fact, a decision that would dictate the course of events at Cape Hatteras for more than two centuries.

Surveyors were sent to Hatteras Island with what must have seemed an impossible list of specifications for the prospective lighthouse location. Foremost, it had to be close to the terrestrial point of the Cape, the demarcation of where land ended and the submerged shoals began. Secondly, the lighthouse also had to be situated on the highest ground possible, boosting its woefully inadequate 90-foot stature so the rays of its flickering, porpoise-oil fueled lamps were able to reach the extremities of the outer shoals, 10 miles away. "It is supposed that there is no part of the American coast where vessels are more exposed to shipwreck, than they are in passing along the shores of North Carolina," declared the U.S. Congress in 1806. At Cape Hatteras and its shoals, "hardly a season passes that does not afford the melancholy spectacle of stranded ships…and it is fortunate indeed if the friendless mariner escapes with his life."[20]

If the surveyors who searched for the "head land of Cape Hatteras" thought they would find something similar to a 100-foot high, New England-like promontory, they were sorely disappointed. What they found at Hatteras was more like a farmer's notion of a headland—an unplowed portion of a furrowed field—certainly nothing like a cliff high over the ocean.

The third condition on the surveyors' list was that the lighthouse location had to be accessible by water so construction materials, including the large blocks of granite and brown sandstone, and later supplies and vast quantities of oil, could be delivered safely. Deliveries were certainly not going to be made on the ocean side of the Cape—one of the most exposed, dangerous and unforgiving coastlines in the world, hence the need for the lighthouse in the first place. Materials would be shipped through Ocracoke Inlet, 15 miles to the south, sailed outside the shallows of Pamlico Sound, transferred to shoal-draft vessels, known as "lighters," along Cape Channel and then landed at Back Landing Creek, nearly a mile from the lighthouse location. One spot appeared to fit the surveyor's desires: an unusually prominent, 20-foot high sand dune surrounded by the wide, flat beach and nearly a half mile away from mean high tide. It was as close to a headland as they would find. But the surveyors in 1794 were neither educated in the processes of barrier islands and migratory dunes nor inclined to seek the counsel of the islanders and their wisdom of many generations. The dune, like all natural sand hills on the Banks, was imperceptibly moving southwest but it took decades of observation to know it. The prospective perch for the Cape Hatteras Lighthouse was not going to be a permanent proposition.

The Jennett family estate and its heirs owned the land the surveyors chose. The General Assembly of North Carolina in the 1797 session in Raleigh revived its July, 1794 "act to cede to the United States of America…four acres of land at the head land of cape Hatteras affording the most eligible site for a light-house…in possession…of William Jennett, Mary Jennett, Jabez Jennett, and Aquilla Jennett, all of the county of Currituck, infants under the age of twenty-one years, to whom Christian Jennett, their mother, hath been duly appointed guardian." The Government bought the property for "a fair and full price at a rate of twelve and a half dollars per acre, amounting to fifty dollars." It was the small but inauspicious beginning of many future real estate deals between Hatteras islanders and the United States Government. The lighthouse site was described as follows:

Beginning at a cedar post at John Wallace and John Gray Blount's line, running thence east twelve poles[21] and fourfifths of a pole to a cedar post at the corner of Wallace and Blount's line, thence north, binding on said line, fifty poles, to a cedar post at the corner of Wallace and Blount's and Thomas Farrow's lands, thence west, binding on Farrow's line, twelve poles and fourfifths of a pole to a cedar post, thence a direct course to the first station.[22]

The deed conveying the land owned by the Jennett children to the Federal government was not executed until 1801. By then, the lighthouse had already been under construction for two seasons and its castle-like, octagonal stone rampart was by far the tallest manmade structure on the island. It would not be the last time that an official act was signed-off after construction at the Cape was well underway. The next time produced consequences that were much more serious.

After the Cape Hatteras Lighthouse was finally illuminated in October, 1803, it became the focus of an onslaught of derision and disdain, almost as damaging and relentless as the frequent tropical storms and winter gales. Even before the foundation had been laid, there was concern about the sand hill's instability. Samuel Tredwell, the customs collector from Edenton, North Carolina who disbursed the $50 for the site wrote, "The hill on which the Lighthouse will stand is at present covered with Live Oak and other trees, and it would be well to direct the builder to cut as few of them off as possible particularly on the declivity of it—the trees if left standing will prevent the ground from washing." Builders, even eighteenth century ones, prefer treeless job sites, and so apparently Tredwell's advice went unheeded because by 1810, much of the dune on which the lighthouse stood was devoid of vegetation and the dune itself was rapidly vanishing.

The first keepers fought a constant battle to hold the hill in place. That effort must have sapped their strength because often at night the light at the top of the lighthouse would go out. "The light at Hatteras is very often without any light in the most tempestuous and dangerous weather," wrote John Delacy of Beaufort to the Secretary of the Treasury, William Crawford, in 1817. Delacy added, "It is frequently lighted and kept bright and clear for two or three hours in the beginning of the night and then permitted to go out entirely which it makes it much worse and more dangerous than if there was no light at all shewn [sic]." The fact that the keeper of the light at that time, Joseph Farrow, was moonlighting as the island's official commissioner of wrecks (the man responsible for the distribution of the beached bounty from foundered vessels) added to the intrigue.[23]

Some years later another keeper, Joseph Jennett, became the focus of critics who complained that poor maintenance and dirty reflectors caused the light to be ineffective. These failings were attributed to the keeper's frequent absences while his slave tended the light. Rallying to Jennett's defense was his immediate boss, the local customs collector, R. H. J. Blount, who admitted that Jennett's slave performed "most of the labor of cleaning[,] lighting[,] &c—but under constant personal inspection of the keeper."[24] But Blount's testament to Jennett's constant attention was made from 60 miles away. Other advocates of the beleaguered keeper included his friends, neighbors, fellow harbor pilots, and even Jennett's assistant keeper, Benjamin T. Fulcher. Clearly, Jennett's fellow islanders could empathize with a lighthouse keeper who had a more important and more profitable "day job" and, therefore, could be forgiven for having his slave handle the daily and nightly rituals of cleaning, hauling oil and lighting the wicks of the lamps. Island and mainland politics were not the only factors that clouded the old lighthouse's performance—nepotism, mismanagement and lack of oversight were among the other perennial problems within the lighthouse organization contributing to Hatteras' bad reputation. Bad lamp oil was an excuse offered by the keeper. Lantern fires, poor design, ineffectual equipment, lack of maintenance and persistent sea haze were further reasons why the Cape Hatteras lighthouse was often not visible to seafarers passing deadly Diamond Shoals. Still, no explanation was comforting enough to the masters of ships at sea or acceptable to the owners of those vessels who were often informed their investment had been turned into rubble on the shores of North Carolina.

No one complained more vociferously or with more credibility than George W. Blunt, publisher of the nineteenth century navigator's bible, the Coast Pilot. Blunt's organization received observations and reports from shipping companies and their captains, providing up-to-date information about new maritime obstructions, changes in shoals and inlets, deviations in magnetic fields, variances in sailing instructions, missing aids to navigation and the performance of the nation's lighthouses and lightships. Cape Hatteras was written-up most frequently. In 1850, Blunt posted a notice to his subscribers citing the observation of a colleague: "The light is a notoriously bad one, and so far as can be judged from external appearances, it is badly kept. On at least one night in October the light was out for three hours. There is no point on our coast with which I am acquainted that requires a

Augustine Fresnel's first light-house lens hardly resembles the "modern," Scottish-refined version that has since been identified with the Frenchman's name. Courtesy of Thomas Tag, Great Lakes Lighthouse Research, Dayton, Ohio.

better light than Cape Hatteras," expounded Blunt. "The lights at Hatteras, Lookout, Canaveral, and Cape Florida, if not improved, had better be dispensed with, as the navigator is apt to run ashore looking for them," reported a U.S. Navy officer. In no small measure, the complaints about Hatteras, and other Southern lighthouses, had far reaching implications. For at the same time, Congress, having heard enough about superiority of European lighthouses and the poorly managed U.S. lighthouse establishment, created a new administrative office to direct the nation's lighthouse service. The U.S. Light House Board was mostly made up of military men associated with maritime issues and they started their work in October, 1852. Among their first tasks was to improve the embarrassing light at Cape Hatteras.

George Blunt's persistence and the maritime industry he represented were finally rewarded in 1854 with the installation at Cape Hatteras of the most technologically advanced illuminating apparatus designed to improve the intensity of a lighthouse lamp—a Fresnel lens of the first-order, manufactured in Paris by the firm, Henry-Lepaute.

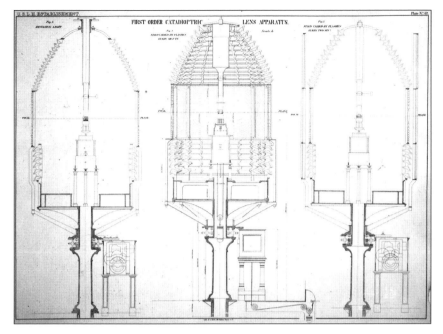

First-order cata-dioptric lens apparatus. National Archives.

French genius Augustine-Jean Fresnel had already gained recognition for his theories of light refraction in the early nineteenth century, and while other scientists had been searching for ways to improve the brightness of wicks, lamps and reflectors for France's lighthouses, Fresnel concentrated his efforts on focusing the light source and casting it in a powerful beam. Circular magnifying panels, or bull's-eye lenses, at the level of a lamp had the expected effect of intensifying the light, but the greatest percentage of radiating photons were lost. The French inventor then developed rows of angled mirrors above and below the central belt of magnifying lenses to reflect more of the emmited light to the horizon.

Fresnel had improved lighthouse optics, but he needed a manufacturer that was skilled in large, clockwork mechanisms—his hollow, barrel-shaped lenses needed to rotate in order to flash. He found the ideal partner in the famous French clock-tower maker of Henry-Lepaute. Together, Fresnel and Henry-Lepaute & Company, revolutionized the world's lighthouses. Two Scottish engineers later improved Fresnel's reflecting mirrors with upper and lower belts of

In 1806, William Tatham described the Hatteras tower as "an architectural eyesore, made from two kinds of stone,". Assistant Engineer of the 5th Lighthouse District, George B. Nicholson drew this sketch of the original Cape Hatteras lighthouse, on October 24, 1870. The drawing shows the brick addition above the middle segment of stone. Fewer than four months later the tower was destroyed to prevent it from toppling accidentally.
Courtesy National Archives.

prisms, called cata-dioptric panels. The result was an optical array of hand-polished, crown-crystal prisms that collected radiant light and bent its rays on a beam that could be aimed at the horizon. It looked like an upturned basket, made not of wicker but of glass, with a light on the inside. The Scottish version of Fresnel's apparatus captured all but 17 percent of a lighthouse lamp while the old, inefficient and problem-prone system of multiple lamps and parabolic reflectors wasted 83 percent of its light.

Initially, Fresnel and his clock-tower maker created six different sizes of apparatus, called "orders." The largest and most powerful, a first-order lens—averaging 12 feet high and more than 6 feet in diameter—was designed for important seacoast lights, the visibility of which was essential for navigators far out to sea. The smallest orders were installed in harbor and channel lights.* An almost unlimited number of flashing characteristics could be derived from varied numbers of center flash panels, rotating speeds and colors, affording gov-

*Only seven orders, or sizes, were used in U.S. lighthouses.

ernment planners a choice so that two or three adjacent beacons could be distinguished easily by mariners at sea. By the mid-nineteenth century, Fresnel's invention with its Scottish refinements had become the world's preferred lighthouse illuminating system, but the Frenchman never got to see his creation at work. He died in 1827.

In a dense forest in the Champagne Region of France, northeast of Paris, lies a tiny, medieval village that can claim to be the source of virtually every Fresnel lens in the United States, if not the world. There were many glassmakers throughout France, but only the artisans of Saint-Gobain understood the precision optical quality that was needed for Augustine Fresnel's creation to succeed. They not only understood the quality, but they also knew how to produce it, as they had since the seventeenth century under the guidance of Jean Baptiste Colbert, minister to Louis XIV. Saint-Gobain's mastery of silicates was well-established, and Fresnel needed no more evidence than the Hall of Mirrors in the Palace of Versailles.[25]

At Saint-Gobain, near the river Oise, raw masses of glass—bricks or billets—were re-melted in cast iron molds, each formed to produce a specific prism shape for a specific position on the apparatus frame. More than one thousand prisms comprised a first-order lens. The rough glass was cooled and tempered into true, crown-crystal. Machine-work completed the rough grinding to render the proper angles, and each prism was given to a peasant laborer to hand-polish it to absolute clarity. Most Fresnel lenses have a distinct green tint that can be traced to the iron oxide in Saint-Gobain's sand used to produce the glass. Although efforts were later made to eliminate the tint, it never affected the optical quality of the glass.

The result of the efforts of Monsieur Fresnel, the lens-manufacturing firms Henry-Lepaute, Lemonnier and Sauter, Barbier & Fenestra and Letourneau & Co., and the glassmakers of Saint-Gobain produced one of the world's most refined, artistic and functional devices of the nineteenth century. Of all their products, the rotating, first-order Fresnel illuminating apparatus of more than 1,000 crown-crystal prisms and bull's-eye lenses was the crown jewel at the top of a lighthouse, an exquisite chandelier. When it arrived on the island of

A "Diamond in the Sky." A 24-panel, first order Fresnel lens identical to the lost 1854 Cape Hatteras Lighthouse Fresnel lens. U.S. Lighthouse Society photo.

Hatteras from Paris in 1854, the Henry-Lepaute lens was considered a marvel no less remarkable than the steam engine.

However, the amazing lens would only make the Hatteras light brighter, not taller, so in 1854 the Light House Board also appropriated funds to add to the already ponderous, granite and sandstone tower, a brick addition increasing the lantern's height from 110 feet to 150 feet above sea level. The lighthouse, once dubbed "an architectural eyesore, made from two kinds of stone," now looked even worse. Yet, despite its aesthetic and structural shortcomings, the Cape Hatteras Lighthouse was finally visible to ships beyond "death's doorstep," the Diamond Shoals.

Three

Buying Blankets in the Summer

At dusk on a springtime evening in April, the same day he received his orders from Governor Ellis, Benjamin Fulcher did something he had not done during his six months as keeper. He stayed home with his family.

Prior to that fateful day, Fulcher, like all dutiful lighthouse keepers, ate an early supper and then set out to climb his tower to light the wicks of the oil lamps. Some keepers were lucky—at most, they only had to ascend a couple of stories. Those luckier still never had to leave their own house in the instances where the beacon was part of the same structure. Hatteras keepers were the toughest of the lot. To reach the lighthouse from the keeper's quarters prior to 1862,* men like Fulcher had to trudge across 300 yards of soft, wet sand (a shallow pond, actually) through all kinds of perils and hazardous weather—gale force winds and flood tides, blinding blizzards, lightning strikes, thick swarms of mosquitoes and biting flies. They next had to climb the equivalent of a 15 story building up a creaking, wooden stairway, lugging heavy oil containers to the top. In the worst of storms, Fulcher remained in the watchroom, directly below the lantern room, while the tower swayed and vibrated, and glass storm panes rattled, buffeted by the unfettered wind. Many nights passed when lighthouse keepers questioned their choice of professions. It was not a job for the faint-hearted.

Now, a new risk confronted Benjamin Fulcher.

---

*In 1862, a boardwalk was constructed between the keeper's house and the lighthouse so that the keepers could go to work without getting their feet wet.

The keeper's quarters of Benjamin Fulcher as depicted in 1863. This frame house, built in 1854, survives to this day. Champney drawing courtesy of the Outer Banks History Center.

On the porch of the wood framed keeper's house 900 feet away from the stone and brick tower, Fulcher probably sat and wondered what the future would bring. Would North Carolina join South Carolina and the other Southern States in the Confederacy? When would the lighthouse be lit once again? Would he and his assistant keepers continue to be paid? Should he continue his daytime rituals of maintaining the myriad of items associated with the keeping of a lighthouse? There were so many uncertainties.

In 1861, lighthouse keepers were generally guided through their daily activities by publications of the Light House Board, including Instructions and Directions to Guide Lighthouse Keepers and Others Belonging to the Lighthouse Establishment; and Management of Lens Apparatus and Lamps. In his groundbreaking book, *America's Lighthouses, An Illustrated History*, Francis Ross Holland, Jr., retired National Park Service historian and author, compiled the following description of a keeper's day:

To perform their main task of keeping the light burning from sunset to sunrise, the light keepers had to…by ten o'clock in the morning…clean and polish the lens, clean and fill the lamp, dust the framework of the apparatus, trim carefully the wicks of the lens lamp, and if required, put new ones in and see that the lamp was ready for lighting in the evening. Also, the keepers were to clean the copper and brass fixtures of the apparatus as well as the utensils used in the lantern and watch room, clean the walls, floors and balconies or galleries of the lantern and sweep and dust the tower stairways, landings, doors, windows; …and alternating the lamps inside the lens every fifteen days.

However, nowhere in the manuals did it say what a light keeper was to do when he was ordered by his state's governor to cease lighting the light. So as Ben Fulcher missed his first sunset over Pamlico Sound from the top of the lighthouse in many months, he wondered what was next. With no midnight watch scheduled in the top of the lighthouse, he might have been able to spend the entire night lying in bed—a rare opportunity for a lighthouse keeper. It must have been an odd and restless sleep. What Fulcher could not have imagined was that the answers to most of his questions would not be long in coming.

The news came to residents of Hatteras Island from members of the State Militia, including the Independent Grays of Pasquotank County, who landed on the docks near the inlet in late May. The State of North Carolina officially seceded from the Union on May 20, 1861.

To the residents of Raleigh, the announcement was conveyed by a white handkerchief waved from a second floor window on the south wing of the Capitol, signaling the final signature had been placed upon the ordinance of secession by Convention delegates. Immediately, cannons boomed, a one hundred gun salute was fired, followed by the playing of the "Old North State." The peal of church bells was heard throughout the city as a wild celebration ensued and "all sorts of extravagances were indulged in."[26]

Inventory of property removed from the Light House at Body's Island

4 boxes contents unknown.
6 " Lens.
5 tool chests.
2 lamps with chains.
8 pieces of brass + tin attachments to lamps.
Weight 12 pieces + wheel.
2 lanterns.
1 bag contents unknown.
5 lamp feeders.
3 tin buckets.
3 " cans contents unknown.
2 clocks.
1 piece casting (brass)
1 glue cup
14 broom, brushes, etc.
4 tin cups + lamp
4 cans oil and boat } belonging to Marshes L.H } left in care of Mydgett.

Inventory of articles removed from the Body's Island Lighthouse. National Archives.

On the Outer Banks, a more subdued reaction must have taken place, for as in the War of 1812, North Carolina's barrier islands would soon be on the front lines—a fact fully appreciated by its residents. The likelihood of maintaining even a marginal standard of living was uncertain since the economy of the Outer Banks was as fragile as the islands themselves. No matter how the war would play out, money and food would be in short supply for some time. Former Federal employees, such as lighthouse keepers and their superintendents, were the first to be affected. If Benjamin Fulcher thought that extinguishing the light of the Cape Hatteras Lighthouse was unthinkable, what had already occurred up the Banks was even worse.

At Elizabeth City in April, District Superintendent of Lights L.D. Starke, was reactivated as a Colonel in the state militia. Starke, probably a perceptive and practical man, thought that extinguishing the state's lighthouses was not enough. They needed to be completely disabled. Starke apparently recognized the possibility (and rightly so) that the lighthouses would not remain in the South's possession very long. On April 30, 1861, well before North Carolina had seceded from the Union, Starke sent a junior officer to Oregon Inlet to assist keeper Samuel Tillett with the complete removal of all the components of the third-order Fresnel lighting apparatus at the Body's Island Lighthouse (today spelled as "Bodie"). The men accomplished their difficult task without the skills of a machinist and without the help of hired laborers. The removal of the Bodie lens is the earliest recorded case of such action in North Carolina and one of a few to have occurred under the sanction of military authorities. Extant documents indicate that other North Carolina lighthouses were simply extinguished at that time.

Next, Starke's man travelled to the Roanoke Marshes Lighthouse, a soundside screwpile light nine miles west of Bodie Island, and removed all the important lighthouse property there. In a subsequent letter Starke reported that his officer "visited those establishments and brought to this place a quantity of valuable illuminating apparatus, materials &c, for which I refer you to the accompanying lists or schedules. These are all stored in this Town [Elizabeth City]. There is no oil here but a small quantity was brought here (the supply was nearly exhausted) and this I permitted to be used by Government steamers in need of it."[27]

A month after Colonel Starke's aggressive action to remove the Bodie lens, the Old North State joined the Confederate States of America and Raleigh transferred authority over all of North Carolina's lighthouses, beacons, buoys and light vessels to her new government's Treasury Department. With little time to create a bureaucracy unique to the new Southern nation, the leaders of the Confederacy modeled its administration on that of the Federal government. As such, the Confederate Lighthouse Establishment was placed under the Secretary of the Treasury, Christopher G. Memminger.[28] Memminger, in turn, appointed Navy Commander Ebenezer Farrand to be Chief of the Confederate Light House Bureau. However, there was a profound difference between the two agencies. The Federal progenitor was dedicated to guiding the "friendless mariner" by building and maintaining the nation's aids to navigation. The Southern version was determined to remove or destroy the lights just as quickly as they could. It was already alarmingly clear, the much more powerful Union Navy would soon appear at the South's strategic ports in an effort to cripple her commerce. The Confederate Lighthouse Bureau did not intend to light the way.

North Carolina's geography and its rail and water transportation routes shaped the state's development in peacetime and played the primary role in the military's offensive and defensive movements throughout the Civil War. Strategically, the coast of the state could be divided into three segments: the Outer Banks and the vast inland sea it protected; Beaufort Inlet; and Wilmington and the Cape Fear River. The state's major ports were at Wilmington, which was served by the rail head of the north/south Wilmington and Weldon Railroad, the main artery supplying Virginia; Beaufort and Morehead City and the rail head of the east/west Atlantic and North Carolina Railroad (fondly known as the "Mullet Line"); and Hatteras Inlet, which had, in the decade before the war, surpassed its neighbor to the south, Ocracoke Inlet, as the busiest gateway to the tidewater ports of New Bern, Washington, Edenton, Plymouth, Elizabeth City, and points beyond.

If the Union Navy controlled the inlets, sounds, rivers and major ports of North Carolina, the army would follow with thrusts into the interior with the goal of severing the Wilmington and Weldon Railroad. In addition, the enormous plantations and bountiful harvests of eastern North Carolina would be denied the Rebel armies. Thus, it was no stroke of genius that by the summer of 1861, on the orders of Ebenezer Farrand in Richmond, many of the South's lighthouses, beacons, screwpile lighthouses and light vessels were not only darkened, but disabled too.

Farrand apparently had little confidence in North Carolina's coastal defenses because he wasted no time in ordering the removal of all lights from the state's coast. In early June, the CSA Lighthouse Chief sent out a circular to the superintendents at Wilmington, Beaufort, Washington, Swan Quarter, Elizabeth City and Plymouth.

The superintendent of lights for the Wilmington District, J. T. Miller, was the first to act on Farrand's orders. It was no small feat. Miller was responsible for four principal inlet lighthouses and numer-

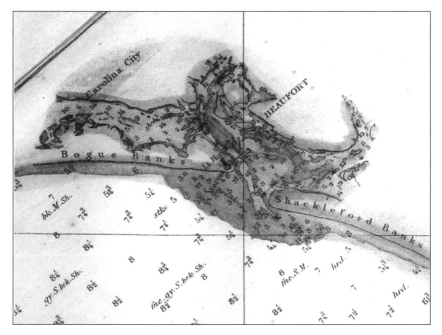

Beaufort Inlet ca. 1858 showing the Harbor lighthouse at Bogue Banks just to the west of Fort Macon. Author's collection.

ous river lights and light vessels. In an 1861 letter, Miller wrote: "By letter of the Light House Board bearing date June 7th I was requested to 'cause all the lenses fixtures and apparatuses of the Lighthouses in my District to be removed to some place of safety with as little as delay as possible and to present to the Department an estimate for the expenses of removal.'"[29]

However, before Miller acted on Farrand's request, he briefed the commanding general of the Cape Fear region, who expressed his objections to the removal of the river lights which were "deemed by him essential for Military and Commercial purposes." At the commander's urging, Miller appealed to Richmond to keep the river lights operating, at least as long as the oil to fuel the lamps lasted (the Confederate Light House Bureau had no lamp oil nor any other of the usual supplies for their lighthouses and had no plans to acquire any). As for the valuable Fresnel lenses, Miller reported: "The lenses fixtures [sic] for the other Lights 'to wit' Cape Fear Light, Oak Island Light and Confederate Point Light being immediately on the Coast I had removed with as much care as possible and placed in the Custom

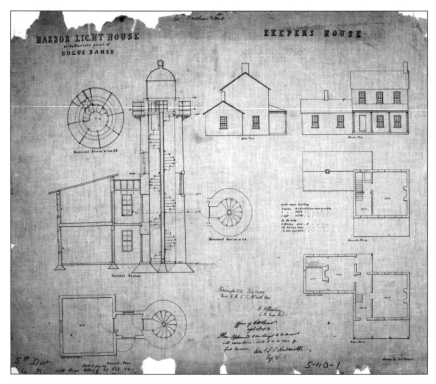

The 1854 construction plans of the Harbor Lighthouse, on the eastern point of Bogue Banks, near the northwest corner of Fort Macon. This was a 50-foot tower, exhibiting a fourth-order, fixed light, and served as a back-range marker in concert with a thirty-foot tower on the southeast corner of the fort. National Archives.

House for safekeeping. The lenses fixtures [sic] &c. of the River Lights still remain in the Buildings and as none of them are now lighted and the Buildings of two of them 'to wit' Campbell Island Light and Upper Jettee Light being occupied by the Military and liable to damage I recommend that the lenses fixtures [sic] be likewise removed. The lenses fixtures [sic] for the above lights are all in good order with the exception of Oak Island Light[,] some damage being done to that light by the Military at Fort Caswell."

Who removed the delicate apparatus from the lighthouses at Bald Head and Confederate Point is not clear, but it can be inferred that soldiers from nearby Fort Caswell performed the function, although not carefully, in the case of the two range lighthouses located on Oak Island's beach. Unlike other lighthouse districts, none of Miller's records have been found, including invoices or payment vouchers for skilled machinists, laborers or for the transportation of the material from the lower Cape Fear River up to the Customs House in Wilmington.

Much better evidence survived the war and reveals the process of removing and storing lenses in the Beaufort District. The presumption that as Confederate troops retreated, they removed the lenses of Southern lighthouses and beacons, is generally incorrect. Early in the war soldiers were less likely to be involved in the "theft" of lenses. They had far more pressing assignments building and arming coastal defenses, and most of the lights had been disabled long before any retreats took place. Since some familiarity with the equipment was necessary for the safe removal of the delicate glasswork and oil-fueled lamps, keepers and their assistants are known to have supervised or at least participated in the task utilizing some outside help. Except in a few instances, it was the intent of administrations in Richmond, Raleigh, and other Confederate state capitals that the lenses should not be damaged or destroyed, since at some point, the South was expected to prevail. When the war ended it would be in everyone's best interest that the lights be reactivated. A letter from Richmond written in November, 1861, anticipated preparations for a time "when the operations of the Lt. Ho. Establishment may be resumed."[30]

This explains why there was a peculiar appropriation made for the purchase of "blankets" by the superintendent of lights at Beaufort in the summer of 1861. The blankets were not to keep the lighthouse keeper and his family warm but to wrap and protect the delicate prisms of a Fresnel lens. According to the bookkeeping records of Josiah F. Bell, Beaufort Collector of Customs and Superintendent of Lights, the removal of lenses in Carteret County occurred on the week prior to June 21. Bell was in charge of the 150-foot tall coastal tower and its first-order, fixed (non-rotating) Fresnel lens at Cape Lookout on Core Banks. Other beacons in the district included the now vanished harbor lights at Fort Macon—the 50-foot tall Bogue Banks lighthouse and its 30-foot tall companion light that served as a range marker for vessels entering Beaufort Inlet.[31]

Superintendent Bell contracted with a Beaufort warehouse owner to store the apparatus from his district at a cost to the Confederate government of $5 per month and paid him $17 at the end of September for storage since June 21. Bell also paid Mr. Asia Waters $25 "for services rendered as Machinist in taking down Lighting apparatus at Cape Lookout & Fort Macon." The voucher to Mr. Waters is particularly instructive because it indicates the Confederate Light House establishment recognized a skilled technician was necessary to safely dismantle the lenses and they valued the property enough to remove it carefully and methodically. Keeper Elijah Willis at the Cape Lookout Lighthouse was on duty at the time and probably assisted the machinist, since he knew the lens best and probably was present in 1859 when the lens was originally installed. Willis was actually retained as keeper (with no lamp to light) through the end of 1861 at his quarterly salary of $75 for the purpose of protecting the public property at Lookout's remote island location. Other disbursements by Josiah Bell in July include: $20.90 to William H. Piver "for provisions furnished to the men employed in removing the lighting apparatus from Cape Lookout and Fort Macon" (although no record of the payments made to the workers seems to exist); and $34.25 for lighterage and $19.25 "for the blankets to wrap up lenses" to J. P. C. Davis of Beaufort. Bell summarized his response to Farrand's orders in a letter written in November stating: "I have in my charge all the lenses and lighting apparatus <u>Complete</u>, of the two lighthouses."[32] Bell underlined and capitalized "Complete" which seems to repudiate the often-repeated reference the Lookout lens was "mutilated" by the Rebels and what remained of it required removal by Union forces before a replacement lens could be installed.

Seventy miles up the chain of low lying sand banks from Cape Lookout, and at just about the same time Josiah Bell was hurriedly storing the lenses of the Beaufort District lighthouses, a shoal-draft, stern-wheel steamer approached Hatteras Island from the middle of Pamlico Sound. She churned the shallow, tea-colored water past Clam Shoal on her starboard side and slipped her anchor in Cape Channel. It was an historic anchorage of sorts. Six decades earlier sailing ships had arrived there with the huge, New England granite blocks that were used to build the foundation of the 1803 Cape Hatteras

Lighthouse. The occasion of the steamer's arrival would become an historic event too. It had been dispatched to collect the magnificent, Henry-Lepaute, first-order Fresnel lens from the top of the "most important lighthouse in America."

The steamer had come from Washington, North Carolina, and was most likely the *Governor Morehead*, a fast transport, stern-wheeler known to ply the Pamlico, Tar and Neuse Rivers during the summer of 1861. Stepping into the steamer's launch were a contract machinist, an extra helper or two and most likely, H. F. Hancock, the 43-year-old Customs Collector and Superintendent of Lights of Washington. They landed on the marshy, soundside shore near Cape Creek and trudged the one-mile distance over the beach flats to the lighthouse on the hill. It must have been an awkward moment for Hancock. He had appointed Fulcher as principal keeper just six months earlier, his hand-picked choice to manage America's most important light. Now the Collector was there to take his lens, and his job. After they discussed the unfortunate events that brought them together, the work party began the arduous process of dismantling the lighting apparatus at the top of the granite, sandstone and brick tower.

The Washington machinist surveyed the job at hand. He had not come unprepared, having been told by Hancock that he would be removing numerous, large, and fragile sections of glass optics from the top of a 15 story building. The lighthouse was a towering structure rarely seen in that day, certainly not in eastern North Carolina. Daunting as the job may have seemed to a man unfamiliar with lighthouses, nineteenth century machinists were highly skilled, generally well-educated and extremely versatile mechanically. It was obvious to the work crew that it would be necessary to anchor a purchase—a block and tackle, as well as a trolley line—deep in the sand somewhere on the leeward side of the octagonal tower.

Stationing the laborers on the ground, the machinist, Hancock, and Fulcher climbed the wooden stairs that wrapped inside the cool stone walls of the tower, and the steep ladders that led up to the hatch below the watchroom. Fulcher, having been present as assistant keeper when the lens was installed by the Light House Board's engineer in 1854, assisted the machinist in formulating the plan. In a reverse of the lens's installation, sections or panels of the lens could be

The view from the modern Cape Hatteras Lighthouse looking south to Cape Point and Diamond Shoals in 1998. Note the person standing on the beach in the lower-left. Author photo.

lowered through the interior from the lantern gallery down into the watchroom, one level below. From there, the glass would be securely wrapped in blankets, carried out on the gallery, hooked onto the hoist and trolley line, which were fastened to the railing of the upper gallery, and lowered easily to the ground.

The men began by attaching a second hoist to the iron braces above the lens, called a spider ring, which tied the base of the dome together and provided a pivot point for the top of the rotating lens. The hoist was positioned above the open stairwell that led down to the deck of the watchroom, so each panel could be gently lowered to the man below.

Few people today have experience in dismantling, reassembling, or restoring nineteenth century Fresnel lenses. Jim Woodward, a lighthouse consultant and civilian lampist for the U.S. Coast Guard, has taken apart and rebuilt as many as 60 Fresnel lenses over his 40-year career. The tools and procedures have not changed in 140 years. "You have to start at the top. There is a bronze ring at the top that

Special estimate for Cape Hatteras lens removal. National Archives.

ties all those panels together, where they meet at the top," describes Woodward. "So you've got to take that ring off. Then I would take out cata-dioptric panel number 1-2. That's a single panel. Then I would rotate the lens 180 degrees, and I would take out the opposite panel, which was probably 13-14. The bronze panels are bolted together so you remove the bolts and then remove the panel."

Each lens panel was stamped with a series of numbers so, as the apparatus was set up by the lighthouse lampist, it would be assembled precisely as it was designed and tested by its Paris manufacturer. The upper and lower corners of panel number one would have a "1" stamped on the left side and the right side would be stamped with a "2." The machinist had only to spin the lens on its bearings to access the next panel, turning 180 degrees to the left, and so on, until he came down to two panels on opposite sides of the frame. "You do that to keep the lens in balance," says Woodward. The bronze upper cata-dioptric panels with eleven crown-crystal prisms were heavy but not unmanageable. In fact, part of the genius of Fresnel's design was the modular structure of the huge, first-order lens—large molded sections, as a whole, would have been impossible to install. "Upper 'cats' in a first-order lens are going to weigh 120 pounds or so," according to Woodward. "Flash panels in a first-order lens are lighter than people think they are—they're going to weigh somewhere between 50 and 70 pounds. It's not so much weight that two people can't comfortably handle any piece of the lens when it's broken down into individual panels. The same is true when you get down to the lower cata-dioptric panels, which are below the flash panels. You would follow the exact same procedure. And it's actually easier as you go down."

"Then you're left with the iron skeleton frame, which is what holds it all together," Woodward continues. "You disassemble the iron frame, and then, at that point, you are down to the pedestal." Either running out of time or deciding the huge lens pedestal was more than they could handle, Fulcher, Hancock and the machinist left the apparatus in the tower. Woodward estimates that the job of removing the lens to the ground took about two days. Boxing it up took even more time.

As careful as the men had been in protecting the components of the Fresnel lens as each section was lowered to the ground, they probably caused the greatest injury to the lens when it was crated for shipment to the mainland. Woodward explains: "More than likely a mechanic, or a lighthouse keeper for that matter, would not have understood the real specifics of how to crate a lens panel, because a lens is very much a self-supporting structure. All those little pie shaped pieces that all have funny angles to them, when you put them all together it's completely self-supporting, and other than the pedestal which carries the weight of it, none of those panels feel each other from a structural standpoint. When you take them apart though, they become very susceptible to damage if you don't know what you're doing. And if you just take one of those panels and lay it in a box and stuff a bunch of cotton around it and put a lid on it, you are going to damage it." Which is exactly what the men did on that summer day in 1861.

The machinist and his helpers, unfamiliar as they would have been with lighthouses, must have been awestruck by the view from the gallery of the 150-foot tall Cape Hatteras lighthouse.[33] To the southeast were the chaotic, crashing waves of Diamond Shoals doing their perpetual dance of death. To the north was the vanished Cape Inlet, and the horizon where the breadth of the island narrowed until it disappeared. The men could also see their steamer, looking like a child's toy boat, five miles to the northwest.

Talking about the ominous events of the day as they worked inside the lantern, Fulcher, Hancock and their assistants must have expressed some apprehension about what they were doing despite their loyalty to the Southern cause. Taking the lens out of the lighthouse was no trifling matter and, whichever side prevailed in the conflict, restoring the old lighthouse to its intended purpose would not be easy. In fact, removing the lens was such a serious business, that Fulcher and Hancock would both, in less than a year, flee their homes with their families for the greater safety and anonymity of inland hideaways.

Before the job of removing the Hatteras lens was complete, Fulcher sent his second assistant and some men down the beach to retrieve the sixth-order lens from the little beacon near Cape Point. The beacon's lens was small enough that the men were able to place it in a single wooden box.

Onto horse drawn carts, hired from a nearby resident, were loaded cotton-lined wooden boxes containing the bronze framed glass panels, prisms and bull's-eye flash panels, lamps, tools, light keeper's implements, assorted brushes, spare wicks and glass chimneys, oil cans, copper sheets and any other implements associated with lightkeeping that were no longer necessary in a tower without a lens. Back up the broad, bare beach like a funeral cortege, went the procession of men, horse-drawn carts and the heart of the most important lighthouse in America on its journey into history. Later, when Benjamin T. Fulcher watched the diminishing wake of the stern-wheel steamer as it carried the lens of Henry-Lepaute out of Cape Channel on its way across Pamlico Sound, he bid farewell to his brief career as a principal keeper for the Confederate States of America Lighthouse Establishment—or any lighthouse organization for that matter.

The steamer made stops at Royal Shoal and Pamlico Point, removing the lenses from two light vessels and a quaint, two-story house on iron stilts. With its cargo of five Fresnel lenses, the *Governor Morehead* steamed west up the Pamlico River (following the same course taken by Sir Walter Raleigh's 1585 expedition and Blackbeard the Pirate in 1718) to the town of Washington, where the spoils of war were unloaded and carried to the warehouse of John Myers, 67, merchant, shipbuilder and loyal Southerner. He charged no rent to the Richmond treasury for the honor of hiding the Cape Hatteras lens on his property and may have been willing to pay for the right to do so.[34]

Unlike keeper Elijah Willis at Cape Lookout, it is not known if Fulcher was paid to remain at the Hatteras lighthouse to watch over the public property there.[35] If not retained, he probably considered returning full-time to his lifelong profession as a harbor pilot. Two months later even those prospects would end for Fulcher, since he was an anti-Union man and a slave owner, but especially because he was known to be the man who took the lens out of the lighthouse. Hatteras Inlet would not be a Confederate-held port for long.

It proved to be a cruel year for Fulcher. His 11-year-old daughter died and his eldest son, George, who adopted abolitionist views while at college, returned to Hatteras to face his disapproving father and death threats from anonymous neighbors. The beleaguered keeper left his government quarters at the lighthouse and returned to his family home in Trent, 5 miles away, and waited to see what would happen next.

Unbeknownst to Fulcher, his place in history would be redeemed by a descendant, a man with piercing blue eyes, who would one day be honored as one of the greatest keepers of all.

Four

WANING DAYS OF GLORY

The citizens of the Confederate States of America must have been confounded about how to behave on Independence Day, 1861. The anniversary was, for the first time, a belligerent nation's celebration. In any event, along the coast of North Carolina there was not much time for holiday merry-making. Military units were feverishly making preparations for the expected arrival of the United States Navy. There was, in fact, a flurry of activity on the sounds, rivers and rail lines throughout the coastal counties of the state. Troops, supplies and ordnance arrived daily at military installations along the Cape Fear River, Beaufort Inlet, Ocracoke Inlet, Hatteras Inlet and Roanoke Island; but far from the quantities that would satisfy the nervous Confederate commanders. At Ocracoke Inlet, the Washington Grays of Beaufort County were busy fortifying the unfinished defenses on Beacon Island that had been initiated for the War of 1812.

Beacon Island—a dry sand shoal, one-quarter mile long, one-eighth of a mile wide and rising barely above mean high tide—is marked on Colonial sea charts dated as early as 1733. In that year, sailing instructions on a map by surveyor Edward Moseley urged mariners wishing to enter Ocracoke Inlet to align the two large beacons there and "bring them in one...[and] steer up along said Beacon Island till you have Thatch's Hole to bear, East by North... and there come up to an anchor

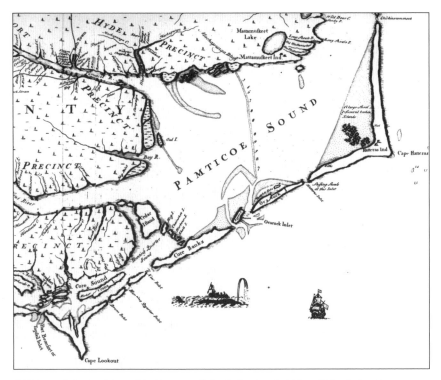

"A New and Correct Map of the Province of North Carolina by Edward Mosely, late Surveyor General of the said Provence," published in 1733. Beacon Island is located between Core Banks and Ocacock [sic] Island. Courtesy of the South Caroliniana Library, University of South Carolina.

in five or six fathoms water."[36]

The two unlighted range beacons referred to on Mosely's map were probably erected shortly after the province of Carolina's assembly passed an act that called for the marking of channels and at the same time also made Ocracoke Inlet the principal port of entry for the region in 1715. Thus, despite the fact that North Carolina's first lighthouse was established at Bald Head Island in 1795, Beacon Island holds the distinction of having the first significant aid-to-navigation in the state. Its "two large beacons" were guiding mariners at about the same time as America's widely accepted first sentinel, Boston Light. The original timber towers were later replaced with a small, two-story wood-frame lighthouse on the southern end of the island that exhibited a sixth-order light.

In 1861, however, North Carolina's leaders were more concerned

"In the middle of the Inlet lies a small Island having two large Beacons on it." The earliest reference describing an aid to navigation on the North Carolina coast can be found on Edward Moseley's map of 1733. Courtesy of the South Caroliniana Library, University of South Carolina.

that Beacon Island repel ships standing in from the ocean across Ocracoke Inlet bar rather than attract them. By early June, five guns had been mounted along the ramparts of the island's Fort Morgan with preparations under way for 12 more. At the same time, the small Fresnel lens was removed from the Beacon Island Lighthouse along with the fourth-order lens atop the Ocracoke Island Lighthouse.

Fourteen miles northeast of Beacon Island the great amount of defensive labor was matched only by an ever increasing anxiety among military commanders over the vulnerability of Hatteras Inlet. The 15-year-old inlet had become, in the preceding decade, the preferred passage through the barrier islands to the prosperous ports of the Tar Heel tidewater region (and the direct route to the soft underbelly of the state). During the summer of 1861, two forts, Hatteras and Clark, were constructed at the southern end of Hatteras Island. The point provided a broad expanse of sand devoid of protection, vegetation and elevation but had a commanding view of the channel through which more tonnage passed per year than through the established port of Beaufort and nearly as much as Cape Fear inlet. Engineers shaped the forts out of sand revetments held in place by slanted wooden planks covered with blocks of sod from island marshes. The polygonal shaped Fort Hatteras was armed with 12, 32-pound smooth-bore guns that were woefully inadequate when matched against the longer range and more accurate rifled guns of the Federal Navy. The first line of defense against a naval attack was the smaller redoubt of Fort Clark, hardly a threatening battery with just five 32-pounders.

There were 350 men of the 7th North Carolina Regiment stationed at the Hatteras Inlet forts by early July, but slaves were doing most of the work. The days were typically steamy and when the sea breeze was nonexistent the insects were unbearable. "The mosquitoes held possession of it by day and night, blackening the air with their presence," wrote Dr. Edward Warren, who was on an inspection tour with Brigadier General Walter Gwynn.

"A sable cloud composed of myriads of these insects…hovered over the head of every living thing that stood or walked upon that dreary shore, and while one laborer worked upon the fortifications another had to stand by him with a handful of brush to keep him from being devoured by them. The poor mules looked as if they had been drawn through key-holes and then attacked with eruptions of small-pox."[37] But not all the days were spent swatting green-head flies and mosquitoes, according to a young infantryman stationed on Portsmouth Island, southwest of Ocracoke. He described men dining on "crabs, bluefish, spots and mullets, besides ham for dinner…saving their cake until later."[38] Another wrote of having "a pleasant time fishing, crabbing, clamming and oystering."[39] But other contemporary accounts tell of troops who passed the long, dreary days drinking whiskey "to an alarming extent."

There was much more activity on the water. North Carolina's "bold and skillful seamen" were organized to crew a ragtag fleet of paddle-wheel steamers, iron-hulled propeller tugs, pilots boats and freight schooners, that comprised what was appropriately named, "The

Mosquito Fleet." No other point along the American East Coast was better suited for the commerce-destroying mission of these privateers. The prow-shaped Outer Banks thrust its islands and protective harbors out into the Atlantic, close to the heavily traveled sea lanes of the Gulf Stream and Labrador Current. There, heavily laden cargo vessels labored around the capes, making themselves attractive targets for the more nimble, but lightly armed, North Carolina Navy.[40] The masters of ships that rounded the Carolina coast at night were drawn even closer to shore, searching for the comforting light of lighthouses at Cape Fear, Cape Lookout and Cape Hatteras. But they were instead greeted by darkness and the panic-inducing roar of breakers on the shoals.

For three months North Carolina's Mosquito Fleet harassed the merchant ships of the Northern states and captured an impressive number of prizes. Where Outer Bankers once depended on Providence and gales to "ground" ships and deposit their cargoes on the beaches to be claimed by all, now they were sanctioned by "letters of marque" to take all that they could—although much of the spoils was reserved for military stores. Brazilian coffee, Cuban sugar, molasses, tropical fruit and salt spiced up the diets of the island's growing population, including hundreds of residents, troops and, surprisingly, the families of wealthy mainland planters, who considered the impending war no reason to interrupt their annual pilgrimage to the beaches at Portsmouth, Ocracoke, Hatteras and Nags Head, for the healthy summer sea breezes and fresh seafood. Unlike summers past, 1861 provided the additional tourist entertainments of fort building, troop drilling and privateering.

Privateering also captured the attention of merchant ship owners up North. The Mosquito Fleet made President Lincoln's "Anaconda" blockade of North Carolina ports seem no more intimidating than a garter snake. By the first of August, the failure of the plan became fodder for the national press. "We learn that the port of Beaufort, N. C., is for the most time perfectly free from blockade," wrote a reporter for *Harper's Weekly*. "There are but three government vessels to look after the entire coast of North Carolina, and from information we received, it would not require a very sagacious privateer to slip in or out of any of the ports of that State." Another New York columnist, alliterative but less objective, wrote: "…the waters guarded by this pestilential inlet became a pirate's nest, from which issued with perfect impunity a swarm of Confederate privateers, who, after a murderous cruise, returned with their ill-gotten booty to sustain the Southern rebellion."[41]

The strategic importance of the Outer Banks was entirely underestimated by military planners until the successes of Carolina privateers could no longer be ignored. Washington considered the coast of North Carolina, for the first time since the reign of pirates Blackbeard and Stede Bonnet, as "the most dangerous stretch of shore in the whole Confederacy."[42] Occasionally, a Federal warship would appear off Hatteras or Ocracoke inlets to observe the defensive works in progress. One Navy Lieutenant reported back to Washington that, "It seems that the coast of Carolina is infested with a nest of privateers that have thus far escaped capture…Hatteras Inlet, a little south of Cape Hatteras light, seems their principal rendezvous. Here they have a fortification that protects them from assault. A lookout in the lighthouse proclaims the coast clear, and a merchantman in sight; they dash out and are back again in a day with their prize."[43]

Here, the historical record becomes confused. Often written is that the Cape Hatteras lighthouse, after having its light extinguished and its lens removed by Confederate troops, was used a lookout and signal tower to inform the Mosquito Fleet of potential prey passing offshore. However, it has been well documented that the majority of privateering raids were launched from Ocracoke Inlet, 27 miles southwest of the Hatteras tower, much too far away to relay timely signals. Furthermore, Hatteras and Ocracoke inlets were often confused or even merged in the writings of geographically confused northerners. However, the Ocracoke Lighthouse was known to have been utilized quite effectively as a signal station for the raiders anchored inside "Teaches Hole" channel. Although once, the signalmen at the lighthouse mistakenly sent the fleet out to intercept a merchantman but then raised the flags spelling "a man-of-war" approaching, which caused a good deal of consternation among the Mosquito captains.[44] The Cape Hatteras Lighthouse may have been used as a lookout tower, but since it was not visible 10 miles away at Hatteras inlet, it was unlikely to be an effective signal post.

Another Outer Banks legend has it that before the commencement of hostilities at Hatteras Island, someone with an extremely good aim and range, fired shells at the 18-foot-wide lighthouse from the rolling deck of a ship at a distance of more than 1,300 yards, blowing out the top 30 feet of the tower. This, of course, could not be true because there are excellent records detailing the condition of the lighthouse after it was recaptured by the Union, and it is clear that the tower had not been damaged by artillery fire of any kind. The legend may have been derived from one of two events that occurred during the Outer Banks' waning days of glory as a Confederate outpost. On July 10, 1861, the former Revenue Cutter turned Federal gunboat, USS *Harriet Lane*, which had been a frequent visitor before the war, appeared at the inlet and fired three salvos from her guns at the forts under construction. The intent was not clear as the shells did no damage, but it may have been for nothing more than to cause excitement among the workers, who until then were distressed mostly about bug bites and running out of whiskey.

The other event that may have fueled the lighthouse-shelling legend came three days later when the crew of the pilot boat, *York*, captured the brig, *P.T. Martin*, out of Philadelphia, but then purposely grounded their prize when the USS *Union* appeared. The *Union* then fired shells into the forest after the *York*'s crew fled.[45] In any event, it is unlikely that a Federal vessel would attempt to fire on the Hatteras tower, since the North was so desperate to get the lighthouse relighted.

The desire to reactivate Cape Hatteras light notwithstanding, some Southern lighthouses were damaged or destroyed by Union shells or resulting fires but mostly because the towers were adjacent to Confederate forts. The lighthouse at Fort Morgan at the entrance of Mobile Bay was one. The Beacon Island lighthouse at Ocracoke Inlet was another.

As the dog days of August progressed, the pickings for the Mosquito Fleet grew thin as merchantmen gave the Carolina coast a wide berth. Payouts by maritime insurers of northern ships mounted (the loss of the *P.T. Martin* was valued at $60,000). The presidents of six northern insurance companies demanded that Navy Secretary Gideon Welles do something. "Any project by which this nest of pirates could be broken up would be hailed with gratitude by all interested in commerce," wrote the shipping executives.[46] The influx of men and materials had also slowed, then reversed itself after the South's victory at the Battle of First Manassas (Bull Run) when the Confederate War Department, brimming with newfound confidence, shifted from a defensive to an offensive mindset.

At the Outer Banks forts, morale was low, ammunition was in short supply and whiskey was hard to come by. The summer guests had gone home to the mainland, presumably to tend to the fall harvest, but maybe because the seacoast no longer seemed a healthful place to linger. There, the ominous quiet, like the still hours before the worst of hurricanes, harkened an approaching storm in the form of a Federal combined amphibious invasion.

The fun and games were over.

"A Foothold on Southern Soil"

At daybreak on Tuesday morning, August 27, 1861, the telegraph office in Raleigh received a startling dispatch for the governor from Norfolk: "Enemy's fleet…left last evening; passed out of the capes and steered south, I think to the coast of North Carolina." The intelligence was little help to the 350-man Confederate garrison at Hatteras Inlet, a day's sail from the closest telegraph wire. By 9:30 that morning, the Federal squadron consisting of the USS *Minnesota, Wabash, Monticello, Pawnee, Cumberland*, the Revenue Cutter *Harriet Lane*, the U.S. tug *Fanny* and the chartered troop transports *Adelaide* and *George Peabody*, ferrying 900 troops were in sight of the Cape Hatteras Lighthouse. While visibility was good, the sea was running and many of the new recruits were feeling the effects of seasickness and probably no small measure of anxiety about their upcoming first operation. By afternoon the fleet was anchored off Hatteras Inlet within sight of the officers and men of the suddenly modest bastions of Forts Hatteras and Clark. The *Harriet Lane* had returned, and this time her mission, and that of her consorts, was clear.

The plan of attack, as described by the commander of land forces, Major General Benjamin F. Butler was, "to land the troops under cover of the guns of the '*Harriet Lane*' and '*Monticello*' while the '*Minnesota*' and '*Wabash*' try to shell them out of their forts. We are then to attack on the land side, and my intention is to carry them with the bayonet."[47] The plan worked, with the exception of a few unforeseen surprises and without the bayonets. The shelling of Fort Clark began at 10 a.m. on the 28th, first by the steam frigates *Wabash* and *Minnesota* and the sloop *Cumberland*. When the return fire from the fort splashed harmlessly in the water 800 yards short of the Federal ships, everyone involved, whether Union or Confederate, would have bet their month's wages on the outcome. The Federal fleet mounted 149 guns to the two fort's total of 18. Within an hour the smoke was so dense that neither side could see the other, but by then the Union gunners had found their range and lobbed shell after shell into the fort.

More than 300 troops from units of the Twentieth New York, Ninth New York, the Army's regular artillery, and Marines from the *Minnesota* were landed two miles east of Fort Clark. Not taken into account was the strengthening onshore breeze and the resulting breakers, which tossed the men, landing craft and artillery pieces hard onto the beach. The commander of the landing party later reported that, "All of us were wet up to the shoulders, cut off entirely from the fleet, with wet ammunition, and without provisions; but still all had one thought—to advance."[48] Advance they did, despite a brief scare when what appeared to be a Rebel cavalry unit suddenly charged toward them but then was quickly discovered to be just a herd of frightened Banker ponies.[49] By 2 in the afternoon, 90 minutes after the Confederates evacuated Fort Clark under the hailstorm of Navy gunfire, the Twentieth New York, wet and thirsty as they were, hoisted a U.S. flag over a captured enemy fortress for the first time since the start of the Civil War.

What followed was a tense night for both sides. Under the threat of weather, the Federal fleet was forced offshore, leaving the Union troops unprotected inside Fort Clark. Fort Hatteras was reinforced with Confederates from Portsmouth Island. Both sides were unsure of the other's intentions. By 7:30 a.m. the next morning the Union warships returned to finish the business of Hatteras Inlet. They fired their shells at Fort Hatteras, "the range fully two miles—just the timing of the fifteen-second fuse. The immense shells could be traced away in the air. Houses were torn to the ground. A legion of fiends could not have withstood such a storm of shells."[50] A Confederate captain

"A legion of fiends could not have withstood such a storm of shells." The bombardment of Fort
Hatteras, August, 1861. Residents of nearby Hatteras village are depicted observing the reduction
of the fort from the safety of gnarled live oaks in the lower left. National Archives.

described the experience inside the fort: "Such a bombardment is not
on record in the annals of war. Not less than three thousand shells
were fired by the enemy during the three hours. As many as twenty-
eight in one minute were known to fall within and about the fort."
By 11 in the morning, a white flag was raised over the fort and the
invasion of Hatteras Inlet was over.

The significance of the fall of Hatteras Inlet was far reaching and
well publicized. An officer of the frigate, USS *Wabash*, who filed
reports for the *Evening Post*, wrote that Hatteras is "a place which
is of such vast importance to us. It is the key of the State of North
Carolina, and to the ports north and south of this... With the possession of this port we can easily keep alight Hatteras lighthouse and
maintain the various lightboats and stations removed by the rebels...

We should keep and hold this place at all hazards." Admiral David D. Porter later wrote: "This was our first naval victory, indeed our first victory of any kind, and should not be forgotten... The moral effect of this affair was very great, as it gave us a foothold on Southern soil and possession of the Sounds of North Carolina if we chose to occupy them. It was a death-blow to blockade running in that vicinity, and ultimately proved one of the most important events of the war."

The bombardment must have made quite an impression on the residents of nearby Hatteras village, who had previously experienced such relentless force only from nature's own fury. Once the smoke cleared, some of the more curious men from the village appeared from their observation posts behind the thick tangles of myrtle and live oak to greet their new (old) government. The Confederate defeat satisfied the Unionist population of Hatteras who welcomed the bluecoats with open arms. Others were not so pleased and quickly carried the news to Southern loyalists up the old sand road to the northern villages, including the first stop at Trent Woods. There, former lighthouse keeper Benjamin Fulcher received the report with resignation but not surprise. He knew what he had to do and probably had already made preparations. With as many of their possessions as they could take away, the family boarded their flats and poled out to Fulcher's pilot boat anchored out in King's Island Channel. Taking an extra measure of precaution, Fulcher steered the pilot boat out by Cape Channel, far from the Federals at Hatteras Inlet. With a fair wind they would have made Swan Quarter in half a day.

The hospitable and beguiling Unionist residents of the local villages must have also made an impression on the northern correspondents accompanying the Hatteras Inlet operation. As a result, their reporting of the aftermath of the engagement was full of post-victory propaganda. One columnist reported that:

> Thousands of the people of Eastern North Carolina are flocking to the captured fortress, and voluntarily subscribing to the oath of allegiance to the United States. White flags are displayed at every conspicuous point; the fort at Ocracoke Inlet, 40 miles to the south of Hatteras, has been abandoned; and every indication is to the effect that the Union sentiment

Keeper Enoch Ellis Howard
standing at the base of the
Ocracoke lighthouse in 1893.
Howard was a Unionist who
replaced William Gaskill
as keeper in 1862 and who
served for 35 years, one of
the longest tenures in the history of the U.S. Lighthouse
Service. National Archives.

is predominant and only required the dispersion of the rebel
in arms to find expression...The heart of [North Carolina's]
people were never with the traitors at Montgomery and
Richmond, and, as we have already said, she will leap back
gladly to the bosom of her mother, whenever the military
despotism that weighs her down shall be lifted by the Federal
arm.[51]

In reality, far fewer people took the oath of allegiance—between
56 and 250, depending on the source—although a year and a
half later, 77 men from Hatteras Island enlisted in the First North
Carolina Union Regiment, compared to just 13 who had joined the
Confederate service. Probably, Hatterasers saw the Federal occupation

of their island as a potential economic boon or, at the least, they hoped that by taking the oath their homes, personal property and livestock would become exempt from foraging troops. Neither expectation was realized, and the islanders were quickly disappointed when the hungry and bored Union garrison stole anything that was edible on two or four legs. A greater indignity occurred later when captains of Federal vessels hired and paid former slave boatmen and pilots to guide their vessels through North Carolina inlets. Still, a few island men held out hope for a job as a light keeper.

At Ocracoke and Portsmouth islands, residents and Confederate soldiers alike must have been disconcerted by the incessant thunder-like sound—thump, thump, thump—that was heard for two consecutive mornings from the direction of Hatteras, 15 miles up the beach. In Ocracoke's unique language they would have been feeling "right quamished" (ill in the stomach), especially the Washington Grays, who only three months earlier had set out amid tremendous fanfare on their exciting adventure.

The day after the surrender of Hatteras Inlet, the locals observed the unexpected retreat of the remaining Confederate forces from Fort Morgan on Beacon Island, and at Portsmouth, with "nary" a Union combatant in sight. Some Confederate troops had left to reinforce the outmanned defenses at Hatteras Inlet and arrived on the first night of the two day siege. Despite Fort Morgan's strong defensive position—beyond the range of the Union Navy's guns—the awful sound coming from over the northeast horizon panicked the fort's commanders. When the Confederate gunboat *Ellis* arrived with eyewitness accounts of the pummeling of the Hatteras forts, the Fort Morgan officers considered their situation hopeless and ordered the guns spiked and the fort abandoned. An ordnance sergeant disagreed with his superiors' assessment and called it "the most cowardly evacuation ever known…a most disorderly thing."[52] The brief debate among the Confederate officers within the fort has been described by one historian as the "Battle of Beacon Island."[53]

From the gallery of the extinguished Ocracoke lighthouse, Keeper William Gaskill was disgusted when he saw a white flag fluttering in the breeze over Portsmouth Island. "Damn cowards!" he must have thought. Gaskill was 49 years old, married and had five children. In June, the keeper took the lens out of the lighthouse as he was ordered, along with the one on Beacon Island, and now he was in imminent danger of prosecution by the Yankees. On September 2, with no other choice, Gaskill gathered his family and boarded a schooner for Hyde County, appropriately named since it was a good place to hide. On the unusually crowded streets of county seat, Swan Quarter, Keeper Gaskill of Ocracoke must have found sympathy in the company of Keeper Fulcher of Hatteras.

Worried about how he would be able to provide for his family on the mainland, Gaskill wrote a letter to North Carolina Governor Henry Clark:

> Dear Sir. I have enclose my account for keeping the light at Ocracke [sic] Lighthouse which I would be very glad that you will attend to it and see it paid as soon as can be convenit [sic] as Mr. Dewey the Collector of the port of Ocracke [sic] he said for me to stay there and I would be paid. So I stayed untill [sic] the 2nd of Sept. and I am going back as soon as the Yankees leaves Hatteras. So attend to this matter if you please as I am very much needy and you will oblige yours. [signed] William S. Gaskill.[54]

Gaskill's claim was forwarded to the Confederate Secretary of the Treasury, Christopher Memminger, by Governor Clark, who wrote, " I believe his claim is correct & I have supposed that your Department is the proper one to audit & pay it." If Gaskill thought he would soon be paid, he was disappointed, for in late November he submitted two invoices to a Justice of Hyde County—one made out to the United States of America for "keeping Ocracoke Lighthouse from the first of January 1861 up to the twenty-six of the above date [April]. Amount due me $128.88." The second invoice requested payment from the "Confederate States of America to Wm. S. Gaskill for keeping the Light at Ocracoke from the twenty six of April 1861 up to the Seckoned [sic] of Sept. of the above date. Due me 138.89." It is not recorded whether Keeper William Gaskill was paid by the Richmond government, but there is no doubt that the U.S. government never compensated the keeper who vandalized his own lighthouse.

Gaskill was not alone in his financial frustrations. Hanson R. Ruark, keeper of the Price's Creek range lights on the west bank of the Cape Fear River, sent a demand for payment to the Collector of Customs at Wilmington, North Carolina for his service through Nov. 27, 1861, when the two lights were extinguished by order of the Collector. Ruark's claim fell on deaf ears, perhaps because he waited until 1863 to send his request. Most lighthouse personnel throughout the Southern coast faced similar difficulties and some even appealed to the U.S. Light House Board after the war to be paid reparations for the loss of personal property as a result of military action—something that hundreds of thousands of Southerners would have also appreciated. As late as 1869, Ruark apparently hired an attorney in Smithville, North Carolina (now Southport) who presented his client's case to the Federal Government. The Light House Board tersely refused to consider any claims by Ruark or any other keepers for unpaid salaries or lost property "arising out of the rebellion on the basis that the Board had no authority to do so."[55]

Six

"WITH THAT INSANE LOVE OF PURPOSELESS MISCHIEF

With Hatteras Island in their possession, Union troops had achieved their foothold on Southern soil, but the lighthouses (and lightships) of the Outer Banks were still not safe from destruction. In September, 1861, a small sailing cooner with two African-American men aboard, arrived at the federal garrison at Hatteras inlet with a startling report. Miraculously, the men had escaped from Roanoke Island in the middle of the night and sailed 38 miles across the open, and sometimes, dangerous waters of Pamlico Sound. They risked their lives to deliver the news that the Bodie Island Lighthouse had recently been destroyed by Rebel raiders.[56-1]

The loss of the Bodie tower was appalling to the Union Naval commander at Hatteras but the threat to North Carolina's lighthouses was not limited to just Confederates in the early months of the war. On September 16, a small detail was sent out from Hatteras Island to "explore and subdue" the Confederate fort at Beacon Island. Previous intelligence indicated that the Union men would find no resistance. Indeed, after months of engineering, mounting of guns, labor, sweat and countless pints of blood lost to mosquitoes, the Rebel stronghold of Fort Morgan was captured by the simple act of an Union officer stepping foot on the wooden pier at the southern end of the little island. Lieutenant J.G. Maxwell's men of the USS *Pawnee* finished destroying what armaments

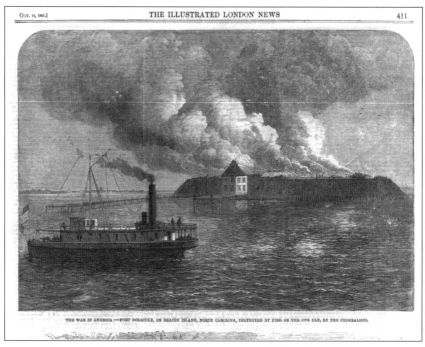

THE WAR IN AMERICA :—FORT OCRACOKE, ON BEACON ISLAND, NORTH CAROLINA, DESTROYED BY FIRE ON THE 17TH ULT., BY THE FEDERALISTS.

"The torch was applied to the bombproofs and magazines, and also to the lighthouse on the island. The conflagration raged furiously all night, the light being plainly visible thirty miles distant." The Federal propeller tug, *Fanny*, stands by. Author's collection.

the retreating Washington Grays had not already damaged. As the troops went about torching platforms and smashing the gun pivots they admired the fort's construction of "earth covered barrels of sand, the large bomb-proof shelter and magazine."[56-2] According to the *Illustrated London News*, "The torch was applied to the bombproofs and magazines, and also to the lighthouse on the island. The conflagration raged furiously all night, the light being plainly visible thirty miles distant." After nearly a century and a half as the home of North Carolina's first lighthouses, Beacon Island would never again guide mariners entering Ocracoke Inlet.

Not yet finished with the aids to navigation there, Lt. Maxwell's men then set fire to the light vessel that was posted between Beacon Island and the inlet, and then set it adrift.* They next sank several derelict vessels loaded with stone in the inlet in an attempt to block future forays by blockade-runners or privateers.[57] Since the first days of the blockade, it had been the desire of Washington, D.C., strate-

---

*The Ocracoke Inlet lightship had been removed from its station and used by the Confederates as a supply vessel.

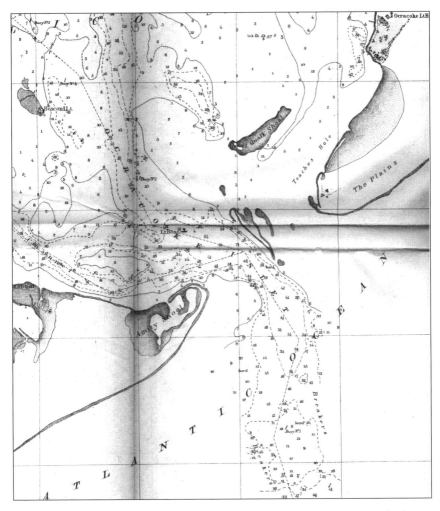

Ocracoke Inlet in 1858. In the upper left is Beacon Island. Just above the tip of Amity Shoal is
the Ocracoke Inlet Lightship. At the upper right is Ocracoke Lighthouse. Author's Collection.

gists to use the hulks of old schooners to block the channels leading
into North Carolina's ports, especially those leading into Pamlico
Sound. However, anyone with practical knowledge of Outer Banks
inlets would have thought the idea ludicrous. The force of water flowing in and out with the tides (and storms) had made short work of
countless foundered vessels over the centuries. One gunboat's pilot
tried to reason with the commander of the North Atlantic Blockading
Squadron by observing, "from my experience and knowledge of the

bottom, which is shifting sand, I deem it entirely impractical." The admiral's rebuke was imperious and typical of an impatient, if not ill-informed, superior: "What the department wishes is to have its orders executed if possible. I attach, myself, but with little consequence to the opinions of pilots or other persons."[58]

Throughout the war, Confederate and Union forces purposely sank vessels, including lightships, to block rivers and inlets and then later spent time and money to raise, recover or remove them. It is no wonder that Captain Horatio Williams of Ocracoke at the outbreak of hostilities, sailed his beloved schooner, *Paragon*, far up the Roanoke River and sank her to keep his proud little ship from the indignity of being another wasted obstruction of the stone fleet.[59]

B ack on Hatteras, the Federal troops left to garrison the forts at the inlet began the shocking adjustment to life on the beach, although some may have been warned by their prisoners who had spent the summer there. There was not much for the men to eat, and foraging quickly became a sore point between the islanders and their guests. The stores of tropical fruit discovered on board a couple of prizes captured by Confederate privateers did little but make the men sick. The thrill of victory vanished quickly once the bluecoats had a look around. A correspondent for *Frank Leslie's Illustrated Newspaper*, clearly unfamiliar with the barrier island environment, had this to say about Hatteras:

> It seems scarcely probable, but it is nevertheless a fact, that this miserable sterile strip of land which our gallant troops regard as "a slip of a desert," is the birthplace and home of nearly 1,000 persons, who make a living by fishing in the Pamlico Sound. The only vegetation this barren place affords are dwarf shrubs and bushes, which are truly a most miserable apology for trees. Nevertheless they are gratefully accepted. Captain Parisen of the 9th regiment, says, that when he visited Fortress Monroe [Virginia] after the stay of some time at Hatteras Island, he was positively impressed by the enormous altitude of a tree near Hampton, which was only thirty feet high!

Soon after the destruction of Fort Morgan, the attention of the garrison at Hatteras Inlet was directed to the north, where there was an increasing Confederate presence on Roanoke Island. On September 29, based on faulty intelligence, Colonel Rush Hawkins of the Ninth New York Volunteers and commander of ground forces on Hatteras Island, sent 600 troops of the Twentieth Indiana Regiment to establish a forward base at the village of Chicamacomico (south of the Bodie lighthouse and the abandoned Rebel fort at Oregon Inlet) to discourage a Confederate counterattack. Calling their post, "Camp Live Oak," the Twentieth Indiana settled in for what proved to be a short visit. The residents of Chicamacomico were, nevertheless, happy to have the Union troops there to protect them.

Where one end of Hatteras Island was considered a "slip of a desert," the other end was oddly thought of as an "Eden." One soldier with a literary bent, wrote about what he found at Chicamacomico:

The island contains some twelve houses, about 60 people; is three miles long and half a mile wide. It is a wild spot, and notwithstanding the white sand that covers most of its surface, is luxuriant with vegetation and a heavy growth of small timber. The trees are loaded with wild grapes, and the persimmon tree yields its fruits bountifully. Huge box trees, such as decorate the borders of our gardens, thrive in wild beauty. Whortleberry bushes are as thick as grapes. It reminds one of Robinson Crusoe and the Island of Juan de Fernandez, this semi-tropical life in this lone island, the men gathering grapes, fruitful as those brought from Canaan; oysters may be had upon the beach for the trouble of picking them up; and a contraband that followed us from Virginia, will do for the man Friday. To give still more resemblance, we have goats, pigs, chickens and ducks for our Robinson Crusoes to take care of.[60]

The preceding report notwithstanding, the Twentieth Indiana brought only one day's supply of provisions, and they anxiously awaited the Federal supply vessel, *Fanny*. But before the steam tug could off-load her cargo, she was engaged and captured by the *Curlew*, a former Albermarle Sound passenger steamer armed with a field piece at her bow. The acquisition of the *Fanny* was a modest retribution for the Confederate's loss of all their Outer Banks fortifications, but it was in fact "the first capture made by our arms of an armed war-vessel of the enemy [during the Civil War] and dispelled the gloom of recent disasters."[61]

Fanny's captured cargo, intended for the Union troops at Chicamacomico, was described as including 1,000 overcoats, 1,000 dress coats, 1,000 pairs of pantaloons and 1,000 pairs of shoes. There was no mention of food. Presumably, the quartermaster who dispatched the supplies for his "Robinson Crusoes" intended for them to be, at least, well dressed. In any event, the Confederate soldiers on Roanoke Island ended up being the ones who wore the Federal clothes. The more valuable product of the *Fanny* capture (besides the *Fanny* herself) was the intelligence gleaned from the Federal prisoners regarding the size and intention of the Federal force at Chicamacomico, which did much to agitate the commanding officers at Roanoke Island. It appeared to them that the Twentieth Indiana was preparing to launch an attack. Consequently, on October 5, Colonel A.R. Wright and Commodore W.F. Lynch took the initiative and organized six of their steamers, some from the Mosquito Fleet, towing barges loaded with troops from the Eighth North Carolina and the Third Georgia Infantry, and set out for Chicamacomico to roust the Federals from their camp. What ensued was the well-documented "Chicamacomico Races," which amounted to two days of Yankees and Rebels chasing each other up and down the Banks but accomplishing little of strategic value. It did cause the men to become very thirsty and tired, and it also dislodged the frightened residents of Chicamacomico who had only recently taken the oath of allegiance to the United States. A soldier with the Twentieth Indiana described the experience:

> The sun was shining on the white sand of the beach, heating the air as if it were a furnace…The first ten miles was [sic] terrible. No water, the men unused to long marches, the sand heavy, their feet sinking into it at every step. As the regiment pushed along man after man would stagger from the ranks and fall upon the hot sand.…But the most sorrowful

"…The most sorrowful sight of all was the Islanders leaving their homes from fear of the enemy."
Day one of the Chicamacomico Races. Outer Banks History Center.

sight of all was the Islanders leaving their homes from fear of the enemy. They could be seen in groups, sometimes with a little cart carrying their provisions, but mostly with nothing, fleeing for dear life; mothers carrying their babies, fathers leading along the boys, grandfathers and grandmothers straggling along from homes they had left behind. Relying on our protection, they had been our friends, but in an evil hour we had been compelled to leave them. We still toiled on, the heat most intense, and no water. Hunger was nothing in comparison with thirst. It was maddening. The sea rolling at our feet and nothing to drink.[62]

Leading the men of the Third Georgia down the island, Colonel Wright had it in his mind to "demolish the light at Hatteras if we do no more." Despite Wright's desires, he made the tactical mistake of not ordering ashore his North Carolina troops, who had been following in boats parallel to the soundside shoreline. His hesitation cost his men the chance to cut off the Yankee retreat. "Had we landed we would have taken them [Twentieth Indiana] all prisoners and blown up the Hatteras lighthouse. Bad Generalship on the part of Colonel Wright prevented it," wrote a disgusted Tar Heel soldier. In fairness, the broad shallows and shoals on the west side of Hatteras Island made it difficult for the Eighth North Carolina to get close enough to land. Fortunately for the lighthouse, darkness intervened. When the Confederates made camp at Kinnakeet, six miles north of the unlighted tower, it was as far as they were going to get. By midnight, the exhausted Union troops arrived at the lighthouse after marching 28 miles. "Here we found water, and using the lighthouse as a fort, we encamped for the night, and woke up next morning feeling like sand-crabs, and ready, like them, to go into our holes, could we find them," wrote an Indiana soldier.

The next day reinforcements and the shallow draft gunboat, *Monticello*, chased the Southerners back up the beach. Before retiring to Roanoke Island, Colonel Wright and his men passed the rubble of the 90-foot tall Bodie Island Lighthouse.[63] He failed in his primary mission to topple the Hatteras lighthouse, but Wright must have found some satisfaction in having previously destroyed the three-year old lighthouse at Oregon Inlet. His accomplishment, however, was unfortunate for the graceful tower.

A report describing the destruction of the Bodie lighthouse made its way to Washington, where it landed on the desk of Treasury Secretary, Salmon P. Chase. Chase was the ex-officio president of the Light House Board and although, in the span of 30 days his department had reclaimed four Southern lighthouse towers—Cape Hatteras, Bodie Island, Ocracoke Island and Beacon Island—two had been totally destroyed (one by the Union Navy). The rate of loss was alarming. Lenses and lamps could be replaced but if 50 percent of the 100 or more Southern light towers were destroyed, it would take the government a century to replace them. On October 17, Chase sent a letter to the War Department requesting that something be done to protect the Cape Hatteras Lighthouse. One immediate result was that some junior officers of Colonel Hawkins' detachment on Hatteras began questioning local residents living in the vicinity of the lighthouse about the lens and lamps and who was responsible for their disappearance. As for getting the lighthouse relit, because of organizational changes made by President Lincoln within his Cabinet

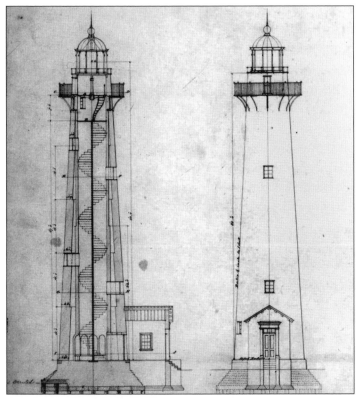

The 1858 Bodie Island Lighthouse (the second at that location), which exhibited a rotating, third-order lens manfactured by Lemonnier, Sauter & Co. of Paris. The graceful tower was destroyed by Confederate troops retreating from Hatteras Island to Roanoke Island in 1861. The lighthouse was located on the south side of Oregon Inlet, not part of Bodie Island at all, but the northern extension of Hatteras. National Archives.

and senior general staff, six months passed before anything was accomplished.

Changes were also taking place in the Confederate Light House Establishment in Richmond. A few weeks after the loss of Hatteras Island to the Union, Treasury Secretary Memminger appointed Thomas E. Martin, previously a clerk in the Lighthouse Bureau, to be Chief of the Lighthouse Bureau ad interim, replacing Commander Ebenezer Farrand, who returned to service with the Confederate Navy.[64] Martin took over a Lighthouse Bureau that, in effect, had no operating lighthouses. Martin's duties—besides fielding letters from keepers wanting back wages—were to keep track of all the lighthouse property that was, by then, scattered about in storehouses throughout the Southern coast. In November, Martin sent out a circular to all of his lighthouse superintendents requesting them to prepare and send an inventory of all lighthouses, beacons, light vessels, buoys and employees in their districts. The letter began on an optimistic note:

> It is desirable to have in the possession of the Bureau, as far as possible, correct information of the Lt. Ho. Property in the Confederate States so that when the operation of the Lt. Ho. Establishment may be resumed the actual wants in the various districts may be more easily ascertained.[65]

From Elizabeth City, W.C. Davis answered Martin that all of the lights in his district were extinguished and "Body's Island Light at Oregon Inlet" had been destroyed; lenses, lamps and other property were stored in the Customs House and, "it would be well to have someone there to look after the property." No letter responding to the circular from Superintendent H.F. Hancock appears to have survived, but it is known that the lenses from Hatteras and the Pamlico Sound were safely ensconced in the warehouse of John Myers & Sons at the Washington waterfront. Beaufort Superintendent Josiah Bell reported having, in his charge, all of the lenses and lighting apparatus of the two lighthouses there, as well as some buoys, but that one was left in the harbor to assist small craft. The three buoys on the outside bar of Beaufort Inlet were another matter altogether since they were large and dangerously close to the ship(s) of the Union Blockading Squadron. Bell estimated it would cost $100 to retrieve them, which he accomplished a month later with the exception of the most seaward buoy, which was "in such a close proximity to the Blockade that it was deemed impractical to undertake to get it." The remaining outer buoy was apparently the most expensive to retrieve since the final cost for the other two was just $18.

At Wilmington, Customs Collector J.T. Miller informed acting-chief Thomas Martin that aside from the extinguished and dismantled lanterns along the Cape Fear River, "Buoys have either 'broken adrift' or been removed by the Military authorities. The two Light Vessels in this District are the '*Arctic*' formerly stationed on Frying Pan Shoals and the 'Horse Shoe Shoal' light vessel. The '*Arctic*' is in fine condition and could be used at any moment, the latter requires some repairs. I have been informed that the '*Arctic*' has been transferred to the War Department but I have received no official communication to that effect," concluded Miller.

Her keel laid at the Philadelphia Navy Yard in 1854, the wooden hulled *Arctic* began her career as a Navy vessel. She was well known for her successful expedition to rescue American *Arctic* explorer, Elisha Kane, whose party had been trapped in ice off the coast of Greenland. In 1859, the *Arctic* was transferred to the Light House Board and she was assigned relief duty as a lightship in the Sixth District. Lightships of the period, like the *Arctic*, were stout ships, but they were not designed for permanent station-keeping like the bulbous, heavy keeled vessels of the modern era. Consequently, the *Arctic* was eyed by the Confederate Navy as a potential warship. At first it was thought that she could be "fitted-up" as a privateer, but those plans were abandoned. In a follow-up report to the Confederate Lighthouse Bureau, J.T. Miller wrote from Wilmington, North Carolina, that "Capt. Muse of the Navy Department now in command of our waters requests me to say that [the *Arctic*] would make a most excellent Gun Boat and would respectfully call the attention of the Department to the subject." The *Arctic*'s destiny, in fact, was to become an ironclad floating battery, armed with three guns in 1863, but just prior to the imminent siege of Fort Fisher the *Arctic* was sunk, ignominiously, as an obstruction in the Cape Fear River on Christmas Eve, 1864.[66]

Prior to her service in the CSS Navy, *Arctic* spent most of her time in relief of the old and leaking Frying Pan Shoals lightship. Captain Muse of the Confederate Navy Department had plans for her too, but they were not so glamorous as a gunboat. Customs Collector Miller informed the Lighthouse Bureau in Richmond that "the 'Frying Pan,' being very rotten and of very little use has been taken by the military authority, loaded with stone and is now anchored opposite Fort Caswell, ready to be sunken in case of emergency."

The Frying Pan Shoals lightship presents an excellent example of how the reasoned action of one side in the war was twisted into fodder for the propaganda machine of the other. The following account appeared in an early February edition of *Frank Leslie's Illustrated Newspaper* of an event that occurred on December 30, 1861.

> It will be remembered that sometime ago the rebels, with that insane love of purposeless mischief and malignity which has characterized them, stole the lightship from the Frying-Pan Shoals and anchored it, having, of course, destroyed the beacon, at the entrance of Cape Fear river, directly under the guns of Fort Caswell, being only about 150 yards distant from it. They commenced cutting ports in the stolen vessel, and were about to put heavy guns in her for the purpose of offensive operations.[67]

Knowing the Confederate's assessment that the lightship was "very rotten and of very little use" it is hard to imagine the Frying Pan being armed for offensive purposes. Nevertheless, she posed a perceived threat to the enemy who made plans to attack and sink her before the old hulk could inflict injury on the United States Navy. Capt. O.S. Gleeson, commander of the U.S. steamship *Mount Vernon*, dispatched two boat crews, commanded by H.J. Sturges and Alick Allen, masters of the U.S. Navy, and John P. Foot, to sneak over to the stone filled derelict to set her on fire. The newspaper story concluded:

> The night, although starlit, was exceedingly dark. The gallant men rowed in silence from the *Mount Vernon*—which was stationed about three-and-a-half miles from Fort Caswell—and reached the lightship undiscovered. In a few minutes the vessel was in flames, while our gallant men rowed off under heavy fire from the fort, which commenced as soon as the first flame was seen by the rebels, but which did no damage. The ship blazed all night, and when morning came not a vestige of her remained.[68]

Seven

BURNSIDE AND FEAR
SWEEP THE LOWCOUNTRY

Winter had set in—the first of the war—and it was time to turn one's attention to survival, not from the evils of the enemy but from the elements of nature: the cold shrieking wind and bitter rain, sleet and snow, and the quenchless fury of the sea. The nighttime Southern coast was dark, save for two dim, flickering steamer lamps that had been placed in the Hatteras lighthouse and the little beacon on the Cape. The sea lanes were empty as far as the eye could see, the Slue Channel across Diamond Shoals surrendered to Neptune's tempests. At Beaufort Inlet and the entrances to the Cape Fear River, gray-clad soldiers garrisoned in their respective earthen and masonry forts and blockading Union sailors at their moorings, peered at each other through the gloom. It was a time to wait.

But some ambitious men thought otherwise, men with visions of glory, of victory, of aggrandizement. One such man was Colonel Ambrose E. Burnside who conceived a plan to deliver and land up to 15,000 men to penetrate the sounds of North Carolina, "with a view to establishing lodgments" and the ultimate goal to threaten "the lines of transportation in the rear of the main [Confederate] army, then concentrating in Virginia."[69] Burnside convinced his former Illinois Central railroad boss and current general-in-chief of the Union armies, George B. McClellan, that his plan was what the North needed after the disaster at Bull Run (First Manassas). The operation was approved, and Burnside was promoted

The *Harper's Weekly* depiction of the Burnside fleet at Hatteras Inlet in January 1862.
Courtesy North Carolina Collection, UNC.

to General. The scheme had already succeeded.

The far-reaching orders later sent from McClellan to Burnside for the nation's "first major amphibious force" included: protection of the position at Hatteras Inlet; the capture of Roanoke Island and its entire Rebel force; the possession of the bottom ends of the Albermarle and Chesapeake Canal and the Dismal Swamp Canal (effectively cutting off Norfolk from the Confederacy); the capture of New Bern and the railroad to Goldsboro; the capture of Fort Macon and the opening of the port of Beaufort; and, if all went well, the destruction of the strategic Wilmington and Weldon Railroad, which was the vital supply line to the Confederate Army in Virginia. Remarkably, Burnside accomplished nearly every goal he was given except for the destruction of the Wilmington and Weldon. Even that might have been achieved but for the fact he, and much of his army, had been reassigned to help McClellan in Virginia. But because of later disasters in his career, Burnside is best remembered for his mutton-chop whiskers that added "sideburns" to the nation's lexicon.

Into the worst weather imaginable steamed and sailed Burnside's "motley fleet" of more than 80 vessels, bits and pieces from the emaciated

Union Navy—barges, tugs, coasting schooners, passenger and freight steamers, transport rafts, scows, colliers and water transports. Departing Newport News on January 11, the armada ferrying 11,000 seasick men bounced and pitched across the Graveyard of the Atlantic and over the tombs of lonely sunken ships. To silence his men, who grumbled about the unseaworthiness of their transports, the general rode aboard the smallest vessel in the fleet, the little propeller-driven tug Pickett.[70] Burnside's stature among his men was hard earned. "[The wind strengthened] to a terrible gale…. At times, it seemed as if the waves, which appeared to us mountain high, would ingulf [sic] us," Burnside later wrote.

Not all at once, but eventually, the expedition arrived at Hatteras Inlet, two days after they put to sea, where they next endured two weeks of furious gales while trying to enter the Pamlico Sound. Burnside's ships hove-to on the inside of the inlet's outer bar along Oliver's Channel, through which the Pamlico Sound alternately filled or emptied millions of gallons of water four times a day on the tides. When the wind and the tide were in opposition, the inlet boiled in a mass of confused, breaking seas. When the wind and tide worked together, the raging "8 to 9 mile-an-hour" current strained the heaviest anchor chains, causing some vessels to steam throughout the night "backwards and forwards" to avoid colliding with another vessel. Not all were successful. "This morning a steamer came crashing down upon us, running her bow into the afterpart of the 'New York,' and ripping clean off the after cabin…. Soon after, another came thumping away at our bows, smashing things," wrote a Massachussets soldier.[71]

Clinging to their rolling decks, recruits, both green in experience and complexion, sized up the beach their predecessors had fought valiantly to gain, a "lonely God-forsaken [place where] the water is never still and fair weather is never known; storms and seagulls are the only productions."[72] The observer was not entirely correct. Shipwrecks were also a prolific product of the Outer Banks and had been for nearly three hundred years. In January 1862, the sea claimed the Burnside Expedition's troop transports City of New York and Zouave, the floating battery Grapeshot and the horse carrier Pocahontas. One soldier wrote in his diary, "Of all forlorn stations to which the folly and wickedness of the Rebellion condemned our officers Hatteras was the most forlorn…This is the kind of soldiering that makes the boys think of home and of their mother."[73]

During the month of January, vessels of the Mosquito Fleet came down from Roanoke Island to observe (from a safe distance) the travails of Burnside's fleet as it slowly organized itself. Commodore W.F. Lynch, commander of Confederate Naval forces on North Carolina's sounds, anticipated the consequences of the potential fall of Roanoke Island in a letter to Navy Secretary Stephen Mallory, "Here is the great thoroughfare from Albermarle Sound and its tributaries, and if the enemy obtains lodgments or succeeds in passing here he will cut off a very rich country from Norfolk Market." The sensational news of the menacing Union flotilla also reached the tidewater towns along the Neuse, Pamlico, Pungo, Roanoke and Chowan rivers. On January 18, a New Bern newspaper reported that a steamer captain had sighted "42 gun-boats and 2 sailing vessels in the harbor at Hatteras." Another headline read, "An attack [is] thought to be certain."[74]

At Washington on the Pamlico, townspeople, who only nine months earlier had turned out to shower their fearless soldiers with flowers and patriotic speeches, were now resigned to an unthinkable invasion of "vile [Yankee] feet treading the soil of the Proud old North State."[75] There were additional concerns among the leaders of the town because on the waterfront were two Confederate gunboats under construction, one intended to be ironclad and mounted with six guns. Also, in the brick warehouse of John Myers and Sons, not far from the town docks, rested an inconspicuous pile of wooden boxes and loose bronze castings that constituted the Fresnel lens from the Cape Hatteras Lighthouse (among others). There had been rumors around town that Yankees were asking questions on Hatteras Island about the identities of the people involved in the theft of the lighthouse apparatus and its present hiding place. Someone suggested they look for it in Washington. When he found out, John Myers knew that sooner or later he and his sons would be paid a visit by Abe Lincoln's army.

Final preparations were unenthusiastically underway at Roanoke Island for the inevitable encounter with Burnside's force. The same problems that frustrated the commanders of the Outer Banks forts were being confronted again: a dire shortage of arms, ordnance, troops, morale and, most of all, time. Brigadier-General Henry Wise who was assigned command of the Confederate forces on the island in December later reported the condition of his stronghold: "The infantry were undrilled, unpaid, not sufficiently clothed and quartered, and were miserably armed with old flint muskets in bad order. In a word, the defenses were a sad farce of ignorance and neglect combined, inexcusable in any or all who were responsible for them."

Because the main shipping channel between the Pamlico Sound and the Albermarle Sound passed on the west side of Roanoke Island, through the shallow Croatan Sound, most of the island's defenses were positioned there, with four forts nearest the northern end. In anticipation of the Union Navy's determination to cross into the Albermarle, Commodore Lynch ordered the scuttling of schooners and the sinking of piles to block the channel between Fort Forrest on the mainland and the Roanoke Island forts. Nine privately owned vessels were seized from their owners and were loaded with stone or sand and sunk during 10 days at the end of January.

One of the vessels Lynch wished to get his hands on was the Roanoke River Lightship, which, though darkened, was on station at the mouth of the Roanoke River near Terrapin Point. This caused Joseph Ramsey, Customs Collector of the Plymouth District, much anguish because the lightship had recently been "made sharp" (refitted) at a cost of more than $1,000. "The use of the Roanoke River light Vessel…has been broached to me at different times. I have replied in the negative, unless advised to her use for that purpose by the Lt. House Bureau. At all events," as Ramsey protested in a February 7 letter to his superiors in Richmond, "…if it becomes necessary to use her either there or in this river for such purpose, all her fixtures that may be of use hereafter such as lamps & their masts, standing rigging, hatches &c. should be removed & such as could not be stored, be sold. I hope a sufficiency of vessels and pilings can be procured for all purposes without the necessity of her use…" Ramsey need not have worried. On the same day that he was composing his letter to Richmond, Burnside's ragtag armada had appeared over the horizon through the early morning fog, south of Roanoke Island, and within 24 hours began landing more than 10,000 men in opposition to Wise's even more motley 5,000-man army.

After a brief, but at times spirited, engagement, Burnside's overwhelming force swept over the small island. It took just half a day. Truthfully, the Confederate officers in command of Roanoke Island had given up weeks

Soldiers of the Ninth New York Regiment (a.k.a. Hawkins' Zouaves) storm a Confederate battery on Roanoke Island on February 8, 1862. Author's collection.

earlier and were further convinced their situation was utterly hopeless when all of the Federal fleet finally made it through Hatteras Inlet and into the calmer waters of Pamlico Sound. Brigadier General Wise was not even on the island during the attack. He was laid up in a Nags Head hotel with a painful bout of pleurisy. The capture of Roanoke Island was another feather in Burnside's favorite slouch hat and a catastrophic blow to the Confederacy. Three months later, Norfolk was evacuated by the Rebels, in part because of the loss of Roanoke Island, the Albermarle Sound, and its connecting canals to the Chesapeake, yielding to the North a great industrial navy yard and control of the extremely important James River waterway to Richmond.

Burnside's expedition next moved to squash the Mosquito Fleet, which had retired up the Pasquotank River to Elizabeth City after expending all its ammunition in the first hours of the battle of Roanoke Island. The Federal Navy easily penetrated Commodore Lynch's stone fleet blocking the channel through Croatan Sound. The owners of the scuttled schooners could not have been too pleased. Within 24 hours, the Mosquito Fleet was no more. Elizabeth City was captured, but not before some panicked townspeople, with the help of retreating Confederate troops, set fire to their property, burning two city blocks and other buildings on the perimeter of the town. Union troops attempted to put the fires out. Elizabeth City was completely deserted, a "dead town...dead as a graveyard."[76] Curiously, when the Federal soldiers combed through the storehouses, shops and offices of the town in their customary search for food, military supplies and documents that could provide valuable intelligence, they failed to find the lenses and lamps that had been removed the previous year from the Bodie Island Lighthouse and the Roanoke Marshes light. Just two months earlier, it had been reported that all of the material was stored in the Elizabeth City Customs House. Where had the apparatus gone?

Over the next two weeks, other minor operations swept through the Albermarle region and eventually up the Chowan River to the little port town of Winton, a strategic site thought to offer potential as a base for maneuvers on the Weldon railroad or to Norfolk. The first attempt to take Winton, led by Colonel Rush Hawkins and Navy Commander Stephen C. Rowan, caught their fleet of eight gunboats in a near fatal trap, but on the second incursion into the town, the Rebel force withdrew. A search of the town found that most of Winton's buildings were being used as military storehouses and quarters. Hawkins ordered the structures torched, but the fire consumed much of the town. "Court houses, churches, beautifully furnished dwellings with velvet carpets, pianos, &c., all sharing the same fate," wrote a Union private.[77] Just six months earlier after occupying Hatteras Island, Colonel Hawkins, desiring to promote the Union cause and allay fears that the U.S. Army intended to pillage and plunder private property, issued a proclamation to the citizens of North Carolina. "We come not to destroy, but to secure peace and uphold the law of the United States....Loyal citizens can enjoy their homes and property without fear of molestation."[78] The Hawkins proclamation did not save the citizens of Winton who, apparently, were not loyal enough.

The burning of Winton, and to a lesser extent Elizabeth City, sent a tidal wave of panic to the coastal towns along the "great thoroughfare" of Tar Heel sounds and tributaries, where a mass exodus commenced of those families with the means to travel to more secure inland communities. New Bern was the second largest port town on North Carolina's great inland sea, and the residents expected, even before the fall of Roanoke Island, that they would be the next objective of Burnside's rampage of terror and they were correct. The regularly scheduled westbound train on the Mullet Line (the Atlantic and North Carolina) from New Bern to Goldsboro was filled to capacity with the city's well-to-do, taking with them whatever valuables and keepsakes they could manage, and more trains had to be brought down to accommodate the crowds. The citizens of New Bern "fled so quickly that they left doors banging in the wind, family portraits in front yards, a piano in the middle of the street."[79] William Loftin, one of 4,000 Confederate soldiers awaiting Burnside's arrival, watched the fleeing New Bernians with disgust and wrote to his mother that they were "the worst frightened Dam set I ever saw in my life."

At Washington, North Carolina, one could visualize a scene similar to New Bern except that, without a railroad, the terrified, evacuating towns-folk rushed to the wharves. It was not the first time Washington residents had felt anxiety about an enemy on their doorstep. During the War of 1812, British troops landed on the Outer Banks and when word reached the waterfront town, Mrs. Thomas Blount sent a hastily scribed letter to President James Madison's wife, Dolley: "We are in hourly expectation of the British coming up here...I am so frightened that I scarce can write, the men flying to armes [sic] and the drums beating."[80] The same senti-ments might have been expressed in 1862 except that the white women and men of the town were mostly "flying" to friend's and relative's homes further inland, while runaway slaves were flying the other way—to free-dom in the east. Almost every day since January, the stern-wheel steamers, *Governor Morehead* and *Colonel Hill*, made runs on the Tar River between Washington, Greenville and Tarboro. Troops and supplies were being sent down river, while families, furniture and trunks of clothing went up.

Among the concerned citizens of Washington was the 36-year-old town physician, David T. Tayloe. He had keenly read the local secessionist newspaper, the *North Carolina Times*, keeping up with the disappoint-ments on the Outer Banks and making tentative plans in case of an emer-gency. He was likely to have been at the waterfront when the remnants of the Washington Grays returned home with their tails tucked between their legs, after the fall of Hatteras. Tayloe, like most men of the town, was first and foremost motivated to provide for the safety and well being of his wife and children. The bright, young doctor had been well educated. He graduated from the University of North Carolina in 1846, at age 20,

left: Colonel John Hargrove.
Courtesy Hargrove family, all
rights reserved, used by permission.
above: David T. Tayloe, MD.
Courtesy Tayloe family, all rights
reserved, used by permission.

and received a medical degree from the University of New York three years later. Tayloe was once described in a who's-who of Civil War military history as a "man of broad culture, an accomplished scholar in the classics and fond of poetry, philosophy and history." He was also considered "a devoted Southerner and a loyal North Carolinian." It must have been an unpleasant business for proud, patriotic Southerners like Tayloe to have to turn and run, to abandon his family home, his possessions and the medical practice he had worked so hard to build. Nevertheless, it hardly required a man of letters to plainly see what was ahead for his town.

Winton was the final outrage, the only proof anyone needed to know that wherever Burnside's men went the utter destruction and defilement of personal property would follow. Evacuation seemed the only recourse. As it happened, it was Tayloe's wife, the former Mary Elizabeth Grist, who suggested a place for the family to go, a place well inland. Mary Tayloe's aunt, Mary Williams Grist, had been married for 12 years to a wealthy, aristocratic plantation owner named John Hargrove, and they lived at

Hibernia, outside Townsville, North Carolina, in Granville County, near the Virginia border.[81] The fondness between aunt and niece was not the only bond that brought the two families together—the 47-year-old John Hargrove and the younger doctor had become good friends as well.

Before the disaster at Roanoke Island, the two Marys had probably corresponded about the prospect of the Tayloes' having to leave Washington. Mary Grist Hargrove offered Hibernia as a refuge. Making the 180-mile journey would be no simple matter, especially during the war.

Sometime during the months of January or February, the Tayloes, along with David's mother, Sally Ann, packed up their clothes, family heirlooms, important papers, children's toys and some food for the journey and carried it all by wagon to the steamer dock off of Front Street. A shoal draft stern-wheeler then took them up the Tar River to the inland port town of Tarboro. At Tarboro, after an overnight stay of a day or more, the family then transferred their belongings to the train station for the short rail spur to Rocky Mount. At Rocky Mount, they boarded a car on the crowded Wilmington and Weldon line heading north, and then changed again at Weldon for the Raleigh and Gaston line. Finally, at Ridgeway, in Warren County, the Tayloes changed trains yet again, this time for the Roanoke Valley Railroad, a spur line that terminated at Clarksville, Virginia, but which also ran through Townsville. Once at the station at Townsville, they would have been met by John and Aunt Mary, who would have come with a sufficient number of carriages, wagons and slave hands for the six mile journey to Hibernia, the Hargrove plantation. The arduous journey would have taken at least a week, possibly longer. At Hibernia they were quartered at the modest Clifton-Hanks house, unremarkable except for being rumored to be the birthplace of Mary Hanks, the mother of Abraham Lincoln.[82] Once the Tayloe family settled in, David Tayloe returned to Washington to continue tending to the sick, and possibly the wounded, for as long as he could. The Southern loyalist doctor at least felt more comfortable with his family at Hibernia—especially since his wife, Mary, had announced her Christmas surprise. She was expecting their second child.

But what if the Union army would someday reach Townsville? Tayloe must have thought to himself, *Well, that was unlikely to ever happen.*

Eight

The Federals Landed in Washington Yesterday

A t his command headquarters on Roanoke Island in February, General Ambrose Burnside finally got the recognition he had been seeking. Before him on his desk was a bundle of salutatory letters from the President, Congress, the Secretary of War, and numerous legislative assemblies of Union states, offering commendations and praise for his victories on the coast of North Carolina. The news of the fall of Roanoke Island and the destruction of the North Carolina Navy relieved Abraham Lincoln. The victory in North Carolina also awakened the North from its despondency over the tragedies at Manassas and Leesburg, corruption within the War Department and McClellan's glacial advances toward Richmond. To his credit, Burnside did not spend too much time enjoying his newfound fame. Also on his desk were charts of the Pamlico Sound, the Neuse River and the approaches to New Bern. His general orders were but half completed.

F our significant events took place during a three-day period in early March, 1862. On March 9, the historic first engagement between two ironclad warships, the USS *Monitor* and the CSS *Virginia* (formerly Merrimac) at Hampton Roads lasted for four hours at close range, with no clear victor but with disastrous implications for wooden warships. The captain of the USS *Potomac* later wrote that "the face of naval warfare looks the other way now—and

General A.E. Burnside at camp, most likely outside of Fredricksburg after his North Carolina operations. Library of Congress photo.

the superb frigates and ships of the line…are very much diminished in their proportions." Captain John A. Dahlgren (later Rear Admiral) put it more succinctly: "Now comes the reign of iron." Two days later President Lincoln, frustrated by McClellan's indecisiveness, demoted the exceedingly cautious General from general-in-chief to the commander of only the Army of the Potomac. Also, on March 11, the chairman of the U.S. Light House Board, Rear Admiral William B. Shubrick, dispatched an engineer named W.J. Newman to Cape Hatteras to determine what would be necessary to re-establish the lighthouse. Hatteras Island was still considered part of the front lines of the war and Newman's safety was an issue. Shubrick expressed his concerns in a letter to the Union officer commanding at Hatteras Inlet: "[Newman] will call upon you to which your assistance in the matter and this Board will be under many obligations to you if you will furnish him with the necessary protection and facilities for making an examination of the Lt. House tower, lantern and building with a view to a speedy relighting of that important point."[83]

Finally, on the same day of McClellan's demotion and Shubrick's letter, General Burnside launched his expedition to New Bern with a combined Army, Navy and Marine force of 12,000 troops and 13 warships and transports. Much of the experience and one ironic similarity that occurred in the capture of Roanoke Island contributed to the effectiveness of the New Bern operation: amphibious landings were again made from raft-like launches towed by shoal draft steam vessels; Naval gunboats again shelled the shoreline in advance of the landing parties; Confederate soldiers again retreated without hesitation; and, like General Wise during the Battle of Roanoke Island, the Confederate general in overall command of the Confederate forces at New Bern, R.C. Gatlin, was confined to his quarters with an illness during the entire engagement. The battle for New Bern did result in greater casualties than the relative few for both sides at Roanoke Island with 578 Confederates killed, wounded or missing and Federal losses between 440 and 471.[84] New Bern was fully occupied on March 14, 1862, two days after Union troops landed on the southern shore of the Neuse River.

If the white citizens in neighboring Eastern North Carolina communities were vexed by the stories that Union troops torched the towns of Elizabeth City and Winton (accurate or not), what happened after the fall of New Bern represented the worst imaginable ignominy—an uncontrolled sacking of the town that lasted for two days, conducted by runaway slaves and poor whites, joined by drunken and disorderly sailors and soldiers of Burnside's fleet. Furniture, china, jewelry, money, clothing, carpets, garden implements and foods were carried off in enormous quantities. General Burnside finally stationed guards about the town and threatened the thieves with incarceration, regardless of race, if caught plundering. Even before it was brought under control, Southern sympathizers and Confederate spies had delivered the horrific details of the pillaging of New Bern to the authorities at Washington.

With the fall of New Bern on March 14, the evacuation of Washington became a military, rather than a predominantly civilian stampede. Arms, ammunition, naval stores and official military documents were hastily gathered and taken down to the waterfront. The Confederate defenses lining the approaches to the town along both banks of the Pamlico River were then abandoned and all of Beaufort County's

Secretary of the Treasury
Salmon P. Chase. Chase was
ex-officio president of the
U.S. Light House Board.
Library of Congress.

gray-clad troops boarded the same two steamers that had previously
taken the townsfolk up the Tar River in the direction of Greenville.
Among the citizens who had already departed was H.F. Hancock, town
druggist, former U.S. Collector of Customs and current Confederate
Lighthouse Bureau District Superintendent. Hancock's hurried escape
suggests he believed his duties as Superintendent were finished, since the
lighthouses in his district no longer functioned; or possibly he feared he
was subject to Federal recrimination for supervising the removal of the
Cape Hatteras Lighthouse Fresnel lens; or perhaps Hancock worried
for the safety of his wife and six children. It is even conceivable that he
was a Unionist at heart and wanted the lens back in Federal possession.
Whatever was occupying Hancock's mind during the late winter of
1862, he left town in such a hurry he overlooked an extremely important responsibility. Before departing Washington, Hancock neglected to
see to the security of the Cape Hatteras lens, still stored in the Myers
warehouse on Front Street, probably the first place a curious Union
soldier would look after landing at the town docks.

That the Cape Hatteras lens remained hidden in the Myers building was a piece of intelligence already in the possession of General Burnside, probably learned and conveyed by African-American freedmen in the service of the general.[85] The recovery of the lens was not a specific goal listed on Burnside's general orders, but for months it had been the fervent desire of Treasury Secretary Salmon Chase.

Since the previous autumn, Chase had made persistent appeals to the military authorities to recapture the lens so the lighthouse could be re-established. In fact, since the disappearance of the lens, there had been a high degree of curiosity and concern among the various branches of the Federal government, the lighthouse establishment and the maritime industry that resulted in an almost "grail-like" quest to find the highly valued, and symbolic apparatus. Other southern lighthouses were without their lenses too, but the Hatteras tower was the first to be recaptured and it was also widely considered to be the most important to the merchant fleet. The Presidents and officers of the principal insurance companies of New York had protested to Secretary Chase that Cape Hatteras was "a very important point on our coast and it is desirable the Light be re-established as speedily as possible."[86] Shortly after the battle for New Bern, General Burnside learned of the rapid withdrawal of Rebel soldiers from the defensive positions protecting the approaches to Washington. It seemed a good time to go to Washington and collect the Cape Hatteras lens for its rightful owner, the United States government, and maybe, another feather for old Burnside's slouch hat.

On Thursday afternoon, March 20, a small expedition consisting of three shoal-draft gunboats and an army transport steamer slipped their moorings in the Neuse River for the 16-hour journey to Washington. The naval contingent was commanded by Lieutenant Alexander Murray aboard the USS *Louisiana*, while Colonel T.G. Stevenson lead eight companies of the Twenty-fourth Regiment Massachusetts Volunteers. En route, the warships passed some of the dubious accomplishments of the Confederate Light House Bureau. Protruding from the river's surface were masts and lanterns of the light vessel formerly stationed at the Neuse River entrance and the two boats at Northwest Point and Southwest Point of Royal Shoal, all ineffectively sunk in the channel of the Neuse. They also passed the extinguished screwpile lighthouse at

A scene similar to Washington's waterfront in March 1862. The side-wheel steamer shown is much larger than the stern-wheel river transport *Governor Morehead*. National Archives.

Pamlico Point. If the sailors and soldiers of the Washington expedition needed any additional justification for their mission, navigating the ink-like darkness of the Pamlico Sound and the dangers of its unmarked shoals should have provided sufficient impetus.

At the time, the lower sections of the Neuse and Pamlico rivers would not have been completely without navigational aids. Despite the ongoing war, the first of spring was shad season, when millions of the valuable food fish made their annual spawning runs up into the two freshwater estuaries. In previous years, thousands of slave boatmen and fishermen, organized in small to moderately sized groups, would have worked the waters with dragnets, often fishing 24 hours a day. In 1862, however, the antebellum rhythms and routines of the Carolina tidewater region had been turned upside down by the incursion of Federal troops and the mass exodus of runaway slaves. Still, the men of the Washington expedition would have heard the distant strains of chanteys being sung and seen the occasional glow of lanterns bobbing from the low decks of fishing cooners, periaugers and shad galleys, manned by fishermen who had one leg still shackled in slavery but their eyes focused on the ever-closer horizon of freedom.

At about the same time the *Louisiana* and her consorts were steaming out of the Neuse River, the wharf at Washington was in a frenzied state of activity as men struggled to launch the unfinished Confederate gunboat from its stocks, so it could be towed up the Tar River and out of Union hands.[87] With her boiler kept stoked for a potential quick departure, the sternwheeler *Governor Morehead* was tied alongside the quay, nearby.

Just yards away in a brick warehouse on Front Street, 68-year-old John Myers looked with despair and disgust at the large quantity of lighthouse apparatus, including the glass lens from Cape Hatteras. Myers felt disgust because the faint-hearted lighthouse superintendent, H.F. Hancock, should have taken care of the matter. He felt despair because, as a true Southern loyalist, he knew that if the lenses were not taken away immediately the material would soon be back in the possession of the enemy. Myers was not going to allow that to happen. As the Federal gunboats from New Bern neared the Pamlico River, Myers and his three sons had the lighthouse material transferred to the deck of the *Governor Morehead*.

Among the last of the Washingtonians to step on board the steamer bound for Tarboro was the town physician, David T. Tayloe.

Just after daybreak on Friday morning, March 21, the Union flotilla arrived at the Confederate obstructions in the river across from Hill's Point, about five miles down river from the town. After searching for torpedoes or explosive caps, army engineers blasted a channel through the sunken pilings and the three gunboats, with two companies of the 24th Massachussetts and the regimental band, proceeded to the Washington waterfront. There they were met by the mayor of Washington, Isaiah Respess who informed the commanding officers that the town was abandoned by the Confederates and undefended. As the troops disembarked, a curious thing happened. The invaders were welcomed with open arms by hundreds of Washington citizens, many of whom had regaled their hometown Confederate unit, the Washington Grays, less than a year earlier. The townsfolk put on a good face for their conquerors for several reasons. One, according to Commander Rowan, U.S. Naval commander of the North Carolina Sounds, they had been convinced by "rabid secessionists…that we intended to burn the town, and this fear alone may induce many to seem what they are not." Lieutenant Murray was told that there was "a deep rooted affection for the old Union, and not a little animosity to its enemies…not being diminished by the importation of troops from a distant State [Georgia]."[88] The reason that the Massaachusetts troops were able to state that "the reception given our people is more hopeful than any we have yet witnessed in these waters" and that two-thirds of the Washington population, mostly secessionists (including the town doctor), had "seen fit to leave for the interior," according to a correspondent for the *Boston Journal*. A heartwarming reception notwithstanding, the Federals were terribly disappointed by what they did not find in Washington—the first-order Fresnel lens from the Cape Hatteras Lighthouse. Commander Rowan sent the following report to his superior, Flag-Officer L.M. Goldsborough, commander of the North Atlantic Blockading Squadron:

> I have to regret that the lens has not yet been returned. The authorities assured [Lieutenant] Murray that the lens was taken away without their knowledge or consent and carried to Tarboro in a little steamboat. I propose holding the authorities responsible for the return of the lens before I promise protection to the inhabitants… I shall, if possible, ascertain the guilty parties and take all the property I can find that will reimburse the Government.[89]

For a second time, the Federals failed to catch up with the lighthouse lens, this time by just a matter of hours. With the apparatus on its way to the interior of the state, its recovery would become patently more difficult. General Burnside was worried the failure could tarnish his spotless record on the North Carolina coast. To Edwin Stanton, Secretary of War, Burnside wrote, "The light belonging to the Hatteras light-house, which had been in Washington [N.C.] for some time, was removed up the Tar River in a very light-draught steamer, owned by one of the citizens, who was a large property-owner there. Notice has been given him that he must return the light or his property will be seized or destroyed." It remained to be seen whether the new "keeper" of the Hatteras lens could be compelled by threats to return the property. The Light House Board was under intense pressure to re-establish the light at the Cape, many of the complaints coming from George Blunt, de facto ombudsman of navigators and masters of ships plying the mid-Atlantic waters. The Cape Hatteras Lighthouse had been under Federal control for more than seven months, yet still it remained unlighted. At the least, the missing lens was an embarrassment for the government. At the worst, ships could be lost on the Carolina shoals—and, in fact, some were.

The day after the peaceful capitulation of Washington, the *Governor Morehead*, with its prized lighthouse cargo, was safely tied to the wharf at Tarboro. John Myers was already aware that he had become the target of the United States government's ire, the man who would be held accountable for the second disappearance of the Hatteras lens. Myers, nevertheless, felt no fear or remorse. He wrote the following letter to Christopher G. Memminger, secretary of the Confederate Treasury:

> Dear Sir,
>
> At the commencement of the present war all of the Lighthouse fixtures from Pamlico Sound were placed in our store by the Collector of the Dist. of Washington. As he left without removing them into the interior we took the responsibility of removing them from Washington to this place. We suggest that you send a special messenger to care for them as they are not secure here. The Federals landed in Washington yesterday, took possession and declared that if the Lighthouse fixtures were not returned "Myers" property would be held responsible. The property will not be returned.
>
> Respectfully, Your Obedient Servants, John Myers & Sons

As a final expression of his indignation, Myers underscored "will not."

The letter from steamboat owner, John Myers, to Treasury Secretary C.G. Memminger. In closing, Myers emphatically stated that the Hatteras lens would not be surrendered to the Federals at Washington, N.C. Record Group 365 National Archives.

Nine

"I HAVE HAD THE APPARATUS REMOVED TO A GOOD STORE HOUSE"

It would have taken the *Governor Morehead* about 10 to 12 hours with sufficient water under her keel to make the run from Washington to Tarboro. As the stern-wheeler coursed the slow-moving, coffee-colored waters of the Tar, she periodically passed plantation landings along the moss-draped banks of the river, where slaves observed the steady procession of frightened Rebels making their way upstream. The slaves seemed to appear unconcerned, indifferent, even uncomprehending, and must have had to strain to suppress their glee. They were just biding their time. Under cover of darkness, many would slip the tethers of slavery and of their master's bateaus, flats and rafts, for the trip downriver to freedom. On board the steamer, Dr. David Tayloe and John Myers were probably oblivious to the secret plans of the blacks on shore—they were discussing a secret of their own. Tayloe was probably familiar with the steamer's cargo of lighthouse lenses from the Outer Banks and the Pamlico Sound since, he, being the town doctor, and H.F. Hancock, being the town druggist (as well as the Collector and District Superintendent of Lights) surely discussed the infamous contraband that had been hidden in Washington. Tayloe was likely to be embarrassed for Hancock who had displayed bad form by rushing out of town without the lens being secured, and as he listened to Myers complain about having to do the Collector's work for him, the doctor began to formulate a plan.

Upon landing at Tarboro, Myers delivered the lighthouse lenses and lamps to the care and protection of the local Army quartermaster, Captain George H. Brown, and suddenly, the Confederate officer had a real problem on his hands. Brown probably knew little or nothing about lighthouses, but he did know the U.S. government would soon be on its way to Tarboro to retrieve its property. Thus far, except for weekly transfer of troops, munitions and supplies between the rail head and the steamer docks, Tarboro had remained the genteel, architecturally pleasing place it had been since Revolutionary times. With the Cape Hatteras Lighthouse lens in town, Tarboro was likely to be exposed to the same depredations suffered by Elizabeth City, Winton and New Bern—especially considering the threats that had been made against Washington if the lens was not surrendered. Captain Brown wasted no time and took from his desk a pen and paper and composed in a steady, flowing script, the following letter to the Honorable Ebenezer Farrand in Richmond:[90]

Sir:

I have to inform you that I have received the entire apparatus of the Hatteras light at this point and placed it in as secure a place as possible.

The apparatus was removed some time since from Hatteras and stored in the warehouse of Msrs. John Myers & Son at Washington, NC., who have brought it to this place & put it in my charge.

I would suggest that an Agent be sent on immediately to attend to the packing and forwarding the above as the Federals are in force at Washington and threaten the private property of the parties who took part in sending it away if it is not returned. I have been informed that force would be used to possess themselves of it at all risks, and even threaten the destruction of the town of Washington if the apparatus was not forthcoming. The Light fixtures referred to are, as you must be aware, very valuable having cost several thousand dollars.

I therefore deem it important to apprise you of the circumstances in detail.

Your immediate attention as herein requested will doubtless

Tarboro N. C.ª
March 23 1862

Hon E. Farrand
Richmond Va. Sir.

I have to inform you that I have received the entire apparatus of the Hatteras light at this point and placed it in as secure a place as possible. The apparatus was removed some time since from Hatteras and stored in the warehouse of Messrs. John Myers & Son at Washington N.C. who have brought it to this place & put it in my charge. I would suggest that an Agent be sent on immediately to attend to the packing and forwarding of the above, as the Federals are in force at Washington and threaten the private property of the parties who took part in sending it away, if it is not returned, & have intimated that force would be used to possess themselves of it at all risks, and even threaten the destruction of the town of Washington, if the apparatus was not forthcoming. The Light & fixtures referred to are [as] you must be aware very valuable & coming Cost several thousand dollars. I therefore deem it important to apprise you of the circumstances in detail. Your immediate attention as herein requested will doubtless redound to the interest of the Confederate States.

I have the honor to be
Very Respectfully
Your Obt Servant.
G. H. Brown
Capt & A. Q. M. C. S. A.

P.S.
The probable Cost of getting the fixtures to this point will be ninety dollars. The agent that is sent here to superintend the transportation of the above should be provided with funds to defray the expenses.
G. H. Brown
Capt & A. Q. M. C. S. A

Letter of Captain George H. Brown, CSA, a quartermaster at Tarboro, NC, sent to Ebeneezer Farrand, former chief of the Confederate Lighthouse Bureau on March 23, 1862. Record Group 365 National Archives.

redound to the interest of the Confederate States.

I have the honor to be

Very Respectfully,

Your Obt. Servant.

G.H. Brown

Capt., AQM, CSA

P.S.: The probable cost of getting the fixtures to this point will be Ninety Dollars. The agent that is sent here to superintend the transportation of the above should be provided with funds to defray the expenses.

Thomas Martin must have received a telegram from Washington the same day the Hatteras lens had been removed from the town. He had already made arrangements to take possession of the lens when Brown mailed the above letter. Martin dispatched a letter to the quartermaster on the same day, which was presented by his "agent," sent to Tarboro to take care of the lighthouse property. The agent must have been the only man Martin could find on such short notice, a soon to be discovered disreputable character named, J.B. Davidge. It took Davidge the better part of a week to make the rail journey from Richmond to Tarboro and, by then, Captain Brown had begun repacking the lenses for shipment, although at that point the quartermaster was still not sure where the lighthouse property was headed.

The fact that Captain Brown felt it was necessary to pack the lighthouse apparatus in boxes filled with cotton raises an interesting question. Why did the material require additional packing? In June of 1861, Superintendent Hancock listed an expense of $17 for "Boxes, Cotton &c for packing." It is possible that the first packing of the lenses, or the individual cata-dioptric panels, was done poorly or quickly, causing the glass prisms to shift or be loosened during transit. "When you take the panels apart they become very susceptible to damage if you don't know what you're doing," said Jim Woodward, Cleveland-based lighthouse and lens expert. "There are some very specific ways you attach it and wedge it and support it inside a box. The frames will actually splay. They'll start to move away from each other just by the weight of it. If it's laying down, the sides of the panel want to lay down. As soon as that happens, the glass prisms fall out. Neither the mechanic nor the lighthouse keeper would have appreciated the complexities of the crating process. And probably they thought they were doing a really fine job by putting it in a box and filling it up with cotton."

With the repacking of the lenses underway, the Tarboro quartermaster wanted to know from J.B. Davidge what his plans were for the immediate transportation of the property to a place of safety. Davidge seemed to have no plans but to quench his thirst at the local ale house. Captain Brown was incredulous and wrote to Richmond that Davidge "has been unfit to attend to any kind of business since his arrival... I find that his habits are those of intemperance & though a delicate matter I feel my duty as an officer to furnish the department with the facts of the case. I saw Mr. Davidge yesterday and remonstrated with him on his course, urging the necessity of having the apparatus removed to a point of safety as speedily as possible, and he promised to attend to it at once, but today he has made no effort whatever for its removal."

Somehow, between the delivery of the Hatteras apparatus to Tarboro, and Captain Brown's dissatisfaction with the agent from Richmond, Dr. David Tayloe introduced himself to the Confederate quartermaster. Tayloe had apparently been stuck in Tarboro and unsuccessful in his efforts to arrange transportation to his family's safe haven in Granville County. The Washington doctor proposed an idea to Captain Brown that would serve both their needs and those of the Confederate States of America. Tayloe could take the Cape Hatteras lens into Granville County, a secure place, extremely unlikely ever to feel the shoe-leather of Federal troops. Brown thought it a good idea, especially considering the habits of Mr. Davidge, and wrote the acting Chief of the Lighthouse Bureau. "I can get a very responsible gentleman here to attend to the conveying of [the lens] to a place of safety in this state free of charge for his services if you can furnish means of transportation," Brown told Thomas Martin. "It will require a large Box Car as there are about 45 boxes and some pieces of castings. The place I would suggest sending the articles is in Granville county in this State on the Rail Road where they can be stored at a small expense in a good warehouse. I would suggest therefore that a large Box Car be sent

"Duplicate"

Received Tarboro NC. April 12/1862 from Capt S.H. Brown Asst Q.M. C.S. Army, Forty Four Boxes, 1 Two Cases containing the Lens belonging to the Hatteras Light House, also Sixty Four pieces of Castings. Fourteen Pieces of Fixtures & two Sheets of Copper appertaining to the same, all of which I promise to deliver at a point of safety in Granville County N.C. in as good order as received (all risks of transportation excepted).

D. S. Taylor

44 Boxes.
2 Cases.
64 Ps. Castings.
14 Ps. Fixtures.
2 Shts Copper.

to this place at as early a date as possible. The enemy below this point are still threatening property etc. if the apparatus is not delivered up. Your immediate attention will facilitate the matter." The pressure Captain Brown must have felt to move the contraband property out of Tarboro can be discerned in the deterioration of his exceptional handwriting over successive letters to Martin in Richmond. In the meantime, J.B. Davidge disappeared from Tarboro with the money entrusted to him to pay for the transportation of the lens.

Two weeks passed before Martin could requisition a railroad car in Richmond for the single purpose of transporting the Cape Hatteras lens to Granville County. Among the many acute shortages handicapping the Confederacy in 1862 was the serious lack of rolling stock. A shortage so profound, "that many railroad men predicted the utter breakdown of the Southern Roads within a short time."[91] What railroad cars were operating that spring were desperately needed to transport heavy cannon and field artillery, iron plates, fittings, and steam engines for CSS Navy ironclads, and rails for the South's dilapidated tracks—all being forged by the overworked Tredegar Iron Works on the James River in Richmond. The staff of the South's lighthouse establishment most likely searched the yards and pleaded with local dispatchers for anything that could be spared for Tarboro. The car they finally obtained might have been intended for spare parts but it nevertheless rolled, and to Martin's credit, he accompanied it to Tarboro. The fact that the chief of Confederate lighthouses made a special trip to meet Brown and Tayloe is a clear indication of how anxiously the Richmond government wanted to keep the Cape Hatteras lens out of the Union's possession, although Martin may also have been looking for Davidge and his money. Nevertheless, the Henry-Lepaute first-order Fresnel apparatus was much more than an illuminating device for a lighthouse, it had become a symbolic pawn in the war.

Before the lighthouse property was loaded into the box car, Tayloe signed a receipt for material:

Duplicate
Received Tarboro N.C., April 12, 1862 from Capt. G.H. Brown Asst. Q.M C.S. Army Forty Four Boxes & Two Cases containing the Lens belonging to the Hatteras Lighthouse, also Sixty Four pieces of Castings, Fourteen pieces of Fixtures & two sheets of Copper appertaining to the same, all of which I promise to deliver at a point of safety in Granville County N.C. in as good order as received (all risks of transportation excepted).
[signed] D. T. Tayloe
44 Boxes
2 Cases
64 Ps. Castings
14 Ps. Fixtures
2 Shts Copper

Tayloe began what was to become an arduous journey to Townsville in Granville County on April 14. Shortly after the doctor departed the Tarboro depot, Captain Brown wrote another letter to Martin, who had since begun his return trip to Richmond. Brown wrote, "Dr. Tayloe left this morning with the car. I furnished him with transportation ticket for 1

An engine and boxcar near Union Mills, Virginia. The Roanoke Valley Railroad to Townsville crossed similar trestles. Library of Congress Photo.

Box Car cont'ng L.H. fixtures etc. and he had no difficulty at all in getting away from here."

Brown was probably relieved to see Tayloe and the lighthouse apparatus leave town. Enemy informants could have been expected to get word down to the Union lines at Washington or New Bern that the Cape Hatteras lens was no longer held in Tarboro, thus saving the pretty little town from the torches of Yankee rogues. But the Confederate quartermaster assumed too much about Tayloe's avoidance of any difficulties. His box car, which Tayloe later described as being "in very bad order," was transferred to a northbound Wilmington and Weldon Line engine at Rocky Mount and it broke down just eight miles north of the town. All of the cargo had to be unloaded on the side of the tracks while another car was procured. Tayloe was not specific about how long it took, although in a later report of his mission he wrote that "after much delay and trouble I succeeded in procuring another car and transferring the cargo." On the road again, Tayloe next encountered complications at Weldon where he had the second box car switched to an engine headed west for the Raleigh and Gaston line. Apparently, Tayloe was also transporting some of his family's possessions that he managed to remove from his Washington home on the eve of the

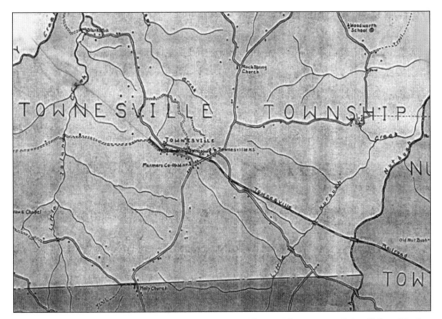

Townsville, North Carolina, depicted in a 1925 map. Hibernia Plantation and the Clifton-Hanks house were located between the "S" and "H" of the word, Township. The old Roanoke Valley Railroad line was rebuilt after the Civil War and is shown on this map terminating in Townsville. North Carolina Archives.

Federal occupation, but the doctor had no official manifest stating the property was his. In the stressful environment of wartime, Southern officials, who were ordinarily gracious and accommodating, became suspicious of everyone and such was the case of the railroad agent at Tarboro, who observed Tayloe loading property into the car other than what was listed on his receipt from Captain Brown. When Tayloe arrived at Weldon he was detained by the agent there who demanded that he pay freight on his personal property "or be compelled to leave the car there." Tayloe attributed his problems in Weldon to "a malicious note to the agent [at Weldon] from the agent at Tarboro." So much for serving his country.

It took Tayloe a full week to make the rail journey from Tarboro to Townsville, a length of time that must have been inordinately slow because the doctor made a point to mention in his report that he "had many difficulties and detentions on the Road." Besides the South's dire shortage of rolling stock, there existed an even greater shortage of rails. Iron that ordinarily would have been forged into track at the Tredegar Works and other rolling mills in peacetime was being wrought into weapons of war and the result was the rapid deterioration of the Confederate rail system. The tracks were in such poor condition in some areas that trains were forced to slow to a crawl, both in an effort to preserve the rails and to keep the cars from being derailed. Tayloe would have experienced such delays. There was a story told by a man who had traveled the Wilmington, Charlotte and Rutherford line during the war who reported that "the speed of the train was so slow and stops so frequent that the train was repeatedly passed by an old Negro laden with farm implements. To each and every invitation from the passengers to get on the train as it overtook him, the Negro politely responded: 'Much obliged, Boss, but I hain' got time.'"[92]

After having his boxcar switched to an engine of the Roanoke Valley Railroad at Ridgeway, North Carolina, Dr. Tayloe finally pulled in to the station at Townsville with the illuminating apparatus of the Cape Hatteras Lighthouse on Friday evening, April 18. It was Good Friday. The lens had by then traversed 240 miles of sound, rivers and Carolina countryside, but its odyssey was far from over. Tayloe's in-law and friend, Col. John Hargrove, was informed of the train's arrival by a slave who heard the distant wail of the steam whistle as the engine crossed the trestle at Nutbush Creek. When the Tayloe and Hargrove families arrived by carriage at the Townsville depot they were surprised to find that the doctor had arrived with the lens of the Hatteras lighthouse in his possession.

Finally reunited with his pregnant wife, infant son and mother after so many weeks, Tayloe took the weekend to rest. On Easter Sunday afternoon, he sat down to write his report to both Thomas Martin in Richmond and Captain Brown in Tarboro. To Martin he concluded: "I trust you will order Capt. Brown to reimburse me for what expense I may have incurred, as I am sure that I do not over rate my services when I say that I doubly earned all I paid out or any advantage I may have gained by the use of the car. I have had the apparatus removed to a good store house in the county and safely stored. I shall return the bills for hauling—removing from one car to the other &c to Capt. Brown. The expense was slight. Hoping that you reached home in safety after a more pleasant jaunt on the Road than I had. Yrs. Very Truly, D.T. Tayloe."

For 140 years the trail leading to the location of the first-order Fresnel lens of the Cape Hatteras Lighthouse ended with Tayloe's words: "I had the apparatus removed to a good store house in the county and safely stored." According to more than a century of published historical records, that is where the lens remained.

Ten

A SECRET DESTINATION

During his slow rail journey back to Richmond, Thomas Martin had plenty of time to think about the narrow escape made with the Hatteras lens. The rapid fall of North Carolina's coastal defenses was alarming. He realized that all the other lenses, lamps, lightships and buoys throughout the South under his supervision were also in danger of being recaptured as the Federals moved inland. Martin proposed to his superior, Secretary of the Treasury Christopher Memminger, that all of the Confederate lenses, lamps and other lighthouse and lightship property stored in warehouses, Customs houses and other facilities be moved inland "to such points as in [the Collector's and Superintendent's] judgement may be secure from the approach of the enemy." Memminger concurred and a circular, ordering such action be taken, was mailed out to lighthouse districts throughout the South. Some lighthouse lenses, in addition to Hatteras, had already been relocated into the interior. A Texas lighthouse lens was rumored to have been relocated deep under the sand.

Pressure continued to mount for the Federal lighthouse establishment to get the Cape Hatteras tower re-lighted. The Board's engineer, W.J. Newman, had safely returned to Philadelphia from the Outer Banks after examining the lighthouse to determine the work and materials necessary for re-establishing the light. Newman was surprised to find the "Confederates" who removed the lens and

"The stairway to the summit is nothing more than a series of heavy wooden ladders and landings, made of yellow pine and most inflammable." Shown is interior of the 1817 Bald Head light-house. The 1803 Cape Hatteras tower would have looked much the same. Photo by author.

lamps from the tower did not take out the base plate, the pedestal or revolving mechanism. Newman determined the old pedestal could be adapted for the second-order lens assigned as a temporary replacement at Hatteras, but security at the station was still a concern.

"The stairway to the summit is nothing more than a series of heavy wooden ladders and landings, made of yellow pine and most inflam-mable," Newman wrote to the Engineering Secretary. "At the base of the tower a large quantity of dry brush is always placed to keep sand from blowing away. Any evil disposed person could in a few minutes, landing in the woods on the Sound Side, collect the dry stuff, fire the stairway, and the man on watch at the top of the Tower would not have a chance to escape." The Light House Board's Chairman, W.B. Shubrick, sent another request to General Burnside asking for guards to protect the tower and for his cooperation and persistence in recapturing the original Hatteras lens. "It has been understood at this office that the lens apparatus formerly in

Federal troops guard the entrance to the Cape Hatteras lighthouse ca.1863, as depicted by wartime artist, Edwin Graves Champney. Outer Banks History Center.

use at Cape Hatteras and which was removed by the rebels, has been taken to Washington, N.C.," wrote Shubrick. "It is highly desirable that this lens should if possible be recovered and if in good order for service it will be put up. If injured it is desirable to take it to New York with a view to repairs."

Burnside, by mid-April 1862, had other priorities, specifically the well-constructed Confederate bastion of Fort Macon that defended Beaufort Inlet at the eastern end of Bogue Banks. The fort was the next strategic objective on the general's orders. Capturing the Hatteras lens would have to wait. However, Cape Lookout's first-order Fresnel lens had been stolen too and was reported to be in the vicinity of Beaufort. Before he left his headquarters at New Bern for the impending siege of Fort Macon, Burnside issued an order for the detailing of guards to protect the Cape Hatteras tower. In a pencil drawing by part-time soldier, part-time artist Edwin Graves Champney, guards can be seen on sentry duty at the base of the lighthouse.

For nearly a month following the capture of New Bern, Federal forces, under Burnside's friend and junior officer, Brigadier General John G. Parke, made painstaking preparations to assault and reduce Fort Macon from its landward flanks to the west, an approach the Fort was never designed to withstand. On April 23, Burnside provided an opportunity for the fort's commander, Lieutenant Colonel Moses J. White, to surrender, but White was not satisfied with the unconditional terms offered and "both parties prepared for battle."[93] Two days later, the attack began in earnest when Federal batteries began to lob the first of more than 1,000 rounds into the fort. Even though White had no chance against Burnside's far superior forces, his men put up a spirited defense and, unlike the embarrassing retreats from Fort Morgan at Ocracoke and the fort at Oregon Inlet, the beleaguered Rebels at Fort Macon held out as long as they could. At about 4:30 p.m. "a white flag [was] displayed from the ramparts of the fort."[94]

With the capitulation of Fort Macon, Burnside's forces controlled almost all of Eastern North Carolina's sounds, bays and most of its major rivers inside the Outer Banks, at least up to the port towns of New Bern, Washington, Elizabeth City and Edenton. For the first time, Federal warships could enter Beaufort Inlet unmolested and supplies were easily landed from offshore and delivered to the railhead of the Atlantic and North Carolina at Morehead City. Union troops filled the streets of Beaufort and set out to find the illuminating apparatus from the Cape Lookout and Bogue Banks lighthouses. General Parke had recently received a letter from Admiral Shubrick of the Light House Board who was still hoping Federal lighthouse property could be located and quickly returned to service. Cape Lookout was considered almost as important as the lighthouse at Hatteras. "It has been supposed that in many cases the Lt. Vessels and apparatus of Lt. Houses have been merely removed from their stations, and that they might be found and recovered upon diligent inquiry," wrote Shubrick. "It is understood further that some light stations…may be re-established by simply restoring the lenses. It is specially desirable to learn the condition of the towers and lanterns at the several stations. This office hopes that its earnest desire to replace the aids to navigation in the waters of North Carolina and elsewhere will serve as to its apology for troubling you with matters so entirely foreign to your present duties."[95]

Parke probably did not mind being troubled by the Light House

Board's "foreign matters" as he was feeling ebullient after his capture of Fort Macon, but he was completely unable to help them. The Fresnel lenses from Cape Lookout and Bogue Banks were nowhere to be found. Thomas Martin's directive from Richmond to relocate lenses to points "secure from the approach of the enemy" had not yet been sent, and the rail line out of Morehead City had been under Federal control for more than six weeks, but somehow the Beaufort District lenses had still been spirited away. The U.S. government was no closer to recovering its lighthouse property. The mystery intensified.

As the port towns of Elizabeth City, Washington, New Bern and Beaufort were captured and occupied by Federal forces, the lines of communication were severed between the respective District Superintendents of Lights and the office of the acting chief of lighthouses for the Confederate States of America, Thomas E. Martin. Consequently, no records, receipts or letters are known to have ever been written or preserved that fully and accurately explain the "who, what, when, where and how" of the inland relocation of the lenses. To be sure, the superintendents destroyed any evidence of their complicity, even if they planned to move upstate as H.F. Hancock did at Washington. There are, however, a series of letters written by Joseph Ramsey, Collector of Customs (and Superintendent of Lights) for the District of Plymouth, North Carolina, on the Roanoke River. These letters provide important clues regarding what might have happened elsewhere, including Beaufort and the first-order lens from Cape Lookout.

Around the first of May, while Burnside's men were rummaging through the Customs House, buildings, and storehouses of Beaufort and Morehead City in their efforts to find the Lookout apparatus, Ramsey wrote a letter to Secretary Memminger of the Treasury in Richmond, reporting the challenges he faced to protect the lighthouse property in his district. His initial letter begins: "Owing to the unfortunate fall of Roanoke Island, much confusion has existed in this section and from the continued expectation of the approach of the enemy I have constrained to remove my family to Hamilton N.C. several miles above on the river and also much of the public property of importance as circumstances would permit… The Roanoke River Light Vessel with part of her fixtures are at Hamilton, part at Williamston 12 miles below & part still remains in the Custom House which as yet I have been unable to remove for want of transportation."

Even before he completed his letter to Richmond, Ramsey's expectation of the enemy was fulfilled as three Federal gunboats steamed up to the Plymouth wharf to present town officials with a proclamation stating that the U.S. Government "was there to uphold the laws of the nation and that all who conduct themselves properly will, as far as possible, be protected in their persons and property."[96] As quickly as they appeared, the Federals departed, but not before suggesting they might soon pay a return visit. Ramsey could not have felt much relief about the gunboats's departure, however temporary, since he seemed to be in the possession of a large amount of lighthouse property and faced almost insurmountable odds at moving it up the Roanoke River. It is especially curious that the Plymouth Collector would refer to multiple lighthouse fixtures in his charge when, prior to the war, the only navigational aid other than buoys within the Plymouth District was the Roanoke River Light Boat. Ramsey's reference could only mean that, at some point prior to the fall of Roanoke Island, the Fresnel lenses formerly in use at the Bodie Island Lighthouse and Roanoke Marshes light (and possibly the Croatan and Wades Point towers), that had been stored at the Customs House at Elizabeth City, were moved across the Albermarle Sound to Plymouth and Ramsey's care.

Joseph Ramsey faced a daunting task and the visit of three more Union gunboats, the *Commodore Perry*, the *Ceres* and the *Lockwood* on May 14, added to his headaches. The Collector was, in fact, suffering from declining health and expressed repeated concern about his condition and for his family's safety. However, unlike his colleague at Washington, North Carolina, Ramsey did not shirk his responsibilities. In the ensuing weeks after the Federal's call on his town, Ramsey retrieved most of the lighthouse property stored at his Customs House and had transported it to Williamston and Hamilton, 30 and 42 miles respectively, from Plymouth. He described his ordeal in a rambling but descriptive May 18 letter to Richmond:

> When steamers were running down to Plymouth, I could get but little of the fixtures transported up the river & those that were, consisted of such articles as were of less value than those being left behind being of considerable weight such as the Lantern &c. In the meantime the road was for considerable times almost unpass-

able yet I received a wagon & cart load to Williamston & upon return of the waggons [sic] empty, it broke down, since then at odd times I have had the articles brought up by land & water. What I could, I have had stored in a warehouse at Hamilton, while others are at Williamston. These I shall endeavor to have brought soon to Hamilton as well as that remaining at Plymouth, if I can get transportation which before, as now, seems to be difficult; no transportation by water as the river is blockaded below Hamilton.[97]

The second Federal expedition to Plymouth led by the USS *Ceres* seemed to be conducted for the express purpose of searching for United States property hidden along the Roanoke River. The search may have been ordered on the basis of intelligence from Unionist informants, and it is possible authorities received information regarding the transfer of the lighthouse apparatus from Bodie Island and the screwpile lights in the sounds. The gunboats stopped briefly at Plymouth and "pushed on up the river" to Williamston, where the Confederate steamer *Alice* was captured with about 20 pounds of "Government bacon" on board. A warehouse was searched, where sailors found iron bolts intended for the gunboat that had been under construction at Washington, but that was all they found—no U.S. property.[98] However, the Federals were careless because part of Ramsey's contraband was there, in Williamston, somewhere. On their way back down the Roanoke River, Lieutenant Flusser of the *Ceres*, apparently dissatisfied with simply "bringing home the bacon," paid another visit to Plymouth. He and his men searched the Customs House and found the lantern from the Roanoke River Light Boat, which Ramsey had said was too heavy for him to remove.

Two weeks later, Ramsey sent another letter to Richmond reporting that during a temporary absence on his part, "the most important items of fixtures have under military orders, been removed to Weldon."[99] At the same time, Ramsey announced his resignation as Customs Collector in order to accept an appointment with the Department of Justice. To his credit, he persisted in delivering the lighthouse property to a secure location. "I have to state that the Lighthouse fixtures as far as possible & with but few unimportant exceptions have been forwarded to Weldon N.C. [on the rail line near the Virginia border] in the care of S. Woodson Venable, Capt. & A.Q.M.," wrote Ramsey to his former superiors in Richmond on July 1, 1862. A single-minded Southern loyalist, he reiterated his dedication once more by stating that "as to the safety of these things at Weldon…the Department is the best judge—I am however willing to do any thing I can to secure their safety." Weldon was only a way station for the lighthouse apparatus. On July 1, Ramsey wrote a remarkable letter, revealing the secret destination not only of the lenses from the Plymouth and Elizabeth City Districts, but most likely all of North Carolina's lighthouse property including the lost Cape Lookout apparatus. Ramsey confirmed his new orders with these words: "I received instructions from the Hon. C.G. Memminger, Secretary of the Treasury, under date of the 31 May last to have the several articles of Public property in my care to be removed to Raleigh."[100] Raleigh! A place secure from the approach of the enemy, at least until General W.T. Sherman arrived in the state.

On July 22, Joseph Ramsey, former Collector of Customs, finally fulfilled his obligation to deliver the lighthouse fixtures and other government property from the Plymouth District to Raleigh. The most significant portions had already been transported by steamer up the Roanoke River to Weldon. The other items in Ramsey's possession, mostly from the lightship, including instruction manuals, a bell, oil cans, blocks and falls, lamps and a compass, went westward by wagon from Hamilton to Tarboro across the perilous Conetoe pocosin. Ramsey barely got away in time as the Union Navy had made another foray up the Roanoke, this time reaching the town of Hamilton, where Lieutenant Flusser captured a small Confederate steamer. In poor health, Ramsey took another 10 days to reach Raleigh via Weldon and Gaston, where he turned over the material to the assistant quartermaster, Capt. M.M. Peirce. More than two months later, Ramsey concluded his final report with an apology: "These articles were delivered in July last but from continued ill health as well as the trouble of moving my family, as I hope, beyond the annoyance of the enemy, is the cause of the delay in rendering the information of accounts sooner." Hopefully, Joseph Ramsey's new duties with the Department of Justice were less rigorous.

Eleven

Triumphs and Defeats

On April 21, 1862, Blatchford, Seward and Griswold, a New York law firm founded by William H. Seward (former governor, senator and Lincoln's secretary of state) and protégé Samuel Blatchford (future Supreme Court justice), sent a letter to Admiral Shubrick of the U.S. Light House Board requesting the firm be provided all available information relative to the "extinguishment of the Cape Hatteras Lt., N.C., by the Rebels."[101] It was three days after Dr. Tayloe had placed the Hatteras lens in a good, Granville County storehouse and almost a year to the day since keeper Ben Fulcher ceased lighting the lamp in the tower. Why the New York law firm, respected for its work on government patents and railroad matters, had become involved in the Cape Hatteras affair is uncertain, but it was most likely at the direction of Seward. Seward had organized a government effort to seek out and prosecute Confederate sympathizers and those people who had been disloyal to the Union in the North. The power-obsessed cabinet secretary, who fancied himself more a prime minister, once boasted that "He could ring a little bell and cause the arrest of a citizen." Whoever extinguished the Hatteras light certainly could be counted among Seward's targets, especially if they were keepers. He regarded them as traitors who had been paid out of the Federal Treasury.

It is conceivable that Blatchford and Seward's witch-hunt was encouraged by George Blunt, pub-

"He could ring a little bell and cause the arrest of a citizen." Secretary of State William H. Seward, senior partner in the law firm, Blatchford, Seward and Griswold, of New York City. Library of Congress.

lisher of the American Coast Pilot and at various times critic and champion of the famous Southern sentinel at Hatteras. Blunt's offices were located at 179 Water Street in Manhattan, near the piers of the lower East River, and not far from Blatchford, Seward and Griswold. Blunt, too, was incensed at the criminal behavior of the Confederates who were destroying lighthouses he and his father had fought so doggedly to improve. Blunt and Seward may have felt that Southern lighthouse keepers—loathsome men who blatantly disregarded their sworn promise to protect lives and property and should have never had the privilege to be keepers in the first place—should suffer some form of retribution as an example to others so inclined.

These are just theories, but, what is without question, is that in the spring of 1862, the suspicions and full weight of one of New York's most powerful law firms, led by one of the Federal government's most powerful leaders, was focused on a poor, old, out-of-work harbor pilot, formerly residing on Hatteras Island. On May 9, Blatchford, Seward and Griswold sent another letter to the Light House Board, this time asking for the name and address of the keeper of the Cape Hatteras

Lighthouse at the time it was extinguished. Admiral Shubrick, although occupied with many other problems at the time, not the least of which was getting Hatteras relit, responded immediately to Blatchford's request. Shubrick's reply was not entirely helpful: "Gentlemen, Your letter of May 9th is received. The name of the Light Keeper at Cape Hatteras was B.F. Fulcher. His address is unknown to this office."[102] As far as can be determined, Blatchford, Seward and Griswold's pursuit of Benjamin Fulcher ended there. The former Hatteras keeper was smart to have moved to the deep, dark tangles of forest and wetlands of Hyde County.

Seward's "little bell" never rang for Fulcher.

Men who were not smart, at least according to the U.S. lighthouse establishment, were the pool of prospective lighthouse keepers who remained among the residents of Hatteras Island. By mid-April 1862, the Light House Board ordered a second-order Fresnel lens and all of its necessary components to be sent to the Cape to be installed on the pedestal from the missing Henry-Lepaute apparatus. At the same time, a sixth-order lens was requested to re-light the 25-foot tall beacon marking the Slue Channel of Diamond Shoals. With confidence the job would be accomplished quickly, New York and Philadelphia newspapers were informed. Notices were published, including bulletins from the offices of the American Coast Pilot, that the light at Hatteras was again flashing. Unfortunately, the reports were incorrect as the shipment of the lenses had been delayed by the heavy demand for moving war supplies. As a result, during the month of May, the masters of ships who put to sea out of Northern ports for the West Indies or to supply the Federal blockade in the South, passed the Outer Banks expecting to see a light at Hatteras that was not there. No doubt, this caused George Blunt much irritation.

The work crew finally arrived at Cape Channel in the Pamlico Sound in mid-May and transferred the lenses in their heavy crates to flats for the four-mile lighterage to the landing near the lighthouse. The uniforms, people and vessels were different, but the actions were almost exactly reciprocal to those involved in the removal of the lenses the previous summer. This time, the cargo also included a year's supply of oil and new oil butts (50-gallon tanks) in which to store it.

By the end of the month, the refitting of the second-order lens was complete and, it was time to recruit new keepers. The Light House Board worried that finding trustworthy and qualified keepers would be difficult. In their opinion, the Union loyalists who remained on Hatteras Island were "too ignorant to be entrusted with the care of so important a Light Station."[103] The Board certainly had no shortage of applicants. The economy of the island had been hit hard. Scores of men, who had prospered as mariners, boatmen or pilots, were sitting home with nothing to do. Many joined the First North Carolina Union Regiment during the following year.

The acting engineer of the Fifth District, W.J. Newman of Philadelphia, was delegated the task of filling the keeper's positions. Newman, being new on the job, was at a disadvantage having to navigate the vagaries of Hatteras Island politics, something of which the former Superintendents of Lights were more familiar. The engineer, no doubt, had to sort through numerous slanders and accusations made among the applicants. Nevertheless, the clerk of works for the Fifth District reported the appointment of keepers and the completion of the lens installation on May 29. Bateman Williams, former lighthouse assistant under Fulcher, was again made an assistant, which means that while Williams might have shared meals with his former boss, he did not share the old man's politics. Abraham Farrow was appointed keeper.[104] The Farrow family had been keepers of the Hatteras light for many years in the early nineteenth century, albeit during the lighthouse's darker period in terms of performance. Engineer Newman may, or may not, have considered the Farrows' checkered past as keepers, but if the U.S. government was going to replace Keeper Fulcher with a Union man, they at least picked one with a good first name.

Farrow moved into the keeper's residence in May, the one vacated by Ben Fulcher the previous summer, and began the difficult task of sprucing up the old lighthouse, neglected for so many months. On an evening in early June, 1862, with the engineer of the Light House Board present, Farrow crossed the soggy flats and walked the sandy path to the 20-foot high sand dune on which the lighthouse stood. Glass polished, lamps fueled and the clockwork counter-weights cranked up to the base of the lantern deck, the Cape Hatteras Lighthouse once again flashed its warning to seafarers of the dangers of Diamond Shoals after having been darkened for more than one year. Even though the Confederates still held the original lens, the Hatteras re-lighting was as significant a victory for the U.S. lighthouse establishment as Grant's turning back of Beauregard at Shiloh. Like their War Department colleagues, the Light House Board and Admiral Shubrick had gained a foothold on Southern soil. The steady flow of communication from the Washington, D.C., organization to their Fifth District Inspectors and Engineers that had stopped so abruptly in April, 1861, resumed after General Burnside took Roanoke Island. The U.S. lighthouse establishment was back in business in the Old North State.[105]

With the Cape Hatteras light re-established, the Light House Board turned its attention to the restoration of North Carolina's other navigational aids, especially those in the Pamlico, Albermarle and Croatan sounds, which were frequently needed by the Navy. Among the first projects was the recovery of three light vessels sunk as obstructions by the Confederates at the entrance to the Neuse River. Shubrick wrote to Commander Stephen C. Rowan, USN, commanding Naval forces on inland waters in North Carolina, directing him to consider, "if just and reasonable," a proposal by the New Jersey Submarine Company to raise the ships at $833 each. Rowan was authorized to enter a contract with the salvage company on behalf of the board, but before he could do so, the New Jersey Submarine Company abandoned the project. The U.S. Navy eventually undertook the salvage, using the wrecking steamer *Dirigo*. In August, the Light House Board agreed to pay $500 to raise the Brant Island Shoal light vessel sunk at Hatteras Inlet. Also in August, a fourth-order Fresnel lens was placed aboard the USS *Minnesota* at New York, bound for immediate use at the Ocracoke Lighthouse.

The Neuse River screwpile lighthouse, which was under construction at the outbreak of the war, was quickly completed during the summer of 1862. As many of the small, channel and shoal lighthouses were re-established, the need for new, loyal keepers became critical and a real challenge for the Light House Board engineers working the district. Admiral Shubrick asked Engineer Jeremy Smith to find Collectors of Customs for the ports of Washington and New Bern who could assume responsibility for appointments, but even these positions were difficult to fill. Eventually, the personnel problems sorted themselves out and, as was the case at Hatteras, there was no shortage of men willing to take the oath of allegiance to secure a regular paycheck. Some men, contemplating a career in the lighthouse establishment, easily convinced local military authorities the only thing keeping a lighthouse from operating was the lack of a keeper. Such was the case involving the commander of Fort Macon, Captain Lewis Morris. In the summer of 1862, Morris appealed to the Light House Board to make a Mr. Thomas Thompson, light keeper at Cape Lookout—a lighthouse without a light! Admiral Shubrick responded to Morris: "As it is not probable that the Cape Lookout Lt. House will for some time be in condition to require the services of a keeper, it is not deemed necessary at this time to submit the subject to the Department as under other circumstances this Office would be glad to do."[106]

The Union-loyalist keepers who applied for work at the isolated screw-pile lights, accepted risks beyond their imaginations. The little self-contained lighthouses on iron stilts surrounded by water, including Pamlico Point and Roanoke Marshes, were not under 24-hour guard by the U.S. Army, unlike the all-important Cape Hatteras Lighthouse, and were vulnerable to Rebel raiding parties. Any men serving as keepers after the Union occupation of the tidewater region of Eastern North Carolina were considered, by their former Confederate friends and neighbors, as traitors to the Southern cause. As times grew more desperate, one man, an assistant at the Croatan lighthouse, filling in for his Unionist keeper, was kidnapped and later held at the Confederate prison at Salisbury, a "dolorous" death trap with a mortality rate of nearly 40 percent.[107]

The year 1862 concluded on a series of indecisive and melancholy events for both the Blue and the Gray. General Ambrose Burnside, who had begun the year with successes at Roanoke Island, New Bern and Fort Macon, was reassigned to Virginia to support his plodding mentor, General George McClellan. Raleigh and Wilmington would have to wait. Within six months, Burnside, like his mentor, was out-generaled by Robert E. Lee and routed at Fredricksburg, a disaster for the great Army of the Potomac and for the ambitious, fuzzy-jowled railroad man. Horrific clashes earlier that year at the Seven Days' Battle near Richmond, 2nd Bull Run (Manassas) and Antietam cost both sides tens of thousands of lives. Even the Light House Board had encountered frustrations and setbacks. In May, a shipment of lighthouse lens apparatus and supplies intended for lights at the entrance to the Mississippi River and the passage to New Orleans, was sent from New York to Boston aboard the USS *Minnesota*. It was to be transferred to a steamer headed for the Gulf. In a classic, bureaucratic boondoggle, the valuable lighthouse property was temporarily placed in a warehouse and subsequently transferred to another ship by a Navy supply officer who shortly thereafter died. Unfortunately, the deceased had not recorded which ship the crates of lenses were on and they went missing for months. Admiral Shubrick of the Light House Board was furious and wrote numerous letters to Gideon Welles, Secretary of the Navy, incredulous that such a thing could happen. "This was a careless transfer of Government property with a value of nearly $1000," the tight-fisted Shubrick wrote to Welles.[108]

Succeeding General Burnside, General John G. Foster assumed command of the Federal army at New Bern. In November, Foster led a 5,000-man force toward Tarboro to intercept a growing force of Confederates who were collecting food from Eastern North Carolina farms for the war effort in Virginia. The General's men ravaged the towns of Williamston and Hamilton, searching under every rock and stealing everything they could. Foster's raid would have certainly resulted in the capture of lighthouse property from Bodie Island and the Albermarle, had it not been for the heroic efforts of Joseph Ramsey. Foster stopped short of attacking Tarboro when the shrill sound of train whistles convinced the wary general that "Confederate reinforcements were arriving almost hourly."[109]

The next month, Foster turned his attention to the strategic railroad bridge over the Neuse River at Goldsboro. With 10,000 infantry, 40 pieces of artillery and 640 cavalry, Foster set out on a crisp winter's march through the pine forests and swamps of Craven County. Near Kinston, the Federals encountered 2,000 Confederate soldiers from units of both North and South Carolina. For a brief but furious period, the Rebels held their own against the Federals' overwhelming numbers. "The balls whizzing past and men falling around," lamented an infantryman from the Palmetto State. "It was a time to try the soul." Eventually, General Foster's superior artillery prevailed, and the Confederates retreated in panic to the Neuse River

"The '*Monitor*' is no more. What the fire of the enemy failed to do, the elements have accomplished." The U.S. Navy's first iron warship, the U.S.S. *Monitor*, surrendered to a winter gale, 16 miles south-southeast of the Cape Hatteras Lighthouse. Courtesy North Carolina Collection, UNC Library.

bridge that had been prematurely torched to check the Yankee advance. Men were trampled, burned, and shot as they attempted to reach the safety of Kinston. The Confederate wounded were rushed to field hospitals where many were cared for by the Surgeon of the 61st North Carolina Regiment, a doctor who was later "distinguished for a zealous performance of duty and rendered most valuable and efficient service in the hospital and on the field" during Foster's raid on Kinston.[110] Had the doctor been captured by the Federals, General Foster might have been able to solve an aggravating mystery—the location of the Cape Hatteras Fresnel lens. The surgeon's name was David T. Tayloe.

Two weeks after Foster's raid, the USS *Monitor* left her moorings near Fort Monroe at Hampton Roads for redeployment to the Federal blockade of Charleston. The prototype ironclad, conceived as an "impregnable steam battery of light draught," was built to wage war against wood-hulled Confederate gunboats on placid rivers and bays, not against the unbridled forces of nature. As the 172-foot, "cheesebox on a raft" was towed out of the Chesapeake Bay by the side-wheel gunboat, USS *Rhode Island*, her crew of 65 officers and men were thankful to encounter a smooth sea and clear skies. Pleasant weather is not unheard of off the Outer Banks in December, but it rarely lasts long.

When dawn broke on the second day, the *Monitor's* deck officers observed the sailor's worst fear, "a red sky at morning." "Cloud banks were seen rising in the South & West…till the sun was obscured by their cold grey mantle," wrote the *Monitor's* acting paymaster, William F. Keeler. A winter cold front approached from the Appalachians and racing before it, southwest winds, the very direction in which the two ship convoy was steaming. With shocking swiftness, the wind increased to storm force and drove before it waves that danced, hissed, and seethed over the low deck of the ironclad. As the ironclad came abeam of the menacing fingertip of Diamond Shoals—"the Cape Horn of our Atlantic coast"—the helmsman, Francis Butts, muscled the wheel to round her up to a course of 240° south by west and directly into the teeth of the strengthening gale. "The vessel was riding one huge wave, plunging through the next as if shooting straight for the bottom of the ocean, splashing down upon another with such force that her hull would tremble, while a fourth would leap upon us and break far above the turret," observed Butts.[111] The one-year-old vessel shuddered, strained, started to ship vast quantities of water through the seam between her turret and deck, and later, through the anchor well. "The water is gaining on us, Sir," cried the men below decks, manning the pumps. Soon, the swirling, cold, green water of the Atlantic smothered the fires of the engine and the huge, four-bladed screw slowly stopped turning. A signal rocket was fired, illuminating the beleaguered warship in its desperate battle with the sea. The *Rhode Island* was hailed. There was no choice but to abandon ship and lifeboats were sent to the rescue. Keeler's observations were seared into his memory:

> It was a scene well calculated to appall the boldest heart. Mountains of water were rushing across our decks & foaming along our sides; the small boats were pitching and tossing about on them or crashing against our sides, mere playthings on the billows; the howling

of the tempest, the roar & dash of the waters; the hoarse orders through the speaking trumpets of the officers; the response of the men; the shouts of encouragement & words of caution.[112]

Forty-seven of the 65 officers and men of the *Monitor* were eventually hoisted onto the deck of her consort, the *Rhode Island*. At 1:15 a.m., the faint glow of light from inside the turret and a little red lantern on the stern of the history-making iron ship were snuffed out, and it vanished into the depths. A sailor on board a lifeboat making his third trip from the *Rhode Island* to the sinking ship said, "As the wind and sea were against me, I made but little progress, yet I continued gaining, until within a quarter mile of the '*Monitor*,' when the light became extinguished; it appeared to settle gradually in the water as I approached her and then it disappeared." "The '*Monitor*' is no more," wrote Keeler to his wife, Anna. "What the fire of the enemy failed to do, the elements have accomplished."[113]

Even if they could have seen the faint yellow glow of the replacement second-order lens of the Cape Hatteras Lighthouse, it would have offered no comfort to the officers and crew of the *Monitor*. A lighthouse is foremost a navigational aid to help mariners determine their approximate location. The officers of the *Monitor* knew exactly where they were. Soon after the news of the ironclad's foundering off Cape Hatteras was published, and for decades after, writers and columnists tried to convince their readers the Confederates who "stole" the first-order lens "with murderous indifference" from the lighthouse, were responsible for the loss of 16 *Monitor* sailors. Nothing could be further from the truth. The "light draught steam battery" should have never been taken to sea, at least not during the winter, and would not have been but for Abraham Lincoln's determination to plug the gaps in the blockade at Charleston.

When the USS *Monitor* left the turbulent surface of the Graveyard of the Atlantic, so ended the equally violent second year of the American Civil War and the search for the lost Hatteras lens.

The Years 1863 and 1864

January 1, 1863, will be forever remembered as the date the Emancipation Proclamation took effect, even though it is mostly forgotten that the proclamation only freed slaves in the rebellious Southern states, not those in the slave-border states that remained in the Union. It also caused deep resentment within the U.S. military, disappointment among abolitionists, and mixed reactions in Europe. Nevertheless, it was a momentous first step in what would become a long, constitutional process.

Also on New Year's Day, 1863, all of North Carolina's hand-polished, crown-crystal lighthouse lenses were still missing. Despite the fact that Cape Hatteras light, the Cape channel beacon, and Ocracoke light were again working, the whereabouts of the state's two dozen first-order, third-order, fourth-order and sixth-order lenses baffled the Federal lighthouse establishment. Despite possessing good intelligence from informants and spies, military authorities had been unable to retrieve the government property as the Confederates rushed to move it inland. The lost lighthouse apparatus had taken on importance well beyond its real value. Even though the apparatus no longer had any strategic importance, the Confederate government was keen on keeping the Federals from repossessing their precious lighthouse property.

Soon after the first of the year, the Light House Board re-established the Cape Lookout light, but with a third-order, instead of a first-order, Fresnel lens.[114] The availability of the largest seacoast lenses

Mobile Point Lighthouse following the bombardment of Fort Morgan during August 1864. National Archives.

was limited and the U.S. Treasury had suspended orders to the French manufacturers for new lenses, out of necessity. Save for the faint golden glow from anchor lights and cabin lamps of the gunboats of the U.S. Atlantic Blockading Fleet, the remaining 4,000 miles of Southern barrier islands, shoals, inlets, bays, harbors and rivers passed the nights in darkness. A few Southern ports, including Beaufort, North Carolina, had been captured early in the war, primarily to establish coaling and supply depots in support of the blockade so that the Federal steamers would not have to return to Northern navy yards to be refueled and provisioned. Other ports taken for coaling stations included Port Royal Sound near Beaufort, South Carolina; Fernandina and Pensacola, Florida; Galveston*; and Sabine City, Texas. In every case, the United States Navy found the lighthouse lenses missing and in some instances the buildings had been damaged or destroyed by the retreating Rebels. Confederate troops had set fire to the pine stairway of the octagonal lighthouse at Tybee Island, Georgia (a scenario that was feared at Cape Hatteras), causing significant damage that could not be repaired until after the war. The Hunting Island Lighthouse between Charleston and Tybee Island was found completely destroyed.

Lenses were also discovered to be missing from lighthouses at Cape Romain, South Carolina; St. Augustine, Jupiter Inlet, and Pensacola, Florida; Pass Christian, Mississippi; and Matagorda, Texas. The Cape Florida lens was claimed to have been destroyed by a "band of lawless persons," while lenses of other lighthouses seemed to have been hidden not far from their stations. One apparatus was rumored to have been buried in the sand.

Southern lighthouse structures (in addition to the Bodie Island

---

*Galveston was captured by the Confederate Navy on January 2, 1863.

Lighthouse) that were damaged or destroyed during the war either by sabotage or by bombardment included the Charleston light on Morris Island and Georgia's St. Simons light. Confederate saboteurs did their best to blow up the tenacious St. Marks light in Florida by placing kegs of powder inside the interior base of the tower but only succeeded in knocking out a section of the wall about 8 feet high and one-third around the tower. The 82-foot tower refused to fall and was repaired after the war. The Mobile Point light suffered an unrelenting rain of shells from Admiral Farragut's fleet during the reduction of Fort Morgan and afterward stood long enough for a well-publicized photograph. Additionally, Rebel raiders destroyed the "magnificent tower at Sand Island" off of Mobile Bay but the fate of its first-order lens was not known at that time.

Most of the South's lighthouses in areas occupied by the Federal Navy were not re-established by the Light House Board until after the war. However, the Cape Henry Lighthouse at the southern entrance to Chesapeake Bay and the Pensacola light were soon back in operation. Pensacola was ordinarily a first-order light but had to exhibit a smaller fourth-order lens for the duration of the war. The U.S. Light House Board simply did not have enough of the expensive French apparatus in reserve to be able to relight but the most important of the captured lighthouses. For the most part, the Board and its Chairman, Admiral Shubrick, were bitterly disappointed in their inability to relight the Southern coast after a few initial successes along the North Carolina coast.

The year 1863 has been described by Civil War historians as a dark time for North Carolina. John Barrett wrote that "defeats on the battlefield were not solely responsible for this gloom. Peace movements, desertion of state troops and enemy raids all combined to make the future look dreary."[115] There was little military action of any significance. Confederates, led by General D.H. Hill, attempted unsuccessfully to dislodge the Federals at New Bern and Washington. Later, General Foster's chief of staff, General Edward Potter, commanded a large cavalry unit for a raid on Tarboro and Rocky Mount with the ultimate objective of taking out a bridge on the Wilmington and Weldon railroad. At Tarboro, the bluecoats found the town undefended. An unfinished ironclad gunboat on the stocks was destroyed, and two steamboats moored in the Tar

River were sunk. Although the Federal officers knew nothing about the steamers, one was the *Colonel Hill* and the other, the transport owned by John Myers and Sons, the *Governor Morehead*, which had delivered the Hatteras lens to Tarboro. No lighthouse lenses were discovered in Tarboro or Rocky Mount, but in the latter, a rolling train was apprehended. It carried a captain and four lieutenants and many military supplies, suggesting, but not proving that George Brown, quartermaster and conveyer of the Cape Hatteras apparatus, may have been captured.

On the Outer Banks, life for the remaining residents and the hundreds of troops holding down the forts of Hatteras and Clark had settled into a routine, albeit a different one from peacetime. After spending the preceding year watching and waiting to see if the Yankees were going to leave the island, 77 Hatterasers, formerly mariners, pilots, boatmen, fishermen and oystermen, presented themselves to the recruitment officer at the inlet and joined Company I, First North Carolina Union Regiment. Previously, acting on a recommendation by Colonel Rush Hawkins, President Lincoln authorized the regiment and suggested that Secretary of State William H. Seward's nephew, Clarence, "would be willing to go and play Colonel and assist in raising the force [at Hatteras]."[116] Since, in the early months, there were not enough Union-minded Hatterasers to form even a company, young Master Seward had to find another source of amusement in 1863. Mostly, the Bankers of Company I, First NC Union Regiment, were used for garrison duty at Fort Hatteras and Fort Clark or as guards at the Cape Hatteras Lighthouse.

On January 3, some of the guards discovered five lifeless bodies, clad in the heavy blue uniforms of the Federal Navy, that had been cast onto the beach near the lighthouse. The dead were taken across the beach flats to a high sand ridge south of the lighthouse and buried in an unmarked grave. At the time, no one knew from which vessel the drowned sailors had come, if they had simply been washed overboard or if their ship had sunk. The soldiers did know there had been a big blow four nights earlier, but it would be some weeks before the news reached Hatteras about how the invincible USS *Monitor* had surrendered to the Graveyard of the Atlantic.[117] The gravesite of the *Monitor* sailors has yet to be discovered.

In February, a unit from the Fifth Massachusetts Volunteers landed at Hatteras Inlet for a tour of duty on that infamous "slip of a desert." Among the men who arrived was a 19-year-old Bostonian who, in addition to his

"The sunset was splendid. Gorgeous crimson and gold clouds. The lantern is an expensive and elaborate piece of workmanship. It is a revolving light with a large copper-silver plated reflection. The glass is very thick and of finest quality," wrote wartime artist, Edwin Graves Champney. He described the replacement, second-order lens at the top of the old Cape Hatteras Lighthouse. This sketch depicts the view from the tower looking north. Note the shallow pond in front of the keeper's house and the plank walkway, which had been constructed during the spring of 1862. Outer Banks History Center.

.58 caliber Springfield, carried a good supply of drawing pencils and paper in his haversack. Edwin Graves Champney was born to be an artist and the War of the Rebellion did not interfere with his craft. Champney must not have spent much time soldiering because in five months he produced a prolific collection of sketches of Hatteras Island life. What was seen through other's eyes as a "barren place [covered only by] dwarf shrubs and bushes...truly a most miserable apology for trees" was seen by the cheerful Champney as a fascinating canvas of ancient live oaks, remains of shipwrecks, proud but weathered homes, windmills and the magnificent lighthouse on the Cape. Champney was a "Matthew Brady without a camera," and he was welcomed everywhere he went to preserve scenes that otherwise would be long forgotten, including the only image known to have been made from the top of the 1803 lighthouse. The young Boston artist was also a gifted diarist. He accompanied keeper Abraham Farrow one evening to light the oil lamp in the top of the lighthouse. "The sunset was splendid. Gorgeous crimson and gold clouds. The lantern is an expensive and elaborate piece of workmanship. It is a revolving light with a large copper-silver plated reflection. The glass is very thick and of finest quality. The revolving cylinder is moved by a clock work…. After it had been lit and the sun had set we descended. The refraction of the sunset on the glass was beautiful. Splendid moonlight evening."[118]

During the spring of 1863, the U.S. Light House Board decided that the second-order Fresnel lens in the Cape Hatteras Lighthouse was insufficient in its purpose to warn ships of the dangers of Diamond Shoals. A new, 24-panel, Henry-Lepaute, first-order apparatus was ordered and received, "combining the latest and highest improvements." The lens and its pedestal were delivered by the Navy in May and were installed under the supervision of 5th District Acting Engineer Jeremy P. Smith of Philadelphia, on or before June 23. Even though the 1803 lighthouse had been fully restored to its condition before the war, that condition was described as poor at best. "There exist those [defects] of construction and form which can never be cured," wrote Engineer W.J. Newman to the Light House Board. "The tower had been built of poor sandstone…and the vibrations during heavy gales are alarming and the cracks in the old Tower are extending. The structure is quite out of date and liable sooner or later to a disaster."[119] Despite anticipating years of work to relight the Southern coast, the Light House Board had already begun working on plans to build a new lighthouse on the Cape.

If North Carolina had fallen into a dark, dreary period of impotent military raids and ambivalent politics, the rest of the North and South had not. Murfreesboro, Chancellorsville, Gettysburg, Vicksburg and Chickamauga were once little-known names that today are known for thousands of stories of bravery, tragedy and unimaginable suffering and death. North Carolinians read the news of the calamitous conflicts beyond their state's borders that were siphoning off the lives and limbs of tens of thousands of Tar Heel sons—4,033 casualties at Gettysburg alone, more than a quarter of all Confederate killed or wounded on those Pennsylvania pastures.

Along the Roanoke River Valley at Hibernia, named for the Green Isle of poets, Colonel John Hargrove joined the rolls of Tar Heel fathers who felt the rebellion's battlefield's sting. His 19-year-old son was killed at Ream's Station near Petersburg. His sorrow was heart-rending. Hargrove may have become the custodian of the much-sought-after Cape Hatteras Lighthouse apparatus, but the proud aristocrat probably felt like he had lost or would lose all of those things that he valued the most, his first-born son and a successful plantation that he had labored years to nurture. His friend and "adopted son-in-law," Dr. David T. Tayloe, battle-hardened surgeon of the 61st North Carolina, returned to Townsville when he could and commiserated with Hargrove about the loss of his son, William Triplett Hargrove, and the course of the war.[120]

Tayloe could speak of his own painful loss, for Washington, North Carolina, had been shamefully pillaged by retreating Federal troops when Confederate General Hoke laid siege to the waterfront town. Washington's worst nightmare came to pass. What had been feared and anticipated since Winton had finally befallen the attractive town on the Pamlico River. For three days, "gangs of men patrolled the city, breaking into homes and wantonly destroying such goods as they could not carry away. The occupants and owners were insulted and defied in their feeble indeavors [sic] to protect their property."[121] Fires were set and quickly spread unfettered. Rising above the roar and crackles of the inferno, the bell of Dr. Tayloe's church, St. Peter's Episcopal, was heard tolling its own death knell as flames danced beneath.[122] Washington was later described as a "ruined City...a sad scene—mostly...chimneys and Heaps of ashes to mark the place where Fine houses once stood, and the Beautiful trees, which shaded the side walks, some burnt all most to a coal."[123]

Strolling among the oak- and cedar-lined lanes of Hibernia plantation, Hargrove and Tayloe must have certainly lamented what additional depredations were ahead for the South and for North Carolina. The two men also had to consider the future of the pile of wooden crates and bronze castings hidden in a storehouse nearby. Hargrove and Tayloe were probably aware the Quartermaster Department had assumed control of North Carolina's lighthouse property and much of it had been sent to Raleigh. However, they had heard no word from Richmond, or from anyone else, about what, if anything else, should be done with the apparatus. In fact, on February 5, 1864, Thomas E. Martin, sole employee of the Confederate

States of America Lighthouse Bureau, was transferred to the office of the first auditor of the treasury. Southern lighthouses were extinguished, damaged, or destroyed, lenses removed and hidden, and lightships sunk. Martin had done his job so well there was nothing left for him to do. Hargrove and Tayloe were also fully aware the Federals had already re-established the lighthouse at the Cape. The two Southern gentlemen might have hoped that maybe the Yankees had given up on the Hatteras Henry-Lepaute lens, and it would remain forever forgotten among the sparsely populated, rolling hills of the Roanoke River Valley.

Before 1864 ended, two final acts of vandalism were committed by desperate Confederate raiders against North Carolina's lighthouses, partly in retaliation against the traitorous keepers who were working for the Union. In April, daring saboteurs eluded Federal patrols and crossed Core Sound to Cape Lookout, where they placed two kegs of gunpowder in the base of the lighthouse and lit a long fuse. Their crude plan did not take into account the basic engineering principle that the base of a lighthouse, with millions of pounds of weight pressing downward, is its strongest part. The explosion demolished the wooden stairs, but the sturdily built tower remained intact.* Finally, in October, crew members from the Rebel steam ram, CSS *Albermarle*, attempted to capture a Federal dispatch boat and blow up an ammunition schooner, but they failed. They next turned their attention to the Croatan screwpile light, which had been re-established with a Unionist keeper. The assistant keeper was taken hostage and the lighthouse was torched.

The endgame had begun. General Grant had commenced his long siege of Petersburg. In the South, there was a gathering storm, one that carved a swath of destruction rarely seen in the annals of war. Atlanta had been reduced to rubble. "The heaven is one expanse of lurid fire; the air is filled with flying, burning cinders…the city…exists no more as a means for injury to be used by the enemies of the Union." Columbia shared a similar fate. At the center of the cyclonic mass was the eye of the storm, an Ohioan by birth and a Louisianian by choice. Known as "Cump" in his youth and "Uncle Billy" to his men, he was the reluctant but earnest warrior, William Tecumseh Sherman, and he was advancing toward North Carolina.

---

*The Cape Lookout Lighthouse was said to be slightly bulged. The Tower remained unlighted until engineers were able to rebuild the stairway.

Thirteen

"THE RAVAGES OF SWORD, FLAME AND PILLAGE"

I t seemed all of the South would perish.

> Poor, bleeding, suffering South Carolina!...
> Her time had come. The protestations of
> her old men and the pleadings of her noble
> women had no effect in staying the ravages
> of sword, flame and pillage...Beautiful
> homes...which had been the pride of the
> owners for generations, were left in ruins...
> Everything that could not be carried off
> was destroyed. Thousands who had but
> recently lived in affluence were compelled
> to subsist on the scrapings from the aban-
> doned camps of soldiers...Livestock of
> every description that they could not take
> was shot down. All farm implements, with
> wagons and vehicles of every description,
> were given to the flames.[124]

Although these words were written in a letter
from a Confederate soldier, Southern newspapers,
such as the *Fayetteville Observer* and Raleigh's
Daily Progress, had described, week by week,
in equally vivid details, the horrific advance of
Sherman's 60,000-man march through the South.
The sobering accounts did not escape the attention of John Hargrove, master of Hibernia and
caretaker of the apparatus from Cape Hatteras.
What had seemed impossible two and a half years
earlier, that Granville County soil could ever suffer

the leather soles of Federal boots, was now almost a certainty. It did not take a military strategist to be able to trace a straight line between Sherman's army and Richmond and see that it passed right through Townsville and Hibernia Plantation. Hargrove surely realized the possibility that Sherman would pass by Hibernia and the Hatteras lens might be discovered. It had to be taken away. But where?

Momentous events passed with increasing rapidity. On the fifteenth of January, the formidable bastion of Fort Fisher, the last of the great Confederate coastal defenses, fell under the withering bombardment of Admiral David D. Porter's armada and an amphibious assault by 10,000 soldiers, sailors and marines under Major-General Alfred H. Terry. The largest combined American force to be assembled under one command to that date and unmatched for 79 years until D-Day. The siege lasted for three full days and two nights during which 100 shells per minute poured into and around the Rebel ramparts. Porter later estimated that his fleet expended 50,000 shells, resulting in a half ton of metal and explosive for every linear yard of the fort. "It was beyond description, no language can describe that terrific bombardment," said Confederate General W.H.C. Whiting.[125] The Cape Fear River, Richmond's carotid artery, was clamped off. Throughout the war the river had kept the Confederacy alive, conveying much of its arms, munitions, lead, food, clothing, shoes, blankets, medicines and hard currency from European ports. General Braxton Bragg, who was soon vilified for sacrificing Fort Fisher and the Cape Fear port to save his army for a better day, quickly evacuated Wilmington. "[Bragg] is too fond of retreating or too fearful of being taken by the enemy," wrote D.A. Buie.[126] Whiting was less generous. On his deathbed from wounds suffered during hand-to-hand fighting, he stated the loss of Fort Fisher was due "solely to the incompetency, the imbecility and the pusillanimity" of General Bragg. On February 22, Wilmington was occupied without a fight and without being reduced to ashes. It was George Washington's birthday.

Two weeks after the Federal occupation of Wilmington, General William T. Sherman, with the Fifteenth Corps, rode his mount across the North Carolina state line south of Hamlet. Some of the columns of artillery, supply wagons and pontoon trains stretched 25 miles from end to end. Would North Carolina feel Sherman's wrath of "collective responsibility?" It was the question on every Tar Heel's mind. The official answer was, "no," and the reason was the general thought that the state had large numbers of pro-Union citizens. His orders to his army read: "All officers and soldiers of this command are reminded that the State of North Carolina was one of the last states that passed the ordinance of secession, and from the commencement of the war there has been in this state a strong Union party...It should not be assumed that the inhabitants are enemies to our Government, and it is to be hoped that every effort will be made to prevent any wanton destruction of property, or any unkind treatment of citizens."[127] The unofficial answer was, "yes," for a 60,000-man army and its attendant livestock and refugee train are not easily managed nor fed. The practice of foraging by "bummers," independently roaming bands of self-serving looters, rapists and murderers who "committed every sort of outrage" in Georgia and South Carolina, was mostly restricted in North Carolina. Small detachments led by trusted officers were sent out from the main columns for the express purpose of filling the troughs and plates of the army and not the pockets of lawless marauders.[128] Nevertheless, the new conduct of Sherman's army provided no solace to the panicked people of North Carolina. Clouds of yellow-green pine pollen wafting through the air have always heralded spring throughout the Carolina coastal plain. In 1865, the pollen was replaced by the thick clouds of burning pine forests and fresh sap ignited by bummers solely for the pyrotechnic thrill.

Sherman's next objective was the strategic railroad junction at Goldsboro, but in his way was the tattered, starving, battle-worn army of General Joe Johnston, determined to put up a fight. The progress of Sherman's left wing, 14th and 20th Corps was blunted temporarily along the Cape Fear River at Averasboro. This had Johnston's desired effect of separating the Union general's two main columns. On March 19, at Bentonville, though undermanned and not fully positioned, Johnston's army attacked the Union left. While nearly half his force was engaged by Johnston, Sherman and his right wing marched on to Goldsboro 20 miles away, unaware that the large Confederate force was in the field and on the offensive. Sherman's army was rusty,

City Point, Virginia, headquarters of General U.S. Grant and the Army of the Potomac in the spring of 1865. Library of Congress.

not having fought for months and was later judged to be better conditioned for marching, burning and looting than for shooting. Johnston's men, on the other hand, while serving without pay, were fighting for pride. Bentonville was North Carolina's largest Civil War battle and one of the last of the war. The Confederates lost the conflict in terms of casualties, but gained a good measure of confidence after so many humiliations and disappointments. Unfortunately for Johnston's men, their newfound confidence would only serve them in their old age when they told stories of how they stood up to Sherman's great army because Bentonville was their last stand. Historians have questioned Sherman's decision not to pursue Johnston and end it then and there, but the general's destiny led him elsewhere, and undoubtedly, it saved thousands of lives.[129]

On March 23 and 24, Sherman's army rolled into Goldsboro after marching nearly 500 miles from Savannah. Having divested the countryside of beasts of burden and vehicles, almost none of the soldiers traveled on foot, and a good thing too since most were shoeless. "Nearly everyone has his own coach, cab, buggy, cart or wagon, drawn by horses or mules—blind or lame—colts or old worn out horses or mules…General Sherman could now…supply the whole country, pro-

"Well, you are a pretty pair!" Gen. Sherman met with Gen. Grant at this cabin at Grant's City Point, Virginia, headquarters prior to visiting President Lincoln on the steamer, *River Queen.* Shown are Grant, his son, and wife, Julia. Library of Congress photo.

vided they were not choice as to rigs."[130] The army, in fact, resembled more an absurd, city-sized traveling carnival and was accompanied by pet dogs, squirrels, raccoons, and fighting cocks. Tagging along were pretty young paramours, dislocated freedmen, enterprising reporters and herds of sheep, cattle and hogs. "In every column was at least one wagon loaded with geese, turkeys, and chickens, all adding voice to the noisy occasion."[131]

Sherman wanted to continue his march to Richmond via Raleigh, but with his men badly in need of rest and supplies, the general decided to leave his army and pay General Grant a visit at his headquarters at City Point, Virginia, on the outskirts of Petersburg. Sherman boarded a railroad car on the newly repaired Mullet Line to Morehead City, where he boarded the small captured steamer, *Russia*, for the short but restful voyage to the James River. After a brief stopover at Fortress Monroe, the general landed at City Point late on March 27.

Sherman conferred with General Grant about the possibility of coordinating their operations against Lee. Grant suggested they stroll to the dock where the steamer, *River Queen* was tied up, and confer with the President on the final stages of the war. Sherman was taken by surprise at Lincoln's presence at City Point, and the meeting had a profound effect on the general. In his memoirs, Sherman wrote, "Of all the men I ever met, [Lincoln] seemed to possess more of the elements of greatness combined with goodness, than any other." Lincoln, on the other hand, was greatly distressed that Sherman had left his vast force in Goldsboro without its trusted leader. The general assured the President that his 60,000 men could probably survive without him for a day or two. Nevertheless, the anxious Lincoln pressed Vice-Admiral David Porter for a faster steamer than the *Russia* for Sherman's return trip to North Carolina.

Grant and Sherman were resigned to the probability that there was one final, bloody and climatic battle ahead between Sherman's army and the forces of General Joe Johnston, and Sherman expected that it would take place at, or around, Raleigh. The monumental summit ended after the President expressed his heartfelt wishes that the war be ended quickly and without further devastation of the South. It was Sherman's understanding the President wanted to reunite the country "with as little hardship as possible."[132] Within a few weeks, General Sherman would become embroiled with Lincoln's cabinet and the northern media over the generous surrender terms he offered General Joe Johnston, terms Sherman thought embodied his President's convictions. He was unable to verify Lincoln's wishes because two weeks after the City Point meeting the sixteenth President of the United States was dead.

Upon returning to Grant's quarters, the two war weary generals, with the weight of the entire nation upon their shoulders and the lives of tens of thousands of Union and Confederate soldiers at stake, encountered Mrs. Grant. She asked the two men if they had called on Mrs. Lincoln while on board the *River Queen*. "No," said Grant, "I did

The earliest known photograph of the North Carolina Capitol taken around 1860. The man in the top hat is believed to be ex-governor David S. Reid. Courtesy North Carolina Department of Cultural Resources.

not ask for her." Sherman sheepishly, and most likely, falsely added, "I did not even know she was on board." Unimpressed with the two men, Julia Grant chastised them that "their neglect was unpardonable." She exclaimed, "Well, you are a pretty pair!"[133]

Reminded of his manners, rusty after so long in the field, General Sherman boarded the swift steamer, *Bat*, for the return trip to Goldsboro. He passed the Cape Hatteras Lighthouse in the early morning hours of March 29. If the general had been aware of the lost Henry-Lepaute first-order lens, he might have wondered if his massive army would discover its hiding place in the coming days. Abeam of Hatteras Inlet but on a return course to Cape Lookout and Morehead City, the *Bat*'s captain spotted a propeller steamer heading to sea from the Pamlico Sound. The captain hailed the propeller and had her guide the general's transport through the inlet for the faster trip to

New Bern. By nightfall, Sherman was back in Goldsboro.

In Raleigh, the state's political leaders and citizens had obsessively followed newspaper accounts of Sherman's march through the Carolinas and had long been preparing for the city's invasion. It was not just the Union army they feared, but retreating Confederate troops and bands of marauding deserters who had ravaged the state since the beginning of the war, and, by 1865, they had honed their craft. Former Governor Charles Manly expressed the common sentiments of his Raleigh neighbors to another former Governor, David L. Swain: "The enemy as well as our own stragglers and deserters search every house and cottage and Negroes cabins and take everything they find. Between the two fires desolation, plunder and actual starvation await us." As the day of reckoning neared, Manly again wrote Swain: "I think it pretty certain that Johnston and Sherman will both pass over [Raleigh]. Utter and universal devastation and ruin will follow inevitably. There is no difference in the armies as to making a clean sweep wherever they go of provisions, stock and everything dead or alive." Manly was not the only Raleigh citizen who placed all his valuables in wooden chests and buried them in a secluded place on the outskirts of town, but Manly was probably too old for such a laborious task. "It was a terrible job," he said.[134]

Even while dogwoods were blooming and the sweet smell of spring was in the air, the North Carolina Capitol building and grounds were in shambles. Chaos reigned throughout. Governor Vance directed his staff to remove only those state records and historic documents they deemed important, valuable or incriminating for shipment on the North Carolina railroad to secure points to the west. Wagon after wagon of thousands of military stores, weapons, medical supplies, blankets, leather, overcoats, shoes, cloth and farm implements departed Capitol Square in downtown Raleigh for the station on Cabarrus Street.

Since 1862, the Capitol had been unique among all its cousins throughout the South. It served the combined purpose of legislative State House, offices of the governor and Council of State, State Supreme Court, State Archives and Museum, and most unusually, as a military supply depot for the state Quartermaster Department. During the Civil War, a high iron fence encircled Capitol Square. It was the most secure and best-defended building in the entire state of North Carolina, except for the arsenal at Fayetteville or the mint at Charlotte. It was also crowded with politicians, military officers, black servants and ordinary citizens. As Sherman's army closed on the capital city, the Capitol building was stripped of most of its secrets and treasures; most, but not all.

On the floor of the rotunda between the Senate and House of Commons chambers, amid thousands of discarded papers and documents that littered the floor like oak leaves on an autumn day, lay stacks of assorted wooden crates, cases, and old tattered blankets containing strange objects, previously unseen in that area of the state. The unidentified material was not carried out to the wagons with the other spoils of war. There just seemed no point in doing so.

R ichmond had fallen and General Robert E. Lee's ravaged Army of Northern Virginia was in full retreat across the rolling hills and well-heeled horse farms of central Virginia. In Goldsboro, by the time the muster rolls had been tallied, 83,837 officers and soldiers comprised the newly reorganized Union Armies of Georgia, Ohio and Tennessee. For two weeks, trains from the ports of Wilmington and Morehead City delivered tons of food, clothing and war matériel to support the final, apocalyptic confrontation with General Johnston. While his troops rested, General Sherman and his staff studied maps of the route to Raleigh and the central Piedmont of North Carolina, no longer needing to plan the direct route to Virginia.

In Chapel Hill, the pragmatic former North Carolina governor and current president of the University of North Carolina, David Lowery Swain, unimpassioned by politics or military tactics, considered the South's current state of affairs. It was hopeless, a lost cause, that was plain to see. The university president did not want to see North Carolina laid to waste while Jefferson Davis delayed the inevitable. Swain met with ex-governor William Alexander Graham at the latter's home in Hillsborough and discussed a way for the state to suspend hostilities and lay down its arms. After their meeting, Swain proceeded to Raleigh, followed in two days by Graham. Meeting the ex-governors among the jumbled mess inside the Capitol, the Governor agreed to send a peace delegation, led by Swain and Graham, to present General Sherman the following letter dated April 12, 1865:

> Understand that your army is advancing on this capital, I have to request, under proper safe-conduct, a personal interview, at such time as may be agreeable to you, for the purpose of conferring upon the subject of a suspension of hostilities, with view to further communications with the authorities of the United States, touching the final termination of the existing War. If you concur in the propriety of such a proceeding I shall be obliged by an early reply.
>
> Zebulon B. Vance
> Governor of North Carolina[135]

Swain and Graham were accompanied by Dr. Edward Warren, surgeon general of North Carolina, Colonel James Burr, an officer of the State Guards and Major John Devereux, chief quartermaster of North Carolina. As the peace commissioners set out at 10:30 a.m. from the Cabarrus Street station on a special train headed east toward Smithfield and Sherman, General Johnston's army retreated westward, and, as predicted by Charles Manly, passed right through Raleigh, where the Confederates committed their customary crimes. The Rebels, who at the same time were heard to say of the former governors leading the peace delegation that "such cowardly traitors ought to be hanged," intimidated unarmed, innocent residents, and raided their shops. So efficient were the hungry and tattered graycoats, it was said the only chicken they could not get their hands on was the weathercock atop the steeple of Christ Church off Capitol Square.[136]

Sherman's army broke camp at Goldsboro on Monday morning, April 10. The left column consisted of 28,000 men of the 14th and 20th Corps; in the right column marched nearly 29,000 men of the 15th and 17th Corps; and in the center, the 27,000 strong 10th and 23rd Corps. If one had placed his ear to the ground 10 miles distant, he surely would have heard the earthquake-like rumble of Sherman's forces on the move. On Tuesday, the army engulfed Smithfield, where, in the courthouse, the Federals discovered the county archives tossed "in confusion amongst the dirt," foreshadowing what they would discover in Raleigh two days later.[137]

That night, the familiar sounds of a bivouac—muted harmonicas, the crackle of campfires, the whinny of horses, voices engaged in the odd game of cards or checkers and the hushed murmurs of prayers for a safe deliverance—were all hushed by a rider's voice announcing the news that Robert E. Lee had surrendered to General U.S. Grant at Appomattax. "Begod!" hailed an Irish soldier, "You're the man we have been lookin' for the last four years."[138] For the remainder of the night, various regimental bands could be heard, playing across the countryside, the tunes, "Johnny Come Marching Home," "Yankee Doodle," and the "Star Spangled Banner," punctuated by celebratory gunfire.

In the morning, the peace commissioner's train proceeded to its meeting with Sherman with a great deal of difficulty and danger as it passed through the respective lines of Johnston's and Sherman's armies. Twice their progress was thwarted and once, reversed by Confederate General Wade Hampton. Finally, Union cavalry commander H. Judson Kilpatrick apprehended the peace envoy's one-car train. Governor Vance's representatives finally arrived under a white flag of truce at Sherman's headquarters, "dreadfully excited" by the experience of passing through thousands of blue-clad soldiers cheerfully celebrating Lee's surrender and shouting insults at the well-dressed ex-governors. Sherman received Vance's letter, and quickly drafted one in return, and summed it up by stating: "I doubt if hostilities can be suspended as between the army of the Confederate Government and the one I command, but I will aid you all in my power to contribute to the end you aim to reach, the termination of the existing war."[139]

Swain and Graham had left Raleigh fully expecting to be able to return to the governor before dark with Sherman's response. The general had other plans, however, and was intent on sharing his camp's festive mood following Lee's surrender and feted the two former governors with an evening of food, music and "the most considerate and gentleman-like hospitality," in the woods of Johnston County. So, Swain and Graham were detained until the next morning. The events of the past 24 hours must have left the ex-governors unable to sleep easily, having traveled from their comfortable, stately homes to camp out with "Uncle Billy." They were not alone in their sleepless night.

When his trusted and distinguished delegates failed to return to the Cabarrus Street station, Vance feared the worst. His anxiety was further fueled by the widespread trepidation that prevailed on the Raleigh streets. Even the governor's military aides deserted him in their haste to leave town. Subsequently, Vance received word, erroneous but convincing, that Swain and Graham had been captured. The governor despaired for the capital city's fate. A repeat of Columbia? The last of the loads of supplies and state records had been delivered to the station, and at 9 p.m., the last train pulled out of Raleigh with state officials keen to distance themselves from the expected carnage. The streets were now empty and quiet. Vance was alone, the Capitol vacant but for the mess on the floor and the halls eerily silent after so much activity in so many recent weeks. The governor concluded it was best to observe Sherman's next move from the safety of General Hoke's camp eight miles west of town. He wrote a letter to the Union commander authorizing the Raleigh mayor to surrender the city in Vance's absence. Just before midnight, Vance, accompanied by two volunteer aides, pulled the heavy bronze doors closed on the Capitol's west entrance, secured the locks, handed the keys to a loyal Negro servant and mounted his horse for the depressing ride out of the city.[140] As he cantered down Hillsborough Street, Vance must have had a brief chuckle. Inside the darkened sandstone building, the Governor had left Sherman a surprise gift, something the general's government had been looking for the past four years.

The Discovery in Raleigh

Thursday, April 13, 1865, began as a gloomy, rainy, spring day in Raleigh. The muddy streets were deserted. Businesses were closed and houses were shuttered, the city seemingly abandoned. But, huddled inside many of the large, private homes were women, children and Confederate wounded from the clashes at Bentonville and Averasboro. They all quietly awaited their fate. Many had not slept the previous night. Raleigh's residents wondered if the heavy rain would dampen the desire of Sherman's men for burning down their city. It did not appear so from the vantage point of the peace commissioners as their one-car train pulled in to the Cabarrus Street station, which had been plundered and burned, not by Yankees but by retreating Confederate cavalry. As Swain, Graham, Warren, Burr, and Devereux reached Capitol Square they were surprised to be greeted only by Vance's servant, standing under a portico with the keys to the building. No state officials could be found. Their once straightforward mission now became even more complicated. Vance's representatives had to locate the governor to deliver Sherman's letter. Graham was chosen to continue west in search of Vance, but was delayed because of skirmishes outside the city.

Unbeknownst to the peace commissioners, the Raleigh mayor, William H. Harrison, had already gone out to the southern limits of Raleigh to meet General Kilpatrick and surrender the city. Harrison asked Kilpatrick for "forbearance and protection of private persons and private property." The cavalry commander told the mayor that he had already warned Swain and company that if his men met any resistance, "we will give you hell." There was a tense moment when a Texas straggler, busy looting a Fayetteville Street shop, was surprised by Kilpatrick's arrival and supposedly shot at the approaching column of horses. Kilpatrick did not consider the indiscretion "resistance" but did order the execution of the rash young Rebel. By 7:30 a.m., Sherman entered the city with the 14th Corps and immediately established his headquarters in the old Governor's Mansion at the south end of Fayetteville Street, six blocks from Capitol Square. An aide to Sherman described the residence as "a musty old brick building...in derision called the 'Palace.'" Almost all the furniture had been removed, and the house offered little comfort to the well-traveled Union commander. Sherman immediately dispatched a message to General Grant informing him that Raleigh had been received and his army's next objective was to move due west toward Charlotte to block Johnston's Confederates from escaping on the rail lines south. Sherman also ordered his railroad department to expedite the repairs on the damaged tracks between Goldsboro and Raleigh, thus opening the way for future supplies from the coast.

Thousands of soldiers steadily streamed into the capital city during the day and established camps wherever open space could be found: in the four park squares surrounding the Capitol, on the lawns of private residences, on the broad, grassy hills at Dorothea Dix Hospital for the Insane. The morning storm had passed, the sky brightened, and so did the attitudes of some Raleigh residents, who ventured out when the fires of ruination did not appear to be forthcoming. "Will Raleigh suffer the same devastation as Columbia?" the principal of the city's academy asked a young Union lieutenant. George Round wrote of the encounter after the war: "I told him I was not in that part of the army and did not know the facts about that event, but I could assure him that the most stringent orders had been issued by Gen. Schofield, my immediate commander, for the protection of noncombatants and particularly on the subject of fire."[141] Lt. Round was a member of the U.S. Army Signal Corps, and, shortly after reassuring the anxious principal, he was ordered by Schofield to establish a signal station on the dome of the Capitol. When Round arrived at the Greek revival building, he met Captain John Thomas who had also just reported to establish a provost marshal's office in one of the first floor suites recently vacated by the governor and his Council of State.

No one else was present—the two former Governors, Swain and Graham, the Surgeon General, Vance's aide, and the African-American servant had long since departed. "The provost knew as little about it as I. We found the Senate chamber and Representatives' hall, but no Senators or Representatives. Even the Governor and janitor had stepped out," recalled Round. "I could not be certain but the Capitol was a 'Grecian horse,' which at any moment might swarm armed men from its halls and corridors to sweep us from the face of the earth." There were no armed men. What the two Union officers did encounter nearly caused them to stumble as they walked across the second floor balcony of the rotunda between the two legislative chambers—a mountain of lighthouse lenses!

There, on the floor, stacked more than head-high, were boxes, crates, frames, panels of prisms wrapped in blankets, lamps, oil canisters, tools, clocks, buckets and numerous bronze castings, all property of the United States government. In addition, surrounding this impressive array of Rebel contraband on the pine floors of the two adjacent chambers lay a sea of discarded papers, documents, and maps. Pressed for time in the late afternoon darkness, the two officers were unable to closely examine the material littering the floor. Had they done so, they might have recognized on the old, parchment letters and documents, the signatures of Thomas Jefferson and John Knox. In their haste to abandon the city, Governor Vance's staff had done a poor job of culling the important and valuable state archives from those of little consequence. Round and Thomas may not have immediately comprehended what they had discovered, but they were among the first to convey the news that would travel up the chain of command, all the way to the President's administration in Washington. North Carolina's lighthouse apparatus was found.[142]

Among the first to be notified was General Langdon C. Easton, Sherman's "miserably inefficient" quartermaster general.[143] Easton had enough worries. General Sherman had regularly lambasted Easton for his failure to deliver in a timely manner, the food, clothing, weapons and ammunition necessary to keep the great army in motion. "I find neither railroad completed, nor have I a word or sign from you…of the vast store of supplies I hoped to meet here or hear of," wrote Sherman to Easton while they were still at Goldsboro. Logistics being as important as tactics, the overwhelmed quartermaster could jeopardize Sherman's war plans. Now, Easton was being saddled with the responsibility for a pile of lighthouse apparatus.

Maj. Gen. Sherman, probably at Washington, D.C., after negotiating the surrender of Gen. Joseph Johnston's army near Durham. Photo courtesy North Carolina Archives, Raleigh.

"Our people are tired of war, feel themselves whipped, and will not fight," said General Joseph Johnston to President Jefferson Davis on April 13, 1865. Library of Congress.

General Sherman had no concerns for his quartermaster's problems. He had more important things on his mind. He was worried that his Confederate adversary, General Joe Johnston, might extend his army's retreat westward and the great march would continue. Sherman's concerns were eased on his second day at Raleigh, when a courier delivered a message from Johnston asking for a suspension of hostilities in order to "stop the further effusion of blood and devastation of property," and to "permit the civil authorities to enter into the needful arrangements to terminate the existing war." Johnston had, on the previous day, met with Jefferson Davis at Greensboro. Davis opened the discussion by stating that although Lee's surrender was a disaster, "we should not regard [it] as fatal. I think we can whip the enemy yet…" Johnston responded that his men were "tired of war, feel themselves whipped, and will not fight," and desertions were causing his army to melt away "like snow before the sun."[144]

Sunday, April 16, was Easter Sunday. Raleigh church bells pealed and ministers preached redemption. The camps of 84,000 Union soldiers buzzed with excitement over rumors of a Confederate surrender. However, the frivolity did not last long—word had yet to reach the city that on Good Friday, President Lincoln was assassinated.

A meeting was organized between Sherman and Johnston for Monday, April 17. Over the next two days at Bennett's farmhouse near Durham, the two generals reached terms that Sherman felt were fair, expeditious and negotiated with no "more authority than he had good reason to believe had been granted to him."[145] Sherman sincerely believed the agreement embodied the intent of the recently assassinated President Lincoln: that the Union be quickly restored without further hardship on the South. Critics charged that Sherman should not have discussed the re-establishment of state legislatures and that other parts of his agreement were vague or negligent regarding critical political issues of slavery, amnesty for Jefferson Davis and his administration, and the question of the Confederacy's war debt. Innocently, Sherman, the brilliant West Pointer, had stepped into a minefield he would never quite escape. The General dispatched letters to Grant and Chief of Staff Henry Halleck, asking them to present the terms to President Johnson for acceptance and noting that speed was of the essence in order "to get the Confederate armies to their homes…"[146] The letters, in the possession of an officer of Sherman's staff, went to Morehead City by train and then to Washington, D.C., on a fleet steamer.

During the next five days, General Sherman and his troops whiled away their time visiting the various public institutions of the city, including Dix Hospital and the Asylum for the Deaf, Dumb and Blind. The men in blue attended religious revivals, marched in reviews, held organizational meetings for veteran's associations, and generally tried to woo the pretty, young women of the capital city, whose far fewer numbers made the Raleigh maidens pursued and particular. "Is there no such thing as conquering the Southern woman?" sighed a Union officer to a standoffish prospect whose response offered little satisfaction. Among other Raleigh residents who were able to beguile the Federals was ex-governor Charles Manly, who was ready to retrieve his chest of valuables but did not want to do it himself. Manly, who previously wrote of "desolation, plunder and starvation" at the hands of the enemy, befriended Sherman's chief engineer, Colonel Orlando Poe. Poe provided the politician with his carriage and a 10-man cavalry unit to attend to the digging, thus saving Manly from a repeat of that "terrible job."

Correspondents writing for major northern newspapers also roamed the city streets looking for stories to file. Raleigh was viewed favorably among Southern cities, no doubt because peace was in the air and not the cinders and smoke of burning homes and buildings. It became known as "Beautiful Raleigh, the city of Oaks."[147] "The magnificent dwellings in and around the city, with their ample yards and gardens, adorned with choicest flowers and shrubbery, give the city a most attractive appearance," wrote G.W. Pepper, adding, "the Capitol is a substantial building.[148] One of the most visited sites in the city was the grand, old Capitol and the treasure that it housed. In an April 26 issue of the *Philadelphia Inquirer*, another reporter wrote: "In the rotunda, between the two chambers, is stored a vast pile of lighthouse apparatus: costly lamps and reflectors of Fresnel and Argand that were purchased by the United States Government for the coast of North Carolina, and removed by the Rebels at the outbreak of the Rebellion. The glass concentric reflectors of Fresnel are viewed with novel curiosity by the Western men, to whom light-house paraphernalia is something new."

Before long, General L.C. Easton got around to hiring some local workmen to begin the packing of the lenses for shipment down to the coast to be returned to the Light House Board in Washington. As usual, Easton was already too late to prevent some of the prisms from being "borrowed" by young boys of Raleigh, delighted to have such interesting glass objects with which to experiment in the streets. Back in the Capitol, Easton's workmen needed material that would help to cushion the fragile glass of the Fresnel lenses as they were placed in their wooden crates. Cotton could have been appropriated in time, but on the second floor, in the nearby legislative halls, were ample amounts of paper that would serve just as well.

The report from Raleigh about the discovery in the Capitol caused quite a sensation among Northern readers who understood its significance, not the least of whom included Admiral William B. Shubrick, Chairman of the U.S. Light House Board and George Blunt, publisher of Blunt's American Coast Pilot. Not mentioned in the Inquirer story and unclear from military dispatches from Raleigh was whether the Cape Hatteras apparatus was among those found. Nevertheless, the news electrified the Federal lighthouse establishment, which set in motion a seven-year period of finding, recovering, repairing and reinstalling more than 100 Southern lighthouse lenses.

General Sherman's agreement with General Johnston was also causing a sensation in the North. In an atmosphere of exceptional tension after the assassination of Lincoln, a special Cabinet meeting flatly rejected Sherman's terms. In addition, provocative but unfounded rumors of intrigue were

"In the rotunda, between the two chambers, is stored a vast pile of lighthouse apparatus: costly lamps and reflectors of Fresnel and Argand that were purchased by the United States Government for the coast of North Carolina, and removed by the Rebels at the outbreak of the Rebellion." Photo by Tim Buchman from North Carolina Architecture, reprinted by permission of Preservation North Carolina.

spread, mostly by Secretary of War Edwin Stanton, that Sherman had a secret agenda that included selling Jefferson Davis' freedom for "bankers gold." Only one man could have delivered the news to the sometimes volatile Sherman that his agreement with Johnston was invalid and his loyalty to the Union was suspect—his close and trusted friend, U.S. Grant. At 6 a.m. on April 24, Grant surprised Sherman at the "Palace." Sherman was still in his nightclothes. Two days later Sherman and Johnston were back at the tiny, one-room farmhouse west of Durham, and this time both signed an agreement that matched the non-political terms accepted by General Lee at Appomattox. Sherman returned to Raleigh and got Grant to sign off on the new treaty.

Traveling with Grant to Raleigh was the quartermaster general of the United States, Brevet Major-General Montgomery Meigs. Unlike his subordinate, Langdon Easton, Meigs was considered "a genius at supply and distribution, one of the major factors behind the Union's ultimate success."[149] Meigs had signed out from his office in Washington for a special, unexplained mission to Raleigh. It is not clear exactly what Meigs' mission was, but records reflect his only official concern in the North Carolina capital was the disposition of the Fresnel lenses and Argand lamps piled in the rotunda of the Capitol. Clearly, higher powers at the Treasury in Washington were behind Meigs' mission.

On the day Sherman was renegotiating the surrender of the remaining Confederate army, Meigs wrote a report to Admiral Shubrick regarding the lens apparatus. What he found at the Capitol was as incredible as it was distressing. "I learn that some broken prisms or portion of lenses have been seen in possession of boys in the streets, but the greater part of the lens apparatus will, I think, reach Washington in good order," wrote Meigs. "[The apparatus] has been packed by the Quartermaster Department in some thirty boxes, which have been addressed to the Light House Board, Washington, care of Gen. D.H. Rucker, Chief Quartermaster Washington, D.C. and will be sent forward by rail and steamer immediately." What Meigs observed of the packing of the apparatus clearly left the general stunned: "I notice that the workmen in packing the glass used the papers which in the first occupation of this city, or in the evacuation by the Rebels, had been strewn about the floors of the Capitol. Among those remaining on the floor I saw revolutionary documents bearing the signatures of Thos. Jefferson and Charles Thompson, and John Knox. It will be well to have these papers examined by some intelligent person, that all that are of any interest may be preserved. I saw one of 1756—many of '76 to '69."[150]

Still, there was no word of the Henry-Lepaute lens from the Cape Hatteras Lighthouse.

Administration officials in Washington heeded Meigs' advice and Shubrick responded quickly in a letter on May 8: "Your suggestion with regard to the papers contained in the boxes shall be attended to." But Shubrick was not exactly certain who should do the "attending" and sent an inquiry up the chain of command. George Harrington, assistant secretary of the Treasury, wrote back to the Light House Board Chairman: "Your letter of the 15th instant relative to the disposition of papers belonging to the State archives of North Carolina used as packing paper for the Lighthouse apparatus recaptured at Raleigh from the rebels and forwarded to your office by General Meigs, has been received. I have to request that you will cause the paper to be properly arranged and transmitted to this department."

There, the matter seemed to rest as far as the records go, until 1905,

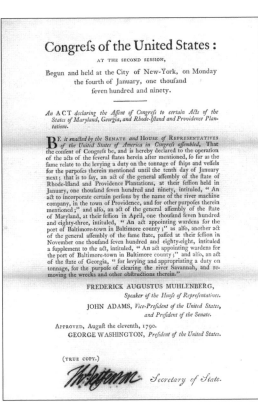

Congrefs of the United States :

AT THE SECOND SESSION,

Begun and held at the City of New-York, on Monday
the fourth of January, one thoufand
feven hundred and ninety.

An ACT *declaring the Affent of Congrefs to certain Acts of the
States of Maryland, Georgia, and Rhode-Ifland and Providence Plantations.*

BE it enacted by the SENATE and HOUSE of REPRESENTATIVES
of the United States of America in Congrefs affembled, That
the confent of Congrefs be, and is hereby declared to the operation
of the acts of the feveral ftates herein after mentioned, fo far as the
fame relate to the levying a duty on the tonnage of fhips and veffels
for the purpofes therein mentioned until the tenth day of January
next; that is to fay, an act of the general affembly of the ftate of
Rhode-Ifland and Providence Plantations, at their feffion held in
January, one thoufand feven hundred and ninety, intituled, " An
act to incorporate certain perfons by the name of the river machine
company, in the town of Providence, and for other purpofes therein
mentioned;" and alfo, an act of the general affembly of the ftate
of Maryland, at their feffion in April, one thoufand feven hundred
and eighty-three, intituled, " An act appointing wardens for the
port of Baltimore-town in Baltimore county;" as alfo, another act
of the general affembly of the fame ftate, paffed at their feffion in
November one thoufand feven hundred and eighty-eight, intituled
a fupplement to the act, intituled, " An act appointing wardens for
the port of Baltimore-town in Baltimore county;" and alfo, an act
of the ftate of Georgia, " for levying and appropriating a duty on
tonnage, for the purpofe of clearing the river Savannah, and removing the wrecks and other obftructions therein."

FREDERICK AUGUSTUS MUHLENBERG,
Speaker of the Houfe of Reprefentatives.

JOHN ADAMS, *Vice-Prefident of the United States,
and Prefident of the Senate.*

APPROVED, Auguft the eleventh, 1790.
GEORGE WASHINGTON, *Prefident of the United States.*

(TRUE COPY.)

Secretary of State.

This original copy of an Act of Congress approved by President George Washington on August 14, 1790, and signed by Secretary of State Thomas Jefferson is believed to be among 1,500 papers returned to the state in 1906.

Courtesy North Carolina Division of Archives and History.

when an effort in Raleigh to catalog the state's archives determined that many of its Colonial records were missing, including the Old North State's only original copy of the Bill of Rights. At about the same time, someone in the U.S. State Department discovered North Carolina's documents on file in that office, but no one knew when, why, or how, they were deposited there. U.S. Senator F.M. Simmons of North Carolina wanted his state's papers returned. However, it was not a trivial matter and ultimately required a joint resolution (S.R. 26) of the 59th Congress to facilitate the transfer. A debate was waged on the Senate floor over two days and some senators of northern states resisted the transfer. Wisconsin's Senator Spooner asked: "I should like to ask the Senator [F.M. Simmons] how did these papers get into the State Department?" Simmons: "I am not able to speak positively about that, but just at the close of the war…the Federal forces occupied the capital of my State, Raleigh." Spooner: "Are these papers a part of the Confederate archives?" Rebellious states were prohibited from possessing Confederate archives. "These are State papers," answered Senator Lodge of Massachusetts. "Are they ancient papers?" asked Spooner. Simmons responded: "Some of the papers are letters from Delegates to the Continental Congress." "That may fairly be considered ancient," said the apparently satisfied senator from Wisconsin. What none of the U.S. senators, nor North Carolina state officials, knew at the time (and did not learn until August 2002) was that the ancient, state papers had also been wrapping papers for Fresnel lenses. In March, 1906, nearly 1,500 documents that had been used to pack the recovered lenses of North Carolina's lighthouses were returned to the state's archives.[151-1]

North Carolina's original copy of the Bill of Rights was not among the papers returned to the state. It reportedly re-surfaced in the 1920s when a New York lawyer, representing an anonymous client in possession of the artifact, contacted state officials with an offer to sell it back to its original owners. The state refused on the basis that it did not purchase stolen property and that the state was, in fact, the rightful owner.[151-2]

E vents transpired quickly after the final surrender at Bennett's farmhouse. Grant and Meigs left Raleigh for Morehead City and Washington on April 27. Two days later, Sherman went by rail to Wilmington for a quick visit to Savannah. General Schofield was placed in command of the Department of North Carolina and a substantial occupying force. The remainder of Sherman's victorious army began the long march to Washington. The 28,000 men of the 14th and 20th Corps crossed the Neuse River at Falls and followed a route north that would take them to the Taylor's Ferry crossing of the 750-foot-wide Roanoke River. More jubilant and orderly than during its days in Georgia and South Carolina, the army still persisted in its foraging habits and cut a wide swath across the countryside. Before reaching the Roanoke, the Federal troops passed right through Townsville and Hibernia Plantation, that remote, insignificant community that was once the hiding place of the apparatus from the Cape Hatteras Lighthouse. The pounding of Granville County soil by Yankee leather shoes had finally come to pass. But in none of the storehouses and barns surrounding Townsville was the Hatteras lens found.

Fifteen

THE IDENTITY OF THE "RALEIGH" LENS

The lighthouse property that had been stored in the North Carolina Capitol was lost.

So reads an index to letters, partially burned in a fire, written to the U.S. Light House Board from its agent at Wilmington, North Carolina. As soon as board Chairman Shubrick received word of the discovery of the lighthouse apparatus at Raleigh, he sent his acting 5th District engineer and inspector, Jeremy Smith, on board the schooner, *Lenox*, to Wilmington, and then by rail to Raleigh, to take possession of the property. Smith arrived in Raleigh after May 1, and found the Capitol empty—no lighthouse lenses or lamps. The provost marshal's office on the first floor of the State House told Smith that they were not certain, as they had been busy keeping order in the city, but that the apparatus may have been shipped to either Wilmington or Washington, D.C., presumably by Sherman's quartermaster. Smith boarded a train and went back to Wilmington, where again he came up empty handed. "On my return [to Wilmington] made diligent search for them but could not gain any information in regard to them," Smith wrote in his report to Admiral Shubrick. Unfortunately for the harried lighthouse engineer, the "Raleigh" apparatus had already arrived in Washington.

At the Washington Navy Yard, on the banks of the Anacostia River, the Light House Board engineering secretary began the process of sorting through all of the material captured by Sherman's army at Raleigh. The board still did not know what lighthouse lenses it had recovered. When the War of the Rebellion began, there were only two first-order Fresnel lenses among North Carolina's nearly two dozen lighthouses, beacons and screwpile towers—the Henry-Lepaute lens at Cape Hatteras and the Cape Lookout lens manufactured by the firm of Lemonnier, Sauter and Company. All of the French manufacturers identified their lenses with the company's name etched on a brass plate at the base of the apparatus. The lighthouses from which the lenses at Raleigh were taken could be identified by their manufacturer. As the crates were opened, the board's staff first discovered that only one, first-order lens was among the third, fourth, and sixth apparatus. If there was only one, which one? Cape Hatteras or Cape Lookout? The workers were, no doubt, holding their breath as they searched for the brass plate among the cata-dioptric panels of the first-order lens.

In the meantime, members of the board and others affiliated with the lighthouse establishment, including officers of the Coast Survey, executives in the shipping industry and the offices of the American Coast Pilot, were all impatient to find out if the Cape Hatteras apparatus had been recovered. The rumor going around was that the lens in the North Carolina Capitol was from Hatteras. George Blunt wrote to the Light House Board requesting confirmation that the "illuminating apparatus taken from the Hatteras Light was reported to be at Raleigh." Blunt's original letter was lost in a Commerce Department fire in the 1920s, but is referenced in an index of general correspondence to the board, dated June 12, 1865. The response to Blunt's letter, copied by a clerk into a letterbook, survived the fire, and in it is the answer to Blunt's inquiry and the identity of the first-order lens recovered at Raleigh. It was the Lemonnier-Sauter lens from the Cape Lookout Lighthouse. The Naval Secretary, Rear Admiral Andrew A. Harwood, in his response to George Blunt, wrote:

> Sir: In reply to your letter of June 12th I have to say that a first-order lens (fixed) originally in use at Cape Lookout, North Carolina, was found by Gen. Sherman at Raleigh and has been sent to New York.[152]

discovered at Raleigh included Bodie Island's third-order apparatus; the fourth-order lens from Bogue Banks Lighthouse near Fort Macon; and numerous sixth-order lenses from the North Carolina sounds.

The reunited but unreconciled nation began the long, painful struggle to heal its wounds, bury its dead, and rebuild its homes, industries and public structures. The Light House Board faced a daunting and pressing task: the re-establishment, repair or reconstruction of more than 100 lighthouses. Southern ports had to be opened quickly to international shipping to facilitate the recovery of the South's destitute economy, and lighthouses were crucial to light the way. Over the summer of 1865, lighthouse lenses were found throughout the coastal regions of the South. A second-order apparatus was discovered at Savannah and was suspected to be from the burned-out Tybee Island Lighthouse. The second-order revolving lens from the destroyed Hunting Island light was found but in "very bad order." In Florida, Keeper James Armouk found and recovered from a local creek, the first-order Fresnel lens from the lighthouse at Jupiter Inlet. Thirty-six cases of lens apparatus were found in a storehouse at Pensacola Navy Yard but not until the June of the following year. Near Gulfport, Mississippi, the lens from the Pass Christian Lighthouse was found, and the third-order lens from the Matagorda Island Light in Texas was exhumed, having been buried in the sand. Some lenses, especially the small, easier to remove and transport fourth, fifth and sixth-order apparatus, were able to be reinstalled with little or no repair, and those lighthouses were the first to be relighted.

Throughout the remainder of 1865, the Southern states continued to be under the control of various U.S. Army and Navy departments, and as lighthouse establishment property was recovered, it was moved to military storage facilities. The Light House Board was overwhelmed by the recovery operation of lenses and had difficulty keeping track of their locations. The process was handled at the highest levels of government. Admiral Harwood, representing the board, wrote to Gen. E.D. Townsend of the War Department on August 16, asking the adjutant general to "…furnish this office with a copy of the W.D. [War Department] order relative to recovery of Lighthouse property scattered over the Southern part of the country."[153] Fresnel lenses from lighthouses that had been completely demolished by Confederate saboteurs, such as the third-order lens from Bodie Island and the first-order apparatus from Sand Island, Alabama, were recovered and returned to the Light House Board's Staten Island, New York, depot. But four months after the cessation of hostilities, Admiral Shubrick and his staff began to anxiously wonder what happened to the most important and most symbolic lens of all, the Henry-Lepaute Hatteras apparatus. It had yet to be found.

During the sultry, dog days of August, 1865, the town of Henderson, North Carolina, began to receive wagon loads of golden, leaf tobacco from the fields of Granville County, to be sold and stored in the auction houses of that increasingly important railroad stop on the Raleigh and Gaston line. For a few months each year, the town had a distinctive, sweet aroma under the baking summer sun. Tobacco was not the only valuable commodity that was being stored in Henderson at that time. During the late summer of 1865, a patrol of Union soldiers discovered the much sought after Fresnel lens from the Cape Hatteras Lighthouse. How and when it was taken there is not known—but it was presumably accomplished by Dr. David Tayloe and John Hargrove of Hibernia. The fact that it was discovered months after the end of the war, after thousands of Federal troops had swarmed over Henderson and Granville County on their way back home, suggests the apparatus was discreetly removed from its hiding place and taken to Henderson when things became more settled. It is possible the boxes of crown-crystal panels and the loose pieces of castings were hidden beneath piles of tobacco on the way to market. Hargrove and Tayloe may have dropped off the lens on their way to Washington, North Carolina, where they attended to the estate of Tayloe's mother, who had died during the war.[154] However the lens made it to Henderson, its passage did not happen without some difficulty. Presumably, Hargrove no longer possessed a labor force, and the railroad tracks that carried the lens into Townsville had long since been removed for the construction of Confederate ironclad gunboats. By wagon, the trip from Townsville to Henderson was about 20 miles over rolling terrain. By water, the trip would have been

Wagonloads of tobacco being transported to auction at South Hill, VA, depicted in this vintage postcard. The relocation of the lens from Hibernia to Henderson may have been accomplished in just such a manner. Author's Collection.

made by poling flats up Nutbush Creek, which flowed from Henderson past Hibernia. Either way, the Hatteras apparatus landed in Henderson unannounced. Its former caretakers, preferring anonymity, assumed that sooner or later the right people would find it.

Unfortunately, it was not found quickly enough. It became known among the townsfolk that some Henderson residents had found and pilfered parts of the lens in the hopes that its return might afford some kind of reward. Times were tough and people were desperate. Nevertheless, the U.S. Light House Board, one of the most staid, close-fisted and humorless bureaucratic organizations that ever served American taxpayers, learned of the lens's discovery and captivity and summoned the full weight of the U.S. Army to descend on the Granville County town and its citizens. On September 13, the newly appointed engineering secretary of the Light House Board, Colonel Orlando Poe, fired off a letter to Brevet Major General Thomas H. Ruger, the commander of the Department of North Carolina at Raleigh:

Sir: Certain portions of the illuminating apparatus formerly in use at Cape Hatteras Lt. House N.C. have been recovered at

Henderson N.C. but other parts of the same lens are witheld [sic] by parties in that vicinity—probably in the hope that a reward will be offered for their restitution. Mr. Simon W. Kitrell of Henderson reports that one H. Harris refuses to deliver up certain parts of this lens now in his possession. The Board would be obliged if you will give such orders in the case as will insure the prompt restitution of this property to the U.S. Lt. Ho. Establishment.

Colonel Poe was familiar with the wily ways of certain Tar Heels. Just four months earlier in Raleigh, the former engineer of Sherman's army was used by Charles Manly to do the ex-governor's dirty work. It is also interesting to note that Henderson historians today surmise that Kitrell was black, and Harris was probably white.[155] Nevertheless, General Ruger did his duty, and after four and a half long years, the well traveled, Cape Hatteras Lighthouse lens was finally back in the possession of the Federal government. Being conveniently located near the railroad, the Hatteras apparatus was sent directly on the recently repaired Seaboard and Roanoke line, to the 5th District inspector of the lighthouse establishment at Norfolk. The source of the lens left the inspector somewhat dubious as to its identity because in a letter to the Light House Board he wrote that he had received the lighthouse apparatus "supposed" to belong to Cape Hatteras. The inspector made a point to emphasize "supposed." The Norfolk agent was ordered to send the lens immediately to the depot at Staten Island.[156]

The Lighthouse Board had no doubt what lighthouse the lens was from.

Sixteen

LENS REPAIRS AND NEW LIGHTHOUSES

At the offices of the United States Light House Board inside the Treasury building in Washington, there was a critical meeting during the autumn of 1865. A steady stream of damaged Southern lighthouse lenses was overwhelming the organization's lamp shops and storage facilities at Staten Island. Chairman William Shubrick solemnly addressed the distinguished members of the board seated around a large table, representing the Corps of Topographical Engineers, the Coast Survey, civilian scientists, the U.S. Navy, the Army Corps of Engineers, and the Secretary of the Treasury. Shubrick's report was discouraging. Chipped, cracked, broken, and missing crown-crystal prisms of many lenses; bent, twisted bronze frames; deformed panels and missing pedestals; represented dozens of nonfunctional illuminating apparatus, and created a crisis for the U.S. lighthouse establishment. The recent war's impact on the nation's aids to navigation was far worse than officials had imagined, and there was not nearly enough money in the department's budget to replace the board's Fresnel lenses with new purchases. Even if they had the funds, it would take years to construct new lenses to relight the Southern coast. A special committee was formed to consider the problem of the "the disposal…of the damaged Light-house apparatus in store at the Depot."[157] The board had a well-earned reputation for being fiscally responsible, and at the meeting on November 17,

The U.S. Light House Board's Staten Island, New York depot. The building on the left was known as the "Old Lamp Shop," where Fresnel lenses from extinguished Southern lighthouses were inspected before being returned to their manufacturers in France. The building on the right was the administration offices of the 3rd District inspector and engineer. Courtesy of the National Lighthouse Museum.

the members decided to try to have the damaged lenses returned to their respective Paris makers to be repaired and refitted.

Initially, it was considered an experiment. Being the cautious and conservative organization that it was, the Light House Board was not entirely confident the Paris manufacturers could repair the lenses for a reasonable cost. "The disposition to be made of the damaged apparatus recovered in the future will greatly depend upon the result of this experiment, and of course the question is an open one," wrote Admiral Shubrick to the firm of Lemmonier and Sauter on the Champs-Elyses. By November 1, the New York depot had received 23 sets of lighthouse apparatus that required substantial repairs, while 12 sets from the Gulf Coast, being small and less susceptible to damage, were given minor tune-ups at the lighthouse workshop at New Orleans.

Among the first nine sets returned to France were the first-order Cape Lookout lens and the third-order Bodie Island lens from North

Carolina. The Board placed a high priority on the repair of lenses from Southern towers that would most benefit the mariner and the temporary third-order lens at Cape Lookout was woefully inadequate for its assignment. The old stone tower at Hatteras received a replacement first-order lens in 1863, so the repair of its original lens was not considered urgent.

In the early stages of what became a multi-year process, the repair orders to the lens manufacturers were very specific about the work required. Possibly the board feared their vendors, being 3,000 miles away, might try to repair more than was necessary (an allowance was made for potential damage during shipping). The memorandum from Chairman Shubrick regarding the Cape Lookout and Bodie Island lenses was written as follows:

> Gentlemen: I have to request that you will make as soon as convenient the following described parts of illuminating apparatus. Upon completion of the work, it should be securely packed, marked "Lighthouse Apparatus," and shipped to the Collector of Customs, New York City, United States, who will pay your bill.
>
> I. First-order, fixed 270°—Cape Lookout. Lens to be refitted with sound prisms in place of 17 which are badly chipped. Astragals, horizontal rings, Crown for lens, Socket, Pedestal Table, Lockers, Balustrade & Wagner Lamps.
>
> II. Third-Order revolving—Body's Island. Lens to be refitted with 65 Sound prisms including 2 annular prisms in place of those which are broken. Astragals, horizontal rings for lens socket, Crown for lens, Pedestal Table, Revolving Machinery.[158]

The other lighthouse lenses, shipped to Paris on November 28, included Cape St. George, Cape San Blas, Sabine Pass and Galveston light, all from the Gulf Coast. One of the nine, the most badly damaged apparatus from Cape San Blas, required 137 new prisms. In case it was not obvious to the Paris craftsmen, Shubrick reiterated the need for expediency and appealed to the Frenchman's altruistic sensibilities:

Screwpile lighthouse at Croatan Sound, North Carolina. Note the sixth-order lens housed in the lantern on the roof. National Archives.

"The question of time is an important one, and it is urged that the repairs be made as soon as possible in order that the apparatus may be re-established upon our Southern coast and the commerce of the world be benefited thereby."

Months passed, the Light House Board waited, and much of the Southern coast of the United States passed the nights in darkness. Then, Commodore C.S. Biggs, USN, 3rd District Inspector at Tompkinsville, Staten Island, New York received a message from Paris. The ship, *Gettysburgh*, was due at the port of New York by the middle of August, 1866. On board was the newly refurbished, first-order illuminating apparatus formerly in use at Cape Lookout. The Board's experiment was about to be tested. The heavily padded crates were carefully unloaded on the depot's pier and hand-carried into the four story brick building that served as the warehouse and lamp shop prior to 1868. Under the intent gaze of Inspector Biggs and his district engineer, the crates were opened. The lens was magnificent. It was perfectly restored. Good as new. The question of the feasibility of repairing the Southern lights was no longer an open one. Over the next few years, the Board even learned to trust their French vendors. Their letters to the lensmakers were no longer specific as to what repairs were needed.

Soon, lighthouses along the Southern and Gulf coasts began to be relighted. Once more, captains and navigators could see the reassuring flashes of their long lost friends. The smaller harbor, inlet and sound-based lights were re-established first. Near the ruins of the once formidable Fort Fisher, the only lighthouse that was renamed during the war—Confederate Point—was relighted, and again called, Federal Point.[159] Five screwpile lighthouses in the North Carolina sounds all received lenses and were relighted during the first year after the war.[160]

Often, the inland waterway lighthouses exhibiting fourth, fifth or sixth-order lenses did not receive the same apparatus that was originally installed because lanterns of the same size were interchangeable. For example, the Oak Island front range light on the Cape Fear River was replaced with a lens recovered from Hunting Island, South Carolina. However, interchanging lenses was not typical for the big, seacoast towers like Pensacola Light or Cape Lookout. With few exceptions, the Light House Board endeavored to return first-order lenses to their original home, matched to their pedestals and revolving machinery. A little more than six months after it was returned from Paris, the first-order Cape Lookout apparatus was carried back to the Staten Island pier to be shipped south. Shubrick to Biggs, March 19, 1867: "You will please forward as soon as possible to W.J. Newman, Esq., Acting L.H. Engineer, Baltimore, Maryland, the first-order apparatus marked L.H.B./L.S. 215—242, recently repaired in France, and now in store at the Staten Island Depot, sending with it all the necessary accessories and supplies of an apparatus of that class, except oil and oil butts. The apparatus is intended for use at Cape Lookout Light Station to replace the third-order lens now there."[161] Apparatus "L.H.B./L.S. 215—242" was the original Cape Lookout lens.

By 1866, the staff of the Light House Board and its employees at district offices along the Atlantic, Gulf and Pacific seaboards were working at a feverish pace. As lighthouses were re-established in the South and new ones were being planned, the recruitment and appointments of keepers and assistant keepers kept the local superintendents and district inspectors busy. They were so busy and so hurried, field offices began to employ, and enjoy, the speed and instant response of the telegraph. Of course, sending a message by telegraph was not free, and many lighthouse establishment employees had not yet learned the virtues of brevity. The reaction of the miserly Board was predictable. By the Fall of 1866, the Board had received so many telegrams that were, in their opinion, "unnecessarily verbose," they sent instructions to their employees stating that "unless there is a crisis that will endanger public property, all communications should be sent by mail, and otherwise, any critical message sent by telegram should and could be done in ten words or less."

The home office of the lighthouse establishment was also having difficulty keeping track of which Fresnel lenses were in France, at Staten Island, or in the holds of ships in between. "Please report what lenses have been received and what lenses have been issued," was one message sent to the New York Depot. "Send list of lenses now in store and in the hands of manufacturers for repair," read another. So as to not overwhelm the Paris manufacturers with too many lenses at once or place too great a strain on federal coffers, the Board parceled out a few orders at a time. The warehouse at Staten Island was still full of damaged Southern lenses at the beginning of 1867. It was not until May of that year that the Cape Hatteras apparatus was finally returned to Messieurs Henry-Lepaute, No. 6, Rue Lafayette, Paris. Shubrick wrote the following to the esteemed lensmaker:

> A lens of the first-order made by yourself and formerly in use at Cape Hatteras Lighthouse, but which was damaged by the rebels during the late war, is sent to you for repairs and refitment. When the repairs are completed you will please ship the apparatus to the Inspector of the 3rd Lighthouse District, New York City, and collect your bill in the usual way.

The repairs were made, the lens was boxed and marked, "Hatteras," and was placed aboard the sailing vessel, *Edith*, for the voyage to New York. It was the second east-west, trans-Atlantic crossing in the life of the Henry-Lepaute apparatus. The *Edith* arrived on October 14, 1868, and the 37 boxes marked "Hatteras" were placed in the general storage section of the Staten Island Depot for future use at a yet-to-be deter-mined lighthouse. Not at Cape Hatteras, there was already a first-order lens there.

The post-war 1860s for the lighthouse establishment were also a pro-lific period of planning, surveying, design, funding and construc-tion of new lighthouses on all three coasts of the United States. Never before, and never after, was the nation's lighthouse service required to manage so many diverse projects at one time. It was, without question, the Golden Age of American lighthouses, brilliantly born out of the darkness of the Civil War. The board set ambitious goals for filling-in critical dark stretches along the East Coast and continuing the decades-long process of lighting the Pacific seaboard from California to the new Alaska Territory. Lighthouses under construction at the outbreak of the war had to be completed. Others destroyed during the war had to be replaced. The Board also committed to retiring the beleaguered fleet of sound- and river-based light vessels, many of which spent the war sub-merged, with more practical screwpile lighthouses and more modern, lighted bell buoys.

Major lighthouse construction projects after the war included first-order lights at: California's Cape Mendocino (completed 1868), Point Reyes (1870), Point Arena (1870), Pigeon Point (1872), and Oregon's Yaquina Head Lighthouse (1873). Florida was scheduled to receive first-order lenses for new lighthouses at Cape Canaveral (1868), at Alligator Reef on Matecumbe Key (1873) and at St. Augustine (1874). Most of the new lighthouses were to receive newly commissioned apparatus from the Paris manufacturers, not refur-bished lenses damaged during the Civil War. Tybee Island Lighthouse, badly weakened by fire during the war, was bolstered by new brick and was raised to 154 feet. Tybee Island is one case of a major lighthouse being assigned the lens of another during the post-war years. The Light House Board sent the repaired Sand Island first-order lens to be installed at Tybee Island during the Spring of 1867 (Tybee Island originally exhibited a second-order light).

Initially, all shipments were routed through the Staten Island Depot for inspection before being sent to designated lighthouses. However,

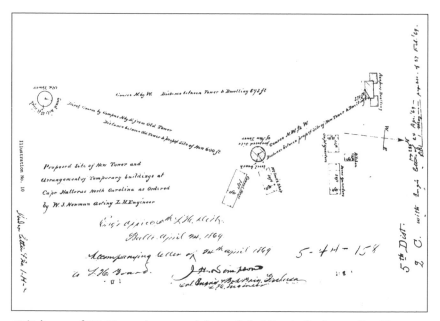

1868 diagram of W.J. Newman's survey and choice of a building site for the new Cape Hatteras Lighthouse approved by his successor, 5th District Engineer J.H. Simpson, on April 24, 1869. The 1803 tower location is on the left, the proposed new tower site is in the middle-right, and the keeper's house is on the far right. National Archives.

before long, the 3rd District employees could not handle the tremendous volume of inbound materials. The board requested apparatus and lanterns for West Coast lighthouses be shipped directly to their respective district engineers. The Paris lensmakers and U.S. manufacturers of the iron lanterns that enclosed a lighthouse's fragile glass optics, were furnished shipping options for Pacific coast lights based on construction timetables and the seasons. If a component was due and ready to be shipped from August through December, it was sent around Cape Horn at the southern tip of South America by a first-class clipper ship. If the fragile glass lenses and heavy iron lanterns were ready in other months, their manufacturers would secure transportation across the isthmus of Panama, shorter but fraught with its own challenges. Not all deliveries were made problem free. Barbier and Fenestra received a letter from the board commending them on "a beautiful piece of workmanship" on the Point Reyes first-order lens. However, the Paris lensmaker's craftsmanship did not go beyond the glasswork—their packing of the lens was sloppy. The board's letter included this reprimand: "It seems it was not packed well, as many prisms are found loose, and some even out of the frame. Fortunately, none are broken. It will take some time to put the apparatus in complete order. While this apparatus seems to be well made, its defective packing rendered it liable to destruction, a state of things not at all satisfactory. It is the most expensive lens ever purchased by the United States, and any injury to it due to defective packing is a grave matter."

O n the North Carolina Outer Banks, there was a question of the destroyed Bodie Island Lighthouse. Admiral Shubrick asked the superintendent of the U.S. Coast Survey, Professor B. Pierce, for his organization's views "as to the propriety and necessity of re-establishing the light at Body's Island, North Carolina, which was discontinued by the rebels in 1861, and not yet relighted." However, the biggest project on the drafting tables in the engineering offices of the Light House Board was the proposed new lighthouse at Cape Hatteras. Because of its location, at the landward end of a large and deadly sand reef, Diamond Shoals, and adjacent to one of the most heavily traveled ocean passages in the world, the new Cape Hatteras tower was designed by the board to serve as a functional and symbolic monument representing all American lighthouses. Originally designed to shine 150 feet above its base, the board amended the plans so the focal plane of the light would be at 180 feet, partly to satisfy the needs of the merchant fleet. No inferior materials or workmanship would be tolerated for "a tower so expensive and exposed as the new one proposed for Cape Hatteras…quality is a much greater object than price," announced the board. Construction was scheduled to begin in the autumn of 1868.

With so much activity going on at the Light House Board offices in Washington, D.C., there were bound to be mistakes. The board contracted with surveyors on both Atlantic and Pacific coasts to iden-tify and acquire the best parcels of land on which to place the nation's new lighthouses. The siting of the numerous West Coast projects occu-pied most of the board's attention. Identifying the location of the new Hatteras tower was practically an afterthought. The choice of locations at the Cape was actually made by default and was justified in the board's Annual Report of 1869:

The site selected bear north by east 600 feet distant from the old tower, and therefore as near it as well could be. The sailing directions will be very slightly affected if at all. It is on the general level of the beach, and therefore secure from the destructive action of the wind, which has always so seriously threatened the foundations of the old tower…The site is also above the highest level of the sea and so far removed from the water line as to render it safe from encroachment from the sea.[162]

It seemed a simple decision, one dictated by practicality. Nevertheless, it was arguably the most serious blunder made by the Light House Board, long regarded as a federal organization that never made mistakes. The Board should have considered issues such as erosion, which had eaten away 1,000 feet of beach in the preceding 20 years. Being located "on the general level of the beach…secure from the destructive action of the wind" simply meant the new tower would not be precariously perched on top of a migratory dune like the 1803 lighthouse. Nor were sailing directions a necessary consideration. The change in the height of the light's focal plane necessitated revised charts regardless of the tower's location.

There were better locations for a lighthouse at the Cape, including the high ground behind the ancient live oaks of Buxton Woods, but no other locations were even evaluated. The final site had been chosen by former District Engineer W.J. Newman, but was not formally approved by the board until after construction had begun. Subsequently, Newman was replaced by General J.H. Simpson.[163] Simpson was a war veteran and a good engineer, but he knew little about Hatteras and its history. When he took over the project, the foundation of the tower, including its improvised and unique pine timber mat topped with huge blocks of granite, was well underway. Simpson had no choice but to endorse the choice of sites. Still, the new Cape Hatteras Lighthouse was considered too important for the board to not be absolutely certain that they had put it in the best possible location, so a committee was sent to Hatteras to see for themselves. They arrived six months after the start of construction and in true bureaucratic fashion endorsed the preceding justifications, featured in the 1869 Annual Report, to justify the site as a good one.

The lighthouse-location boondoggle would produce unimaginable consequences.

Seventeen

The Pigeon Point Connection

The construction of the second Cape Hatteras Lighthouse was completed by the end of November, 1870, two years after it was begun. In May of that year, District Engineer Simpson sent his assistant from Baltimore to Cape Hatteras to examine and measure the first-order lens and pedestal in the 1803 tower to determine the necessary specifications for the iron lantern of the new tower, which had been designed but not yet forged. The assistant concluded that some changes would have to be made to the new lantern in order to accommodate the old lens (the first-order, Henry-Lepaute apparatus installed in 1863). Before Simpson's assistant returned from Hatteras however, the Light House Board sent a message to Simpson in Baltimore and asked him if he would prefer to receive a "new" lens for the new lighthouse. "Originally the Light House Board thought that it would use the lens in the old tower for the new tower...[but] rather than going to the trouble of transferring the old one [,]...the Board said it had on hand a first-order flashing lens with pedestal."[164] District Engineer Simpson accepted. It would take some pressure off his lampist who would have had to expedite the lens transfer between lighthouses to minimize the amount of time the Cape would go unlighted. Now, the old lighthouse could be extinguished one morning and the new lighthouse illuminated at dusk on the same day.

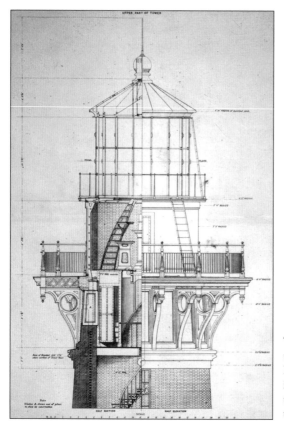

The engineering plans of the upper part of the 1870 Cape Hatteras Lighthouse. The lantern is the level below the roof and the watchroom is below the lantern. National Archives.

The Board shipped the lens to Baltimore by inland waterway from New York and it arrived by mid-June. At Baltimore, the district lampist took measurements of the new lens and found that some minor changes to the lantern would have to be made. It was the same conclusion made of the lens installed in 1863. The lens was repacked and sent on to the Cape, following the age-old route through Hatteras Inlet, up the west shoreline of the island to Cape Channel, onto lighters for the haul across the shallows of Pamlico Sound and ashore at Back Landing Creek. The first-order lens was loaded onto a tram railway and pulled to the building site by teams of oxen, the same route taken by the huge granite blocks and one million red bricks used to build the massive lighthouse.

At the construction site, the process employed eight years earlier, when H.F. Hancock, Ben Fulcher and the hired machinist, removed the original Henry-Lepaute lens from the old lighthouse, was carried out in reverse. The 48 cata-dioptric and 24 bull's-eye panels were wrapped in thick, wool blankets and individually hoisted up the outside of the 18-story structure. At the wide deck outside the watch-room, the panels were received by lampist George Crosman and were lifted, this time just 15 feet, into the lantern room, where they were each bolted into place, one at a time in the huge iron frame. With one panel attached, the lampist rotated the assembly 180 degrees and mounted the opposite panel to keep the fragile apparatus in balance. It must have been pleasurable work seeing the French masterpiece take form, unlike the desperate work performed by the Southern-loyalists in 1861. As their many predecessors had done at the top of the 1803 lighthouse, standing 600 feet away, lampist Crosman and his help-ers would have taken breaks from installing and calibrating the lens. Likely, they stepped out on the gallery to enjoy the stunning view and fresh seabreeze from the top of the new tower. They probably did not notice the Atlantic Ocean lapping, much closer than ever before to the perimeter of the Cape Hatteras Light Station.

There are varying opinions, but the new Cape Hatteras Lighthouse was probably illuminated for the first time at dusk on December 17, 1870. The U.S. Light House Board had built its monument to light-keeping—the tallest brick lighthouse in the world. No one could have imagined then that a time would come when more than half a million people a year would travel from all over the United States and the world to see the lighthouse. Like pilgrims to a shrine, they would come to admire the symbol of steadfast endurance and climb 268 steps to the summit. The imposing edifice became a memorial honoring the courage and daring of seafarers and the compassion of those on shore who would guide them to safety. It would not be the only hallowed ground on North Carolina's Outer Banks. Thirty-three years to the day, and 55 miles to the north of the lighthouse, another remarkable achievement took place—humankind's first powered flight on the perpetual breezes of Kill Devil Hills.

O ver the following weeks, after the new lighthouse began operating, the lampist and the construction crew dismantled the replace-ment Henry-Lepaute lens that had been installed in the old lighthouse

1893 photograph showing the ruins of the 1803 Cape Hatteras tower and the remains of the dune on which it stood. The 1870 tower was located 600 feet to the northeast. This photo was taken near the edge of the surf. North Carolina Archives photo.

in 1863, and packed it up for shipment to the storage facility at Staten Island. Once all of the reusable ironwork and other components of the 1803 tower were removed, the "ponderous" stone and brick structure, teetering above its unstable foundation, was toppled to the ground by three explosive charges. "A large wedge [was blown out] on the side toward the beach & this old landmark was spread out on the beach a mass of ruins," reported the district engineer. The 1803 lighthouse had had a brief but stormy career. Its construction had been a minor miracle at such a remote and inhospitable place. For 60 years, its keepers fought a never-ending and desperate battle to hold the hill on which the light-house stood in place. The lighthouse survived lantern fires, lightning strikes, hurricanes, and slanderous accusations against its keepers. The ill-fated lighthouse, too short and too dim to fulfill its assignment, was cursed by sailors at sea who could not see it. The "Hamilton Tower," as it is often called, was reviled and championed by some of the most influential leaders of the nation's maritime industry. Its lens had been taken and the tower was nearly blown up by Confederate saboteurs. In February, 1871, the worn-out lighthouse was reduced to rubble, an

inglorious and unfortunate end for the historic but beleaguered structure. It, too, became a "lost light."

During the two-year period of construction at Cape Hatteras,
shipwrecks were piling up at another deadly place on the U.S.
seacoast—Pigeon Point, a prominent headland halfway between
Monterey Bay and San Francisco's Golden Gate. The name of the
rocky promontory on the shores of San Mateo County came from the
wreck of a grand and fast clipper ship, the *Carrier Pigeon*, in 1853.
Bureaucratic red tape and the American Civil War postponed efforts
to build a lighthouse on that foreboding and unforgiving stretch of
coast until California newspaper editors championed the cause. Some
wrote scathing editorials aimed at Congress and the Light House
Board, reporting that the public and ships' captains were resigned
to "more inquiries, more reports, more paper, more ink, more tape,
but no more light."[165] The Light House Board, understandably overwhelmed in projects, finally elevated Pigeon Point to a priority status
and secured an appropriation from Congress to begin construction
of the lighthouse in the spring of 1871. The board had not been
completely inattentive. In August, 1869, the Naval Secretary had
dispatched a request to the firm of Henry-Lepaute, commissioning
specifically for Pigeon Point, a new first-order, 24-panel, revolving
Fresnel lens with a preferred characteristic of "flashing once in every
ten seconds." Coincidentally, the flashing interval of once every 10
seconds was the same characteristic as the original Henry-Lepaute lens
from the 1803 Cape Hatteras Lighthouse, and the one that replaced
it in 1863.

Time was of the essence. Construction at Pigeon Point was
expected to take no more than 12 months, and the board did not want
the production of the lens to hold things up. They afforded Henry-
Lepaute multiple options of 10 or 15 second intervals "to enable
you to select that which might be soonest finished." The entire order
included "lamps of the best-kind and every thing else necessary for
one year's supply of the usual articles and fixtures, tools, implements,
&c, as in early orders from this office, omitting, of course, tower-lan-
tern, oil-tanks and oil." The Paris firm was to send the order by way of

Cape Horn directly to Commodore Alfred Taylor, United States Navy, care of the Collector of Customs, San Francisco.[166]

Once again, a war interfered with the Light House Board's plans and the hopes of San Francisco merchants to see a light flashing from the jagged, ship-killing rocks of Pigeon Point. France was at war with Prussia, and the normal flow of communications between Washington, D.C., and Paris was partially interrupted. The Board did not know if its lensmakers were receiving their correspondence. One letter was sent to Henry-Lepaute asking the firm to "acknowledge your two letters of July 28 and July 29 describing your plan adopted for Pigeon Point." Another letter, the copy of which was badly burned in the Commerce Department fire in the 1920s, was sent to the United States envoy at the Palace of Versailles and expressed the board's concern that, because of the war, their letters were not getting through to Henry-Lepaute. "Would you please help us to facilitate our communications?" asked the board.

It was a trying time for the lighthouse establishment, further confused by the comings and goings of illuminating apparatus between the three Paris lensmakers, the Staten Island Depot and the dozens of active work sites along thousands of miles of American coastline. Just how confusing it must have been for the Light House Board is suggested in a letter they sent to one of the Paris vendors at the time. "This office would be obliged to you if, after deducting the above list—from your list—of completed and in hand apparatus, you will send a list—of other apparatus on hand not finished, so that selection may be made according to our wants and the advanced state of the work on each."

It comes as no surprise that no one seemed to know for certain which lens was eventually sent to the Pigeon Point Lighthouse. The first-order, 24-panel, revolving Fresnel lens was manufactured by Mssrs. Henry-Lepaute—a brass plate at the base of the lens confirms its maker—but it did not arrive directly from Paris, but from Staten Island. Apparently, the Board could wait no longer for the new lens to be completed and chose one from its own inventory. The lighthouse's flashing characteristic would provide a clue as to its origin.

When Pigeon Point light was illuminated for the first time on the evening of November 15, 1872, the 12-foot tall, 6-foot wide apparatus began to rotate on its track of bearings. Lookouts on ships riding the rolling Pacific swells off Pigeon Point sighted a brilliant flash of light, and then counted off the seconds: "1-one thousand, 2-one thousand, 3-one thousand..." until they reached 9-one thousand, and saw another brilliant flash. Pigeon Point did indeed receive a Henry-Lepaute lens with the same flashing interval as the Cape Hatteras lenses, flashing once every 10 seconds.

Some mysteries are created by subterfuge, dishonesty or trickery. Others are born simply of collective bad memory and the passage of time. The mystery of the origins of the Pigeon Point lens was produced by a combination of urban legends, outrageous rumors and inaccurate data. In his book, *The History of the Pigeon Point Lighthouse*, Frank Perry masterfully traced the strange sequence of stories that each purported to confirm the history of the lens. "No other aspect of [Pigeon Point's] past has attracted such wide attention as the mysterious early history of its lens," Perry wrote in 1986.

As the decades passed, the theories of the origins of Pigeon Point's lens became more fantastic. The litany of explanations appeared soon after the lighthouse began operating. The *San Mateo County Gazette* reported that the Fresnel lens had once been used in the Cape Hatteras Lighthouse. In 1878, a publication on the history of the county described the fascinating story of the Pigeon Point lens:

> The lens of the Lighthouse has also a historic interest, having formerly been in use on the Atlantic Coast at Cape Hatteras, where it was captured by the Confederates during the War of the Rebellion and afterwards recaptured by Federal forces.[167]

The fog thickened five years later when a Pigeon Point keeper claimed that Confederates had intercepted the shipment of the lens from France, but it was later recovered by the U.S. government. In 1896, an article in the *San Francisco Call* added intriguing facts to the history of the lens. It was recovered from Cape Hatteras after being buried in the sand but was somehow later discovered "in an old warehouse in New Orleans." The truth was becoming evermore elusive.

Twentieth-century accounts have the lens serving lighthouses in New England, at Fort Sumter, which has never been known to have a lighthouse, and most incredibly, a tourist guide to California stated that the lens was buried under a beach by Union troops "to keep it from falling into Confederate hands." [168]

Predictably, the sensational stories about the Pigeon Point lens produced a high degree of curiosity, but little in the way of effort was made to determine the facts. In 1924, George R. Putnam, U.S. Commissioner of Lighthouses,* attempted to clear things up but, in the process, added a new wrinkle to the mystery. Putnam did some research in response to a request by Pigeon Point's district superintendent and wrote the following conclusion:

> You are advised that the lens now at Pigeon Point appears to be the second lens placed in commission at Cape Hatteras Light Station, North Carolina, in 1863, following what is said to have been the destruction of the lantern and original lens placed at this station in 1854. There is also a notation on the records here that the original lens was carried by Confederate agents to Raleigh and was subsequently recovered, but it is difficult to state whether these statements are true or not for the files of the Bureau covering this period were badly burned a few years ago and are difficult of access.

Putnam implied that, although unlikely, Pigeon Point could have received the original Cape Hatteras, Henry-Lepaute lens. Putnam also said the original Hatteras lens had been destroyed along with its lantern during the Civil War. The mystery of "the lost light" became increasingly complex.

---

*The Commissioner of Lighthouses in the U.S. Bureau of Lighthouses was the successor to the Chairman of the Light House Board, which was abolished by Congress to make the organization more streamlined and less military orieinted.

REDEMPTION AND DISHONOR

At Cape Hatteras, through the hard work and dedication of its keepers, the new lighthouse began decades of service and earned its reputation as America's greatest sentinel.

Keepers were often among the first to sight ships in distress at sea, and during the great Christmas storm of 1884, the Hatteras lighthouse crew kept watch over the distressed barkentine, *Ephraim Williams*, as she drifted to the north, five miles off the beach. Throughout the day, observers could see no sign of life on the stricken vessel. Suddenly, a distress flag was raised, a desperate plea for help! Between the beach and the ship, "the surf was the heaviest and most dangerous [islanders] had seen for years."[169] It didn't seem possible that anything could be done. The water was frigid, the waves rose like mountains and the distance was significant. Daunting as its task may have seemed, the crew from the nearby Cape Hatteras Lifesaving Station considered only one course of action. They put to sea. Their little lifeboat faced "a towering and almost unbroken wall of tumultuous water. But away in the offing there were lives in peril which must be saved at any hazard," reads the Annual Report of the U.S. Lifesaving Service. The men soon breached the breakers of the inner bar, but ahead lay the far more treacherous outer shoals. On the beach, spectators watched in disbelief as the lifeboat pitched vertically so the interior decking, ropes and other equipment were plainly visible. In an instant, the intrepid lifesavers of Cape Hatteras vanished into the seething spindrift. In what was later recognized as one of the greatest lifesaving success stories of all time, the surfboat crew from Cape Hatteras Station braved breaking waves never before attempted and rescued all nine sailors aboard the sinking ship. The handwritten report of Inspector Lieutenant C.F. Shoemaker to Superintendent Sumner Kimball of the U.S. Lifesaving Service has become famous:

> These poor, plain men, dwellers upon the lonely sands of Hatteras, took their lives in their hands, and at most imminent risk, crossed the most tumultuous sea that any boat within the memory of living men has ever attempted on that bleak coast, and all for what? That others might live to see home and friends. Duty, their sense of obligation, and the credit of the Service impelled them to do their mighty best.[170]

Among the seven lifesavers who received gold lifesaving medals from the U.S. government for unparalleled bravery was Isaac Littleton Jennett, grandson of the former lighthouse keeper who was once a wanted man, Benjamin T. Fulcher.

Isaac Jennett was not the last of Benjamin Fulcher's progeny to redeem the old mariner's unfortunate past. Other brave lifesavers were born into the family and three granddaughters married Cape Hatteras keepers. But it was Isaac Jennett's brother, Benjamin, who produced a great-grandson of Benjamin Fulcher who grew up to become, arguably, the greatest lighthouse keeper of all, Unaka Benjamin Jennette. Cap'n 'Naka, as he was fondly called, had Ben Fulcher's piercing blue eyes, and he followed in his great-grandfather's footsteps to become principal keeper of the Cape Hatteras Lighthouse on March 16, 1919. Jennette's career spanned a time equally as tumultuous as that experienced by Ben Fulcher. In 1918, the Diamond Shoals Lightship No. 71 was attacked and sunk by the German unterseeboote, U-*140*, creating quite a stir among Lighthouse Service personnel. Unaka Jennette was Captain of No. 71's relief vessel, which was on station elsewhere at the time. Jennette served as keeper through nor'easters and hurricanes too numerous to mention including the back-to-back storms of 1933. Jennette was a young man when the Wright brothers took to the air and when Reginald Fessenden transmitted the world's first music broadcast from a tower at Buxton. Jennette was newly married

Cape Hatteras keeper,
Unaka Jennette, polishing
the central flash panels of
the first-order Fresnel lens.
National Geographic photo
courtesy of the National Park Service.

when a wireless operator at the Cape received the first distress call from the RMS *Titanic*. Along with his neighbors, the middle-aged Unaka Jennette experienced the Outer Banks' version of the Great Depression, although, with a smile, the proud islanders are quick to say, "It didn't bother us at all. We were already depressed—how are you going to get any worse than that?"[171] Good food and good neighbors were plentiful even if cash was hard to come by.

Through it all, Unaka Jennette took care of the lighthouse as if he had built it himself, brick by brick. During his tenure as keeper, the lighthouse always looked as if it were brand new—not a speck of sand on the floor of the entrance or the tower's nine landings. Every brass and bronze component was polished to a brilliant shine, and the keeper's tools and implements were organized so as to impress the most fastidious of surgeons. Still, of all of his daily chores, it was the 24-panel, Henry-Lepaute, first-order lens that Unaka Jennette loved and cared for like one of his seven children. The keeper would polish the glass endlessly, never tired or bored. Even in the 20ᵗʰ century, the Fresnel lens was a stunningly beautiful and awe-inspiring marvel. Cap'n 'Naka was inexplicably proud of the old lens and was always willing to show it off, as he did when National Geographic photographer, Clifton Adams, showed up on the Banks in 1933 to take pictures for a December issue. Jennette could have been photographed in dozens of settings, but he wanted his picture taken while he was polishing the lens.

Unaka Jennette was a man seasoned by salt spray, unrelenting storms and hard times. Not much could worry the stalwart keeper—except for the rapidly encroaching Atlantic Ocean. When his great-grandfather had been the assistant keeper at Cape Hatteras, the high-tide line was more than half a mile away. On the day Jennette became the principal keeper at the lighthouse, the ocean's waves were crashing just 300 feet short of the base of the tower. In 1861, the original Hatteras light was threatened with destruction by the Third Georgia Regiment. During the 20ᵗʰ century, the new lighthouse faced an enemy of a different sort, and one that would not be denied. Like a thief in the night, each time a storm moved out to sea it took a piece of Hatteras Island with it, and a piece of the hearts of the people who lived there.

Erosion and accretion had always been a natural process on the Outer Banks, as it will be for all time. Since the days when Algonquians prospered on the Banks, people knew the wisdom of building their homes and villages on the western side of the island, on the higher ground protected by the ancient maritime forests and along the less-dynamic shores of Pamlico Sound. The first Cape Hatteras Lighthouse was placed on the eastern side of the Cape, necessitated by a lack of technology and stature and the need to cast its flickering light more than 10 miles over the horizon to ships passing Diamond Shoals. The second Cape Hatteras Lighthouse was located through a terrible lack of foresight and an overabundance of pride. The ocean rarely forgives human mistakes and bravado.

For centuries, Outer Bankers thrived from the ocean's bounty—not just from its fish, but also from what was salvaged from countless shipwrecks: livestock, clothing, food, furniture, fuel and building materials. However, the ocean exacted a price for what it provided, and that price was often paid back by Outer Bankers with their father's land. The Cape Hatteras Lighthouse, too, was in jeopardy of being taken by the ocean in exchange for its builders' conceit.

Like a thief in the night, the rapacious Atlantic steadily consumed the ruins of the 1803 Cape Hatteras Lighthouse. Courtesy National Park Service.

The government's response to the dramatic loss of beach at the lighthouse came too late. Some experts would say that an earlier response would not have mattered at all. When it did come, the remedy was actually a government solution to the Depression's rolls of unemployed and destitute workers—an ambitious plan for the Civilian Conservation Corps to build "protective" artificial dunes the length of the Outer Banks, just as was done to please the wealthy owners of beachfront mansions up north. The dunes were expected to stabilize the island's natural migration and facilitate the construction of the Outer Banks' first, and only, paved highway. It worked as planned but, also at a price. The once broad and gently descending beach-face became dramatically steeper as the ocean's fury had no recourse but to claw and carve the artificial dunes away. With a broad, flat beach, storms often flooded the Hatteras light station with relatively minimal damage. Now the ocean had the ability to reach under the lighthouse and threaten its shallow foundation—at least, that was the fear.

Two hurricanes in 1933 forced keeper Unaka Jennette and his assistants to relocate their families to the safety of Buxton village, away from the deadly surf that besieged the Hatteras light station. Before long, the government abandoned the lighthouse too, resigned to the fact

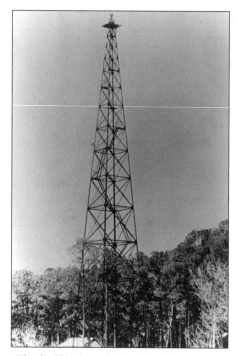

The third lighthouse built at Cape Hatteras began operation on May 13, 1936. National Archives photo.

that an age-old blunder would be punished by the unforgiving sea. An ungainly steel tower, hard to look at and hard to call a lighthouse, was built where the second Hatteras light should have been located, on the high, protected ground in Buxton village.[172] The government's third attempt to build a Cape Hatteras Lighthouse, unthreatened by the sea, seemed to be the charm, but the third Hatteras light was anything but charming. If only surveyor William Tatham, who in 1806 described the original Hatteras light as "an architectural eyesore, made from two kinds of stone," had seen this new lighthouse.

As the sun rose over the horizon on the morning of May 13, 1936, Unaka Jennette, with a heavy heart, extinguished the flame of the incandescent oil vapor lamp and locked off the descending weights of the clockwork mechanism, stopping the rotation of the lens. It was the end of an era.

The sea glittered like gold under low flying puffs of clouds that clearly delineated the western edge of the Gulf Stream. To the south, Jennette may have gazed at the undulating whitecaps dancing over Diamond Shoals, all the way to the horizon. It would have reminded the keeper of the dawn of January 31, 1921, when Jennette and his assistant, James Casey, spied through their looking glass, the five-masted schooner out on the shoals with all her sails set. It was four days before anyone could get close to the mysterious ship. When they finally boarded her, not a soul was to be found aboard. Evidence indicated that the crew simply vanished. From that time on, the Maine-built *Carroll A. Deering* became known as the Ghost Ship of the Graveyard of the Atlantic.

Sunrise from the upper gallery at the Cape Hatteras lighthouse in 1998. Photo by author.

It can be imagined that when Jennette strolled around the parapet for a final time, memories flooded his mind. He might have looked up at the storm panes of the lantern and the iron handholds and wondered how many times he had polished the glass. To the northwest, Jennette would have seen Cape Channel, where the Lighthouse Service side-wheel tenders would appear with supplies, news, and sometimes, a District Inspector. Unaka Jennette was privileged to have been able to start each day with such a view and he probably never failed to consider his blessings. On that last day when Jennette climbed up the steep steps into the lantern to admire the Henry-Lepaute lens, he may have wondered what would become of it. Sunlight often struck the crown-crystal in an explosion of impressionistic colors—indigo, henna, jade. Jennette had not been the first, no-nonsense, island-toughened waterman serving as keeper who paused to enjoy the palate of colors produced by the 1,000 prisms. There were many courageous men who had served his lighthouse and the 1803 tower before it, who swore an oath to never leave their station regardless of weather or other acts of God. Oscar Rue might have come to mind, the keeper who rode out the 1886 Charleston earthquake that rocked the Cape Hatteras Lighthouse "backward and forward like a tree shaken by the wind." Rue wrote to the Light House Board that "the shock was so strong that we could not keep our backs against the parapet wall, it would throw us right from it."[173] Jennette never broke his keeper's oath either. He rode out the worst of hurricanes in the watchroom, 180 feet above the surf.

The view from
an upper landing
inside the 1870
Cape Hatteras
Lighthouse.
Photo by author.

Inside the tower, the handrails of the winding staircase were worn smooth by the strong hands of seven decades of keepers. Jennette had climbed the tower many times—at least two or three times a day for 17 years. Had the keeper computed the figures he would have realized he had climbed the equivalent of more than three million vertical feet—enough to have scaled Mount Everest more than 100 times, not from the mountain's base camp, but from sea level. When Unaka Jennette started the descent down the tower that day in May, 1936, he would never return to the top of the lighthouse.

In the 68 years since the U.S. Light House Board rescued the South's lighthouses from the ashes of the Civil War and proclaimed the new Cape Hatteras light to be the most important, "most imposing and substantial brick lighthouse on [the] continent, if not the world," the proud and resolute spirit of the American lighthouse establishment had faded away.[174] The modern Lighthouse Service classified the 1870 brick tower "surplus."

Five and a half years after the steel "Buxton light" began flashing for the first time, German U-boats returned to North Carolina's offshore shipping lanes, this time with a vengeance. Ill-prepared and under-equipped, the U.S. Navy failed to defend its home shores for the first six months after Pearl Harbor. The enemy inflicted a disruptive and nearly decisive blow to the vital supply lines to the warfronts in Europe. Three hundred ninety-seven ships and almost 5,000 lives were lost to the torpedoes, artillery shells and mines from more than 65 U-boats along the American East Coast

"Cape Hatteras lighthouse is in sight, just as in peacetime, our old acquaintance from the last voyage." U-*123*, shown here returning to France after her first mission to the U.S. East Coast, set a course straight for the Cape Hatteras Lighthouse in March, 1942. National Archives photo.

and the Gulf of Mexico. For six months, the Buxton tower kept flashing at full power, silhouetting darkened Allied ships and cheerfully welcoming the German invaders. U-*123* returned directly to Cape Hatteras after sinking two ships and damaging another on its first mission in January, 1942. Upon arriving in late March, Kapitänleutnant Reinhard Hardegen was comforted by the sweeping beam of the beacon. "Cape Hatteras lighthouse is in sight, just as in peacetime, our old acquaintance from the last voyage," he wrote in the U-boat's diary.

The unlighted, barber-pole striped Cape Hatteras tower was used as a lookout tower by the Coast Guard, reminiscent of the use of the first lighthouse by Confederates in the Summer of 1861, but no U-boat was ever known to have been sighted from the lighthouse gallery. The Hatteras tower was also of interest to a suspicious couple with German accents who were temporary boarders at the home of Buxton postmistress, Maude White. "They would move around the island and then come back and sketch things and then mail them, and from the amount of mail they sent out my mother became suspicious," said White's daughter, Ormond Fuller. "They asked a lot of questions about the lighthouse, too, and we took them out there to see it." Whatever the visitors' intentions, they chose the wrong place to lodge because Maude White was not just an innkeeper and postmistress, she was a secret, U.S. Navy Intelligence "coastwatcher" and she turned her guests in to the authorities.[175]

All the while the Cape Hatteras tower stood extinguished, its Henry-Lepaute lens remained at the top, but without the daily attention and loving care of its former keeper, Unaka Jennette. The bronze and brass gears of the chariot wheel that turned the light a single revolution every four minutes were tarnished with neglect. Sand coated the once shiny, black-and-white tile floors of the landings. Windows were cracked. Paint peeled from the walls. Guano stained the railings of the galleries and rust had begun its destructive process. Worst of all, the pride of Paris and the defunct Light House Board—the first-order illuminating apparatus—began to suffer from abuse. The damage started with minor chips along the precision-ground edges of the crown-crystal prisms and scratches on the finely polished flash panels. It would get worse.

The lighthouse seemed to have gone the way of the Outer Banks in general—useless, forgotten, a relic of the past. In a surprisingly short time, the economy of the islands fell into a desperate situation. Once great menhaden, porpoise, shad and mullet fisheries diminished. Whales grew scarce. Herds of free-ranging livestock died off. Commercial logging of juniper, red cedar and live oaks had played out, and commercial hunting was banned. Piloting and shipbuilding became obsolete, and the Outer Banks' first and most profitable industry, the salvage of shipwrecks, had dwindled with the navigational advances and speed of the merchant fleet. The young people of the islands were forced to leave their ancestral homes for the mainland in search of a better life.[176] Things looked bleak until men with vision rose to the challenge.

Isolated as it was, the Outer Banks for centuries had always had a front seat for the major events and achievements that helped shape the nation—the first English colony, five major wars, the technological marvels of wireless broadcasts and powered flight, America's tallest lighthouses, and a lifesaving tradition that helped to inspire the modern Coast Guard. These things could be promoted to the public and tourism would provide "a new life for the Banks."[177] In a column for the *Elizabeth City Independent* in 1933, Frank Stick proposed that a national seashore park should be developed to preserve the remaining wild and unspoiled beaches and wetlands of the Outer Banks so visitors could come and see and enjoy a unique resource. It was a bold idea that came at a desperate time—the twin hurricanes that sounded the death knell for the Cape Hatteras Lighthouse followed within two months after Stick's proposal. Four years later, Congress approved a bill that formally created the Cape Hatteras National Seashore to be administered by the National Park Service and the Department of the Interior.

The National Park Service set its sights on the "surplus" Hatteras tower as a key destination for visitors to the park and the Lighthouse Service was more than happy to relinquish its responsibility. But before the Park Service could do anything more than clean and paint the buildings of the light station, World War II intervened, and the Coast Guard (which had absorbed the obsolete Lighthouse Service) took over the unlighted tower as a lookout post. Nineteenth century Fresnel lenses were considered anachronisms by the modern Coast Guard and not particularly valuable, except, perhaps, as souvenirs. Sometime after the U-boat terror diminished in 1943, Coast Guard sentries left their post unguarded, and the lighthouse was unprotected from a new enemy—souvenir hunters. It was an ironic fulfillment of a Civil War fear for the 1803 Hatteras light, that left unguarded, the tower could be ravaged by vandals.

Before the war, when the Park Service had considered the value of the historic landmark to tourism, they saw the Henry-Lepaute first-order lens as a potential crown jewel of the seashore park. A Park Service planner wrote "the ascension of the lighthouse tower and the examination of the lens is a thrilling educational experience never to be forgotten." Apparently, not just a few visitors, Coast Guardsmen and residents too, wanted to be thrilled by the lens without having to climb the tower a second time, and they decided to take home sections of the glass. By 1944, two of the center flash panels had been jimmied loose from their bronze frames, and soon after, more disappeared. Years later, it was rumored that visitors to the lighthouse had been encouraged by unnamed Coast Guardsmen to take pieces of the lens, since the government did not expect the lighthouse to survive the waves that were clawing at its foundation. Whether souvenir hunters went about their business with the government's permission is unproven, but it is without question that once word spread the lens was there for the taking, the taking began in earnest. For Outer Bankers who participated, it seemed no less natural than salvaging a shipwreck, except that they were ravaging an elegant work of art that had been lovingly cared-for by their forefathers.

A Coast Guard officer, upon inspecting the early damage, reported to his superiors in Washington, D.C., that although the tower was no longer imminently threatened by erosion and should be reactivated, it was suffering from neglect and abuse. No one seemed to listen and, two years later, the damage was done.[178]

Unaka Jennette had lived a full life by the time he was 64. He had experienced many troubling events over the years—wars, storms, the Depression, illnesses and deaths of family and friends, the erosion of the beach and the decommissioning of his lighthouse, but none broke his heart more than the news he received shortly after the second World War. His magnificent and historic, Henry-Lepaute first-order lens at the top of the Cape Hatteras Lighthouse had been brutally vandalized. Jennette must have felt emotions similar to those experienced by his great-grandfather so many years before when Ben Fulcher was ordered to extinguish the light of the original tower— anger, disappointment, frustration, and especially, disgust.

The Park Service caretaker of historic structures within the Cape Hatteras National Seashore, Horace Dough, reported that "most of the heavy glass prisms that form the powerful lens for the light had been removed from about 28 panels in the lens."[179] Still, the tower was frequently broken into and the senseless, shameful and tragic destruction continued unabated. A tussle developed between the Coast Guard and the National Park Service as to who was responsible, and the parties finally concluded that finding blame would not put the lens back together.

CAP'N 'NAKA'S LENS

If keeper Unaka Jennette had an exceptionally strong affinity for the Henry-Lepaute lens, he never knew why, and neither did his family.

Jennette had a connection to the lens in the 1870 lighthouse because it was also the original illuminating apparatus of the long-lost 1803 tower, the one installed in 1854 and lovingly hand-polished by Benjamin Fulcher. Cap'n 'Naka's lens was the same lens removed by his great-grandfather under orders from the Confederate government in Richmond. It was the very same lens taken by John Myers' paddle-wheel steamer and hidden for nine months in his warehouse at Washington, North Carolina. It was the same lens that was almost recaptured by the Federal Navy but had been taken away to Tarboro along with retreating gray-clad soldiers. Unaka Jennette's lens had been Ben Fulcher's lens and it had ridden the bumpy railroads of the Confederacy to Townsville, where it was hidden for the remainder of the war by Dr. David Tayloe and Colonel John Hargrove. It resurfaced in nearby Henderson, only to have parts of it held captive by local citizens. The lens was finally recovered by the lighthouse establishment and was returned to its creator in France to be repaired. The lens crossed the Atlantic Ocean for a second time to New York and was safely stored for its future use at a lighthouse somewhere in America. On May, 27, 1870, the original Henry-Lepaute Cape Hatteras lens was given its

A bronze lens panel frame with the manufacturers mark, Henry-Lepaute, from the original Cape Hatteras first-order lens. Author photograph.

next assignment—the new lighthouse at Cape Hatteras. The intrepid lens was sent home. When the Light House Board reportedly asked the 5th District Engineer, General J.H. Simpson if he wanted a "new" lens for the Cape Hatteras lighthouse, they meant, "a different one from the one already there in the 1803 tower," but it was, in fact, the old one, the original lens.

After it had been recovered from Henderson, North Carolina, the lens was packed and marked "Hatteras." When it was sent back to Henry-Lepaute for repairs, it was identified as "Hatteras." When it was returned and stored at the Staten Island Depot, it was labeled "Hatteras." And when it was returned to the Cape in 1870, it was still identified as "Hatteras." Admiral Shubrick sent this letter to the 3rd District Inspector:

Unaka Jennette and family in 1962. Photo courtesy of the Jennette family.

Sir, You will please send without unpacking to Gen. J.H. Simpson Lighthouse Engineer, by inland water transportation to Baltimore, Maryland, the whole of the first-order apparatus and fixtures from Henry Lepaute (Flashing eclipse of 10") marked "Hatteras" 1 to 37, numbers and marks of cases, which was received October 14, 1868, and inform Gen. Simpson when sent.[180]

The mystery of "the lost light" is solved. It was never really lost at all.

The question of what lens resides at the top of California's Pigeon Point lighthouse is answered unequivocally by George Putnam's letter in 1924. It concludes:

...the second lens, the one now in commission at Pigeon Point, was discontinued in 1870 when the new (present) tower at Cape Hatteras was established, and there is a record here that it was placed in storage at the General Lighthouse Depot on January 17, 1871, and on August 11, 1871, was shipped to Pigeon Point.

Photo of dismantled Cape Hatteras Lighthouse lens panels taken in 1949. Courtesy National Park Service.

This "second lens"—the first-order apparatus installed at Cape Hatteras in 1863 to replace the original lens—was placed on a clipper ship in New York and sent around Cape Horn for the California Coast. Having served seven and a half years guiding vessels off North Carolina's Outer Banks, the new assignment for the "second lens" from Hatteras, was no less significant. The dark, jagged rocks, blinding fog and Pacific gales on the approaches to San Francisco Bay were every bit as formidable an adversary for a lighthouse as the Graveyard of the Atlantic.

Unaka Jennette's lens had been his great-grandfather Ben Fulcher's lens and it had survived its incredible odyssey, only to be mutilated and destroyed by people who were infatuated with it and wanted to own a piece of it—people who had no understanding or appreciation of the remarkable history of the Hatteras Fresnel lens and who did not respect it. Unaka redeemed the sins of his forefather, only to see his dedication and commitment to his lighthouse and the U.S. lighthouse establishment—one of the great humanitarian organizations in the history of Civil Service—be dishonored and marginalized through a senseless act of vandalism.

The remaining flash and cata-dioptric panels of the Henry-Lepaute lens were dismantled and lowered to the ground for the last time in 1949. Four Coast Guard men and one civilian posed for a photograph with sections of the lens. None of the men appear to be smiling for the camera. Along with the iron frame, the apparatus was boxed and sent to the Park Service facilities at the Wright Memorial at Kill Devil Hills in the care of Horace Dough.

The U.S. Coast Guard redeemed its own mistakes, in a way, and reactivated the Cape Hatteras Lighthouse on January 23, 1950, with a modern, rotating electric beacon. Cape Hatteras National Seashore began operations three years later. As time passed, the long-awaited tourists began to trickle down the newly paved Highway 12. Then the trickle became a flood. License plates from all fifty states would eventually be seen on cars parked at the Cape Hatteras Light Station. A new awareness of lighthouses developed nationwide—practically a religious devotion—and Cape Hatteras was considered the Vatican of lighthouses. Like pilgrims to a shrine, they came—thousands of devotees—to become engaged, get married and otherwise absorb the sense of energy, fortitude and compassion radiated by the light. The Cape Hatteras Light Station became the island community's meeting place and it hosted baseball games, Pirate Jamborees and pony parades. The tower's image became ubiquitous and represented the pride of its community on signs that welcomed visitors into the safe harbors of motels, restaurants and churches. Fishermen caught fish in its shadow, painters and photographers came to capture its image, and surfers from all over arrived to ride the waves at the mecca of East Coast beaches.

During the ensuing years, the ocean came too, with a vengeance, and it washed away the temporary accretion of beach enjoyed during the 1930s and '40s. Storms of unimaginable fury raked the Outer Banks and were named for the day they arrived—the great Ash Wednesday storm, the Lincoln Day storm and the Halloween

Nor'easter of 1992. Each produced open ocean waves more than 30-feet high lasting three days. In 1980, nature delivered a rare March blizzard and under the cloak of swirling snow and saltwater spindrift, the ocean claimed the remains of the 1803 Cape Hatteras Lighthouse. The granite stones of the original tower were not swept away but simply sank into the all-consuming surf. The ocean avenged the first poor choice of lighthouse locations. Would it avenge the new one? The answer was, no.

Through the persistence and dedication of the National Park Service, the genius of scientists and fearless housemovers, and the good graces of the U.S. Congress and the American taxpayers, the Cape Hatteras Lighthouse got a new lease on life. In 1999, the world's tallest, unreinforced brick lighthouse was lifted 5.3 feet onto steel rails and was relocated 2,900 feet to the southwest, placing the lighthouse at the same relative distance from the ocean as when it was first built. It was an historic achievement, no less remarkable in its day than man's first powered flight.

The ocean would not take the 1870 Cape Hatteras Lighthouse, at least not yet. However, 60 miles away on Roanoke Island, stacked on shelves in an unidentified and unremarkable government warehouse, lay the forlorn remains of the ravaged Henry-Lepaute lens, the crown jewel of two Cape Hatteras lighthouses, once a diamond in the sky.

Not all sins can be redeemed. Or can they?

A Melancholy Conclusion?

This is not how a story should end. The mystery of the "lost light" has been solved, but the melancholy conclusion is disappointing and dissatisfying.

The Henry-Lepaute apparatus from the original Cape Hatteras Lighthouse began as grains of sand and silicates from the bottom-land of France's Champagne Region, lovingly fused, shaped and polished into exquisite crown-crystal, assembled into a magnificent chandelier known as a Fresnel lens, and placed in one of the world's most important lighthouses. Now it was reduced to a forgotten collection of chipped and broken glass.

It is hard to imagine how it happened. Certainly, the metamorphosis of the 19th century Light House Board into the 20th century U.S. Coast Guard turned many of the old lighthouse establishment standards, practices and property into quaint but seemingly useless anachronisms. The introduction of electricity made incandescent oil-vapor lamps obsolete, and then, electric motors rendered unnecessary the elegant clock-tower-like rotating mechanisms, perfected by Paris' Henry-Lepaute & Company. Even lighthouses themselves became less vital as the technology of navigation developed. Progress has always been the natural order.

Comparatively small but powerful, rotating aero-beacons finally dislodged Fresnel lenses from the tops of many American lighthouses during the middle decades of the 20th century. Ironically, the beacons, developed for the aviation industry, which was born 60 miles to the north of Cape Hatteras, utilized a technology that pre-dated the Fresnel lens. It was the parabolic reflector, which had been deployed in the nation's first lighthouses. It is understandable that aero-beacons were welcomed by the new "keepers" of lighthouses, the Coast Guard, especially since the lights did not have more than 1,000 pieces of glass that required constant polishing. However, it is difficult to understand why the lovely lenses were so forsaken.

As the first lighthouses were converted to aero-beacons in the mid-1900s, it was not obvious to the Coast Guard, what they were to do with the surplus Fresnel lenses. Some were "sold"* to private collectors and antiques dealers, which was what was done with the lens from the 1903 tower at Cape Fear. At an antique shop in New Hanover County, North Carolina, most of the first-order lens from the Cape Fear Lighthouse has been sold. A few cata-dioptric panels stand forlornly among household castoffs, old bottles and baubles. But the remaining pieces are no longer for sale. A couple of years ago, the enterprising proprietor learned from a customer what the old Fresnel lens would have been worth had it been preserved as a whole. As the dealer discovered, lighthouse lenses are not like automobile parts. The sum is far more valuable than its parts. Now, the Wilmington purveyor of lighthouse prisms wants to buy them back, at double his original sales price.

North Carolina had just two first-order lighthouses at the outset of the Civil War—at Cape Hatteras and Cape Lookout. Each lighthouse lens survived the war, but neither fared well during the Coast Guard's modernization period when Fresnel lenses were removed in favor of aero-beacons.

The Lemmonier-Sauter lens from Cape Lookout, which had been carefully wrapped in the Colonial records of the North Carolina state archives from the Capitol building in Raleigh, served 100 years in the top of the Lookout tower. There, it faithfully and, for the most part, successfully warned seafarers of the treacherous "Promontorium tremendum" or Lookout Shoals. Then, in 1967, at a time when Loran navigation receivers had supplanted lighthouses for navigation among military, commercial and a few private sea-going vessels, the Coast Guard decided to replace the venerable Cape Lookout lens with an unromantic, but brighter, aero-beacon. Soon after, the historic first-order lens

*There are many authorities who doubt the legality of such transactions.

Cape Lookout Lighthouse depicted in a late-nineteenth century photo. The Lemmonier-Sauter first-order lens is shielded from the sun by curtains within the lantern. Courtesy National Archives.

graced the entrance of the Fifth District Coast Guard Headquarters Mess Hall and Base Exchange in Portsmouth, Virginia. No one was aware of the extraordinary history of the artifact—how it mysteriously escaped the clutches of Federal forces on the eve of the fall of Beaufort and was hidden in the North Carolina Capitol, or how it was discovered by Sherman's army. Nevertheless, the Cape Lookout lens guided hungry "Coasties" to the chow line in Portsmouth for many years.

The Cape Lookout lens's own strange odyssey was far from over. In 1994, the Coast Guard transferred the lens to the top of the newly renovated and relocated Block Island Southeast Lighthouse off the coast of Rhode Island. Block Island's own first-order lens had to be removed because it once rotated on a mercury float, used in some towers during the early 20th century, but mercury had been later determined to be highly toxic. The non-profit foundation that had guided the lighthouse's preservation wanted an "authentic" apparatus in its place. The Coast Guard just happened to have one—the first-order lens from Cape Lookout. According to anonymous sources in North Carolina, the Coast Guard first offered the Lookout lens to a state-sponsored museum in Beaufort, but the offer was declined because of lack of space. So, off to Block Island went the lens and the supporters there were thrilled—no matter that the lens's flashing characteristic was different than the original Block Island lens. (It was, in fact, a fixed or non-flashing lens.)

Officials and residents of Carteret County, North Carolina, where the Cape Lookout Lighthouse is located, were outraged and they wanted their lens back. By then, however, they had had their chance and it seemed their plea came too late. The Coast Guard was unwilling to return the lens to North Carolina. "We can't justify returning it for display purposes alone," said an officer of the First District Headquarters in Boston.[181] But a Carteret County Board of Commissioners resolution, passed after Block Island's relighting ceremony, stated that the lens transfer "has taken place without the knowledge of many interested parties." Further, it said that the lens "is one of about two dozen left in this country and is not only an invaluable piece of North Carolina's maritime history, but a valuable artifact of the Cape Lookout National Seashore."[182] More than a decade later, the Cape Lookout lens remains at the top of the Block Island Southeast Lighthouse. Like the Henry-Lepaute lens from the first Cape Hatteras Lighthouse, the story of the Lookout lens has an unhappy conclusion.

The late Michal Schliff, a gifted writer and a brave and supremely sensitive woman who wrote for the Outer Banks' premier monthly newspaper, *The Island Breeze*, wrote that the Cape Hatteras Lighthouse was her teacher. "Everyday, when I come to the lighthouse, I am presented a useful lesson," wrote Schliff. One lesson she eloquently described in a March, 1999, column was "that if I am willing to release my disappointment in not achieving a particular goal, I can discover beauty and fulfillment simply by allowing myself the freedom to look at things from a different angle."

Michal Schliff would have been able to find beauty, fulfillment, and a lesson in the conclusion to the odyssey of "the lost light" of Cape Hatteras. Maybe others can also.

In September, 2002, the National Park Service and the managers of the Cape Hatteras National Seashore made a commitment to lend to the Graveyard of the Atlantic Museum in Hatteras village, the surviving pieces of the original Henry-Lepaute Fresnel lens, as a centerpiece for a major

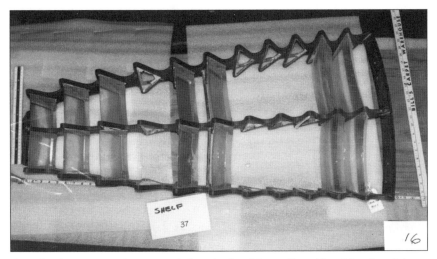

One of twelve upper cata-dioptric panels from the Cape Hatteras Fresnel lens. Note the missing prisms. National Park Service photo.

exhibit at the museum. The Museum has been planned to be a major cultural and educational resource for North Carolina and the Mid-Atlantic region, preserving the remarkable history of 400 years of shipwrecks along the Outer Banks. The foundered and sunken ships of the Graveyard of the Atlantic represent one of the greatest densities of vessels lost in the world. Many unfortunate seafarers met their fate just beyond the reassuring beam of light that radiated through the 1,000 prisms and bulls-eye lenses of the historic Henry-Lepaute lens. In the coming years, visitors to the Graveyard of the Atlantic Museum will be able to view the famous and historic, but incomplete, first-order apparatus up-close. "The identification and authentication of the original 1854 first-order Fresnel lens is of great historic importance and a major contribution to the maritime history of North Carolina's Outer Banks," said Joseph Schwarzer, Executive Director for the museum. Schwarzer adds: "The exhibition is expected to be an ideal introduction to the stunning shipwreck history of the region. As the keynote introductory display, the Henry-Lepaute apparatus constitutes a crucial portion of the Graveyard of the Atlantic Museum collections."

The museum also hopes to be able to recover many of the pieces of Saint-Gobain glass that were removed from the Cape Hatteras Lighthouse. Donors may present the museum artifacts either anonymously or in exchange for recognition near the lens exhibit. No one expects that the

Henry-Lepaute lens can be fully restored, but without question, every additional prism or center flash panel that can be reunited with the lens will contribute to a happier ending to the mystery of "the lost light."

A Fresnel lens was created and manufactured foremost as a machine, but it is also rare in that, unlike most other technological achievements of the past, it has lost none of its aesthetic beauty. A Fresnel lens is an enduring work of art. It may be fitting that this magnificent masterpiece, having survived its astonishing odyssey, will serve future generations as a lesson of genius, dedication, purpose, courage, and compassion.

Not too long ago, Cape Hatteras was graced by a man who embodied the attributes, ideals and spirit of an Outer Banks mariner, lifesaver and lighthouse keeper. This man, and his forefathers, exuded a quiet fearlessness, widespread unselfishness and unbridled bravery. He, and the men before him, were true patriots. His name was Rany Jennette. His father was Keeper Unaka Jennette, and his great-great grandfather was Keeper Benjamin T. Fulcher. Rany lived out his days as a proud member of the National Park Service and Cape Hatteras National Seashore and a beloved member of his island community.

A few years before he died, he described one of his cherished memories as the son of a lighthouse keeper:

> Going to the top at night was a special treat, and it is hard to describe the feeling. The beauty of the prisms that cast thousands of multi-colored lights danced on the deck below. There was complete silence except for the soft hissing of the vapor mantle lamp and quiet whirring of the governor that controlled the speed of the clock mechanism and weights. Everything was spotless, and the odor of the clock oil is something I'll always remember.[183]

Rany never knew the amazing history of his father's cherished Fresnel lens. But if he had still been around to see the lens in its new home in the Graveyard of the Atlantic Museum, Rany would probably have given his trademark greeting to all he would meet.

"Come, if you will, and see."

Epilogue

A NATIONAL TREASURE

"That is possibly the most unrealistic and far-fetched proposal I have ever received in my long career with the Interior Department—you've got to be joking," the national seashore superintendent says, with a condescending grin, to my request to remove the 1854 Henry-Lepaute cast iron pedestal from the top of the Cape Hatteras Lighthouse. Until that moment, we had been having a congenial lunch meeting at an eclectic cafe on Roanoke Island in December 2004.

"Your request has little chance of being approved as long as I am in charge," he says. "That artifact is an integral part of the historic fabric of a national historic landmark and there is no precedent in the history of the Park Service that would allow me to even consider such a possibility."

And so ended, at least for the time, the dream of reuniting the 3,500-pound pedestal with its lens to become part of the most historic lighthouse lens exhibit in America—the once lost first-order classical illuminating apparatus from Cape Hatteras."

Two years earlier, when the first edition of this book was published in the fall of 2002, the National Park Service had agreed to lend to the Graveyard of the Atlantic Museum the surviving pieces of the original Henry-Lepaute Fresnel lens so that the artifact could be publicly displayed and interpreted. Truthfully, none of us involved at the time could conceive of how that might be accomplished. No one even knew for sure how much of the vandalized lens remained in the possession of the Park Service. Estimates of the missing components vaguely ranged from "a few" to "a lot." The only way to know for sure was for the lens to be inspected and evaluated by someone who knew what they were looking at. A call was made to retired Coast Guard lighthouse expert Jim Woodward and an appointment was made for him to visit the government warehouse on Roanoke Island, North Carolina, where the remains of the lens were stored.

In late-February 2003, Woodward got his first look at what was left of the well-traveled and storied Hatteras lens. Upon first glance by the nation's foremost lampist, it was apparent that the apparatus was one of the oldest ever seen in the U.S. According to Woodward, rip-

Jim Woodward examines the Cape Hatteras lens for the first time in 2003. Kevin Duffus photo.

pled edges along the bronze frames are a telltale sign that the Cape Hatteras Lighthouse received one of the earliest lenses shipped from France. "This lens has to be one of the first of three, first-order lenses the government bought after the first Fresnel lens arrived in 1841 for testing," he says in a later interview. Having examined hundreds of lighthouse lenses during his five-decade career Woodward's trained eye can detect the subtlest of clues: "This lens was much more artistic, it is lighter in frame, the glass is heavier. The panels are much more delicate, especially the upper panels of this particular lens which are made of a very light gauge of bronze."

Despite its imposing size and three-ton weight, the Henry-Lepaute lens was a delicately crafted machine. "The little thin strips of metal that hold the prisms in the center flash panels—if you look at them very closely you'll see that they are made of a very fine band of bronze, and very, very, very delicate," Woodward says. And they're held in place with even more delicate jeweler's screws. And that is one of the reasons why it was so easy to vandalize this lens because those very finely threaded jeweler's screws were just easy to rip out."

In addition to confirming this author's belief that the Fresnel lens was one of the oldest in America, during his initial examination Woodward discovered that the destruction of the lens was far worse than anyone had imagined. Of the 960 original crown-glass optics, 688 prisms and bulls-eye lenses were lost or stolen. All twenty-four of the central dioptric flash panels were missing. The dioptric panels were the very heart of the illuminating apparatus and every ten seconds produced a brilliant flash of yellow light as observed by appreciative mariners up to 18 miles at sea.

The news could hardly have been more disheartening. The initial reaction was that there seemed to be no practical reason for proceeding with the reconstruction or display of the historic lens. At best, it would be the most unsightly lighthouse lens exhibit in the world—like a wrecked, rusted Rolls-Royce retrieved from a junkyard for an auto museum.

But remarkably, the skeletal iron and bronze framework of the lens survived in entirety, even though practically all of the finely milled French fasteners seemed to be long gone. If the lens could no longer be appreciated as a "diamond in the sky," its size, artfulness and former function might still be appreciated. In a report and proposal submitted to Graveyard of the Atlantic Museum officials, Woodward wrote: "With a significant amount of skilled labor and proper interpretation, the lens can be reconstructed so that the public will appreciate how careless, thoughtless human actions can virtually destroy a national treasure—a fascinating machine crafted at the pinnacle of the industrial art age."[184]

As it lay forlornly on shelves and in various dusty corners of its U.S. government storage facility, "the lost light" seemed to flicker an ephemeral glimmer of life—a plea to be rescued. There was work yet to do. This "holy grail" of American lighthouses, one of the oldest Fresnel lenses in the nation, having served in two lighthouses, stored in warehouses, shipped across the Atlantic Ocean three times, lovingly polished by generations of light-keepers, pursued by the Union Navy and Army, transported by horse-drawn carts, pole-propelled flats, steamboats and the rickety rails of the Confederate railroad, and once buried or hidden in a storehouse, could perhaps still tell a more expansive and educational tale if it were to be exhibited to the public in its unadorned and ravaged state.

In March 2005, Jim Woodward and his Fresnel lens restoration team, including Jim Dunlap of New York and Kurt Fosberg of Michigan, arrived at Cape Hatteras National Seashore headquarters on Roanoke Island to stabilize, transport and reconstruct the historic Henry-Lepaute lens for its new assignment. On a squally spring day during a typical Outer Banks nor'easter, the men began the process of moving the Henry-Lepaute lens back to Hatteras Island, this time to the Graveyard of the Atlantic Museum ten miles south of its former home at the Cape.

(L-R) Jim Woodward, Kurt Fosberg, Jim Dunlap.
Kevin Duffus photo.

Even though Woodward had inspected and inventoried the lens two years earlier, the lampists anticipated that the artifact might surprise them. "We just about always learn something," Dunlap says. "But a project like this, particularly, we're going to be surprised and we're going to be making discoveries."

Fosberg, the team's metallurgist, and a professional jeweler, took a cursory glance at one of the bronze frames and immediately detected a problem. The metal was wildly warped, abuse apparently suffered after the lens was removed from the lighthouse in 1949. "Do you see that?" he says to Dunlap. Dunlap: "Yeah, oh wow!" The lens team quickly learned that the job would require every skill they had, and more.

Although academically trained archeologists dislike hearing those without degrees claim to be archeologists, Woodward says, that is just what he and his team are: "We are almost forensic archeologists, in a way. Because this lens tells a story, if you know what you're looking at." As it happened, the Hatteras Henry-Lepaute lens had quite a story to tell, even more than its recently discovered lost history. For example, the team was excited when they discovered which prisms had been added to the lens after the Civil War when it had been returned to Paris for rebuilding in 1867. "When we had the panels laid out on the worktables, and you could actually look at the ends of each prism, you could see the color variations between fairly rich green which are probably the original ones, and a kind of yellowish-green which I expect were the replacement pieces," Woodward says.

One of the more enigmatic forensic mysteries later revealed itself to Fosberg, who is particularly alert to subtle degrees of oxidation. Because an advanced amount of rust was visible at the spots where two central flash panel frames were seated onto the lens' base ring, it was evident that those two frames, including their respective 24 prisms and bullseye lenses, were removed from the lighthouse some years before the others. But even more conspicuous—and suspicious—was that the first two panels to be removed were on precisely opposite sides of the lens. "The person who removed those panels had first-hand knowledge of the lens and how it worked," says Woodward. "They knew that for the lens to maintain its balance, they would need to take two opposing central panels out. And it clearly appears this was done a few years before the vandalism began in earnest."

Whoever removed the first two panels remains a mystery. But the list of possible suspects, based on people with access to the building and familiar with the operation of the Cape Hatteras Lighthouse and its historic first-order lens, is a short one, and it includes members of the U.S. Coast Guard and U.S. Navy who took charge of the tower during WWII, and the tower's last keepers. (If one were to speculate too much about the identities of the perpetrators, the likely conclusions could lead to yet another unfortunate postscript to this story.)

Officials of the Graveyard of the Atlantic Museum and the National Park Service were hopeful that as news spread about the resurrection of the Hatteras lens, Outer Banks residents and other souvenir collectors might be willing to return prisms and other parts of "the lost light," in order to restore, as much as possible, the ravaged national treasure. Other rare and valuable items from the Cape Hatteras Lighthouse were also stolen or missing, including the large brass incandescent oil-vapor lamp, and a complete set of U.S. Lighthouse Service light keeper's implements.

But the hoped-for good intentions of those in possession of the

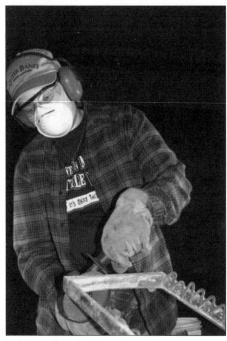

Volunteer Beth Deese uses a sander to clean a bronze frame. Kevin Duffus photo.

government property never materialized, although some islanders were forthcoming with information about anonymous "others" who may have had parts of the lens. As work on the project progressed, a woman informed the museum director that a family on the island had all of the central flash panels. But other islanders' memories seemed to contradict the woman's story. A popular local businessman recalled, as a boy, experimenting with the big "magnifying lenses" from the lighthouse and starting grass fires and frying ants. Even an official with the North Carolina Ferry division discretely claimed to know where a large number of the lens panels were buried.[185] None of the rumors were substantiated.

While community support for the reconstruction of the Hatteras lens may have been irresolute and lackluster, help arrived from elsewhere. Funding of the $85,000 project was provided by the Z. Smith Reynolds Foundation, the Outer Banks Lighthouse Society and the North Carolina Association of Electric Cooperatives. Volunteers from the Outer Banks Lighthouse Society generously donated their time and travel expenses to be able to help rewrite the tragic ending of the well-traveled artifact's story. Some society members came from as far as Connecticut and Maryland.

The volunteers reverently rubbed, scraped and cleaned the metal components to remove years of accumulated oxidation and corrosion. Many of the bronze frame members that had been damaged or warped were reshaped and realigned. All of the extant crown-glass was removed, cleaned, remounted and reglazed. Once the lens components were prepared, reconstruction began. First, the decorative cast iron fan

Outer Banks Lighthouse Society volunteers Bett Padgett, Judy Castleberry and Betty Parrish clean one of the bronze horizontal rings. Kevin Duffus photo.

legs, three horizontal rings and 12 steel vertical columns were fitted together and capped with the upper guide roller assembly, which acts as a "capstone" locking the lens frame together. Next, the lower cata-dioptric panels were fastened in place, followed by the upper cata-dioptric panels. Finally, the vacant center flash panel frames were installed. (See Appendix one, page 218 for a diagram of lens and pedestal parts.)

As the lens began to take shape, the volunteers reflected on their participation in its historic journey. "To be able to work on this lens, knowing all of the places it's been and the many people who've handled it — it is an incredible responsibility," says Betty Parrish of Charlotte. The missing parts of the lens, however, were a sobering reminder of its past. "I think of the possibility that somewhere out there could be the remaining panels and prisms to complete this wonderful exhibit, and that they may be willingly shared with the rest of us, so that the Cape Hatteras lens may once again display all of its magnificent glory for the world to admire," says volunteer Beth Deese. At the conclusion of the lens project, Ms. Deese and the other volunteers were disappointed. None of the missing parts of the lens were returned in 2005, even

The 1854 Henry-Lepaute pedestal as it appeared in the watchroom of the Cape Hatteras Lighthouse in 2006.
Jim Woodward photo.

though it was probable that most of the absent 688 prisms and bulls-eye lenses were located somewhere within 25 miles of the museum.

Although the Henry-Lepaute lens exhibit was more incomplete than supporters had hoped, the "national treasure" was dedicated in October 2005. With the membership of the Outer Banks Lighthouse Society in attendance, the president of the Graveyard of the Atlantic Museum's Board of Directors (the author of this book) said, "It is our hope that this remarkable symbol of America's lighthouse history, having served seafarers in two lighthouses and saved countless lives over two centuries, will serve for centuries more by guiding future generations on a voyage of discovery and understanding of our rich maritime past."

In the meantime, the equally historic and similarly abused Henry-Lepaute pedestal, slathered in dozens of coats of Navy surplus gray paint, remained at the top of the Cape Hatteras Lighthouse, its sole purpose to support the modern U.S. Coast Guard aero-beacon which replaced the Fresnel lens five decades earlier.

Correcting the wrongs of history takes time, but some truly important historical endeavors eventually find a way of prevailing over those who stand in the way. So it was that the Park Service superintendent, who thought it preposterous to reunite the 1854 Henry-Lepaute cast iron pedestal with its first-order Fresnel lens, was given a new assignment. A new superintendant took over, and a new opportunity arose to resubmit the proposal. This time the request was afforded respectful, serious consideration, although it was acknowledged that many difficult challenges would have to be overcome, which included securing the approval of North Carolina's State Historic Preservation Office—removal of the pedestal from the lighthouse had to comply with National Historic Register restrictions.

Since its formation in 1953, superintendents of Cape Hatteras National Seashore have often had to make difficult and controversial decisions. Few have been more contentious than the "move of the century"— the 1999 relocation of the Cape Hatteras Lighthouse a half-mile to a site less threatened by erosion. The proposal to remove the cast iron pedestal from the watchroom at the top of the lighthouse was not without its own mini-controversy. A visitor to the lighthouse heard of the possibility that the Park Service might allow the pedestal to be removed and wrote in his internet blog that the prospect was "disappointing," especially since the artifact was being sent to a museum "that's located within spitting distance of the ocean with absolutely no protection from hurricanes." The blogger encouraged his readers to write to Congress, and at least one individual posted a response stating that they would officially express their "indignant opposition" to the project.[186] Unfortunately, public perceptions these days are often influenced by political activists who don't have all of the facts. For instance, the blogger must have been unaware that the Graveyard of the Atlantic Museum was soundly engineered and built with one-foot-thick concrete walls extending 10-feet below grade and was built above the 500-year flood plain.

Even some volunteer seasonal rangers working at the lighthouse expressed outrage at the prospect of "losing" the pedestal, despite the realities that there was no on-site interpretation of the historic artifact, and tens of thousands of annual visitors to the lighthouse—including off-season tourists, individuals unable to climb a 20-story building and those with disabilities—never get to see the pedestal. Often at odds with the local community on other issues, the itinerant park rangers framed their disapproval of the pedestal's removal on the rationale that it would represent yet another insult forced upon the local community by the ranger's employer, the Interior Department. "As soon as more people hear about what has been decided and what is happening to the pedestal, another hornet's nest of bitterness will take root—and the local residents will be justified in their feelings," wrote a seasonal ranger.[187]

In one sense the ranger was right. Area residents predictably voiced their disgust that "their" lighthouse pedestal was being "stolen" from them and taken to the neighboring village of Hatteras. Remarkably, among them were some who were suspected of possessing pilfered parts of the Federal property.

For a public official to make a choice at odds with public sentiment, he must possess courage and confidence. Much easier and safer would be to defer the hard and controversial decisions to a succeeding generation. However, in August 2006, after much discussion, reflection, planning and public comment, National Park Service superintendent Mike Murray granted the request to remove the pedestal from the top of the lighthouse and reunite it with its lens. According to press reports, Murray did so because he felt the project was in the best interest of preservation and the historic integrity of the Henry-Lepaute lens and its cast iron pedestal.[188]

The work began the day after the lighthouse closed for the 2006 season in October, again supervised by Jim Woodward, assisted by Jim Dunlap and Kurt Fosberg. Woodward had been trained in the lost art of lighthouse lampists by the last surviving lampist of the extinct U.S. Lighthouse Service. It required every bit of Woodward's five decades of experience to figure out how to gently and safely coax the pedestal from the top of America's tallest lighthouse. "From a technical and physical perspective, it was, by far, the most difficult challenge I've ever had to face as a lampist," says Woodward. Later, Woodward estimated he and his team ascended the 268 steps of the 20 story building a total of 110 times during the lighthouse phase of the 18-day project. The three men quickly appreciated the lung capacity and leg strength of the former Cape Hatteras keepers.

Woodward's predecessors, the lighthouse service lampists back in 1870, had the advantage of a stiff-leg derrick to hoist the lens and pedestal components to the top of the unfinished brick tower, weeks before the iron lantern room and roof were installed, enclosing the light.

Jim Woodward prepares for the lifting of the stem and roadway from the clockwork case beneath. Beth Deese photo.

Lowering the pedestal back down the outside of the tower in a similar fashion was not an available option. The Park Service could not allow the risks—or the public spectacle—associated with lowering the pedestal down a trolley-line to the ground, especially with omnipresent, swirling Cape Hatteras winds. The massive artifact would have to be taken down the interior of the tower.

Utilizing chain hoists, the tedious process of lowering each cast-iron component, some weighing upwards of 850 pounds, began by negotiating the narrow spiral staircase that descends from the watch room to the uppermost landing in the tower. Think of carrying furniture down a twisting, narrow flight of stairs. Woodward and his team measured and re-measured clearances, calculated the geometry, and re-hearsed every delicate ballet-like maneuver over and over.

But before lowering could begin, hundreds of French-milled fittings—bronze screws, nuts, and bolts—had to be loosened for the first time since 1870. It was hardly a routine process. Just about anyone who has had to take something apart, especially something old and residing in a marine environment, can appreciate the difficulty. A steady supply of penetrating oil was infused into the seams of the pedestal, and then Woodward's crew waited—and waited. Eventually the 19th century fasteners began to turn, slowly at first, and the pedestal began to come apart. So did its secrets.

One of the first revelations was that a small decorative foot rail that encircled the top of the pedestal was atypical among similar first-order apparatus seen by the modern day lampists. "It suggests that this pedestal may have been exhibited at the Paris Exposition of 1850, the added embellishments a proud display of the manufacturer's expertise," says Woodward, standing in the spacious empty lantern room while a 25-knot wind whistled through an open iron hatch to the upper gallery. If true, this fact further adds to the historical significance of the artifact and increases its age by at least a couple of years.

The Victorian-era decorative elements of the pedestal are perhaps one of the least appreciated aspects of its design. As long as the pedestal of a Fresnel lens functioned as intended and remained in the confined space of the round watchroom at the top of the lighthouse, its ornamental touches would hardly be seen, and even then by just a few keepers and possibly their families. It is doubtful the flair of the French designers was ever appreciated. Later at the museum, as Woodward runs his hand along the structural supports of the three-ton lens, he says: "If you look at the fan legs that the lens is supported on, you'll see that it's not just a piece of cast iron, it's a beautiful fan-shaped piece of cast iron that has all sorts of filigree built into it. There was no structural reason for that, it was just for artistic reasons." In later years, competition between a half-dozen Parisian lens makers led to even more artistic flourishes on the lenses and pedestals—and cost increases. Eventually, the fiscal sensibilities of the U.S. Lighthouse Service prevailed and functional but artistically uninspired pedestals began to be forged by American ironworkers.

As the worked progressed over the next few days, a second discovery presented a darker, more malignant moment in the pedestal's past. To the trained eyes of the lampists, two things became evident. At some time on or before 1936, the lighthouse service installed a modification to the original pedestal machinery—a new, circular roadway on which the steel chariot wheels, supporting the 6,000-pound rotating lens, rolled. The modification covered the original roadway and its deformed indentations, which were carved by years of constant wear from the rolling wheels. But also detected was that something terribly wrong had occurred to the device not too long after, which appeared to have caused an unexpected yet catastrophic malfunction. Broken and bent teeth in the intricate gears of the clockwork mechanism indicated that possibly after the lighthouse service modification was made, the lens came to a jarring, grinding halt, permanently

The pinion gear with missing roller bearings. The bull gear is to the left and below are one of the chariot wheels, frozen in time and paint, resting on the replacement roadway. Kevin Duffus photo.

destroying the pedestal's function. If it could not rotate, the light could not flash and the Cape Hatteras tower ceased being a lighthouse.

Could that have been the real reason, and not the threat of erosion, that the lighthouse was abandoned in 1936? There seemed to be no end to the tragic history of the once "lost" Hatteras light.

How could it have happened? One explanation suggests that the modified roadway appears to have elevated the machinery by an inch or two so that the gears no longer engaged precisely, causing them to be stripped when put into motion. Did the U.S. Lighthouse Service, during its waning years of professionalism and reputation for exacting standards, cause the destruction of its most famous light? Somewhere, possibly in a dusty government file, the truth might still be found.

Historical mysteries notwithstanding, the work of removing the pedestal progressed. Platen, decking, steps, diagonal arms and bull gear, doors, cabinet, stem, chariot assembly, clockwork case, clockwork gears, pinion gear, plates, and base—all components of the pedestal—

were eventually lined up along the circular walls of the watch room, awaiting the trip down the tower. The clatter of the two-ton chain hoist reverberated loudly as each piece was lowered inch-by-inch from landing to landing down the 20-story building. Last to go was the heavy base, a casting not part of the original 1850 French pedestal first installed in the original lighthouse but forged purposely for the taller 1870 tower, boosting the height of the light's focal plane by a necessary two feet.

But there was a problem. The base was too large to pass through the iron door below the watch room. For a moment, uncertainty—but not panic—gripped the modern-day lampists. Was the success of the entire pedestal project hinging on the obstinate base?

The solution was one employed by anyone moving an oversized object through a doorway—removal of the door's hinges. It's easier said than done, though, when the 300-pound iron door hangs on hinges with pins hammered into place 136 years ago. Then came more penetrating oil, more waiting. But the persistence and patience of Woodward and his team paid off. The 850-pound base soon began its inch-by-inch journey down the inside of the tower.

During the ensuing two weeks, layers of surplus government gray paint were sandblasted away to prepare for a new coat of historically authentic, richly-colored forest green. Five panels of prisms, on display for years at the double keepers' quarters and later in the park's bookstore, were also relocated to the museum for inclusion in the exhibit. Then reassembly of the lens and pedestal began. The final component was fastened into place late in the evening on Friday, October 27, 2006. Too exhausted to celebrate, Woodward's team packed up their tools and departed the island the next morning.

Another chapter in the long and tumultuous history of the magnificent Henry-Lepaute first-order illuminating apparatus was about to begin—hopefully a long and stable period of recognition, respect, and admiration.

Also during this time, a couple of island residents who had years ago come into possession of prisms removed from the lens when the lighthouse stood abandoned during the 1940s, brought their artifacts to the Graveyard of the Atlantic Museum so that they may be returned to the incomplete framework of the great lens. One of those good citizens was

The 750-lb. base of the pedestal is lowered one step at a time. Jim Woodward photo.

Mary Elizabeth Gray of Buxton. During a later interview, Gray recalled a happy time during her youth, when the lighthouse provided endless hours of enjoyment on lazy Sunday afternoons.

"I remember when my best friend, Patsy Brown, whose family lived in the keeper's house while her father supervised the CCC camps, and I would dress up in her mother's finest dresses, and we'd play in the lighthouse like it was our castle," says Gray fondly of a time in the late '30s. "We would take each other's dares and sometimes even ride on the lens as it turned. We called it our very own merry-go-round."[189]

And with that misty memory, Mary Elizabeth Gray may have helped to solve a mystery. Apparently, the lens was still able to rotate after the U.S. Lighthouse Service abandoned the tower in 1936. That means that the modified roadway added to the assembly is unlikely to have caused the destruction of the clockwork gears. It must have happened sometime later.

Indeed, a review of the records stored in the Commander's office of the U.S. Coast Guard's 5th District Headquarters in Portsmouth, Va., reveal that as of September, 1943, the Cape Hatteras Lighthouse Fresnel lens, chariot, and clockwork assembly were in "an excellent state of preservation" and "could be put in use in a short time by cleaning and oiling."[190]

A subsequent report, however, written just 13 months later, revealed that the most tragic chapter of the light's intriguing past had begun.[191] Even when Confederate and Union forces fought for possession of the

Hatteras lens during the Civil War, it was well cared for, preserved intact, and largely undamaged. But 80 years later, during a dark period after German U-boats no longer posed a threat during World War II and the lighthouse was left unattended, souvenir hunters began their nefarious work on the lens, removing as many as 600 prisms, 24 bulls-eye lenses, and the incandescent oil-vapor lamp that was the heart of the light. Within four years, the Hatteras lens was destroyed. It was sometime during this period that unknown visitors to the lantern room, someone who possessed a fair amount of strength—certainly not young girls—may have turned the lens with tremendous force, and then engaged the clockwork's brake, violently ripping out most of the pinion gear's roller bearings and breaking and bending the cogs of the clockwork gears. It was a shameful conclusion to the life of a machine that served in two lighthouses and was admired and cared for by generations of Hatteras lighthouse keepers and their families.

"It makes perfect sense," Woodward said in a later telephone interview from Cleveland. "In retrospect, it's the only way the clockwork and pinion gears could have been abused in such a way. The lack of wear following the installation of the new chariot wheel roadway initially made me suspect the lighthouse service engineers were at fault. But if the lens and clockwork were described by a Coast Guard officer in 1943 as being in an excellent state of preservation, the fault for the damage to the pedestal's clockwork lies elsewhere."

Someone may yet discover other lost secrets about the Cape Hatteras Lighthouse Fresnel lens and pedestal and their turbulent past. Perhaps other island residents will "see the light" and return additional prisms or even whole panels of the lens for display. Then again, maybe not.

The historic artifact—indisputably a national treasure and an iconic symbol of Hatteras Island's storied traditions of lighthouse keeping and lifesaving—will never be as it once was. It will never again shine like a diamond in the sky. But no matter. The once forsaken lens and pedestal have now been rescued from the ravages of time, nature, and those who misguidedly claim a right to possess it. Its lost history has been rescued as well, and with luck, "the lost light" will tell its amazing story for generations to come.

THE MEDALLION

The small bronze medallion had been lodged in the corner of a crowded cedar box among faded photographs, exotic coins, subway tokens, military insignia, tattered news clippings, a postcard from a Route 66 motor lodge, a good luck horseshoe, an old watch, and a meerschaum pipe, its mouthpiece encrusted and cracked—family memorabilia kept safe for reasons no one could remember. The bronze medallion had been there for perhaps 40 years or more—waiting to be found. Why it was there, and who it belonged to, had been long since forgotten. The medallion's own story was in imminent danger of being lost forever.

I have felt an inexplicable connection to Cape Hatteras ever since my first visit in 1971. Upon arriving there as adventuresome teenager after riding a bicycle two and a half days from Greenville, North Carolina, I experienced a sensation that I had been there before. Several hundred feet from the lighthouse, I stood atop a pile of tumbled blue-gray granite stones to take a photograph. As the surf swirled beneath my feet, I distinctly recall being struck with a sense of déjà vu, a peculiar familiarity with my surroundings. Then, like evanescent sea foam, the memory soon vanished.

Company G, Ninth Regiment, New York Volunteers, were among 345 Union troops landed on Hatteras Island on August 28, 1861. Author's collection.

Once, during my long, oftentimes serendipitous quest for the long-lost Cape Hatteras Lighthouse Fresnel lens, my research was momentarily sidetracked as I began to review the events that precipitated the fall of the Confederate bastions, Fort Clark and Fort Hatteras, in August, 1861. As the reader may recall, among the U.S. Army units participating in the capture of Hatteras Island was the Ninth Regiment, New York Volunteers, popularly known as Hawkins' Zouaves.

Three companies of the regiment—C, G and H—embarked from Fortress Monroe near Hampton, Virginia, on August 26, 1861, aboard the steamer, *Adelaide*, to participate in the Hatteras expedition. Two days later, the attack on the Confederate forts commenced. In addition to a withering fusillade of shells fired from the Federal fleet, 345 soldiers were landed on the beach through heavy surf, about two miles east of Fort Clark. Among the Union troops who landed there was Company G of the Ninth New York, commanded by Captain Edward Jardine, a trusted line officer on the staff of the regiment's commander, Col. Rush Hawkins.

Despite "great difficulty and danger," Jardine and the men of Company G were some of the first Union soldiers to occupy North Carolina soil—sand, actually—during the Civil War. As the "Army of

Occupation," they survived a tense night without support of the fleet, which, overnight, had stood out to sea due to threatening weather. When the warships reassembled the next morning, the Confederate forces were defeated and Hatteras Island was returned to the Union.

Within the next few days, a detachment of soldiers was ordered by Col. Hawkins (now commanding officer of U.S. forces on Hatteras Island) to go ten miles up the beach to the Cape, to determine why the lighthouse there had not been operating for the past two months. When the men ascended the rickety wooden stairway inside the stone and brick octagonal tower and gained the lantern deck 130-feet above the dunes, they were surprised to discover that there was no light in the lighthouse. The Fresnel lens was missing, but the clockwork mechanism and heavy machinery of its pedestal remained.

While reading these exploits of the Ninth New York, a vague memory of mine was dislodged from where it has slumbered for years unknown—I had once possessed an artifact of the Hawkins' Zouaves, a regimental pin. But where?

A frenetic search eventually led me to the cedar box and the medallion, a two-inch-wide bronze oval which framed a Ninth New York cap, depicting a Zouave's red fez, typically edged in yellow cord and adorned with blue wool tassels. The medallion is correctly known as a reunion membership badge, minted after the war by regimental associations for their members, in this case a survivor of the campaigns of the Ninth New York. I could not remember why I would have the artifact. But my father did, and he shared with me what he knew, not too long before his passing.

The badge once belonged to Michael O'Brien, who had proudly etched his first initial and surname on the flat, back side of the badge. O'Brien, I later learned, was a 17-year-old Irish lad who resided in New York City in the spring of 1861. O'Brien was in need of work, as was his 21-year-old brother, Timothy, and the U.S. Army was hiring. Timothy enlisted in the Ninth New York first. But because Michael was the youngest in the family, he was strictly ordered by the older brother to stay home to care for their mother. On June 5th, the younger brother ran among an enormous crowd gathered along Broadway as citizens of the city cheered the colorfully attired regiment marching toward their awaiting transport docked at Pier 4. Leading the regiment were the national colors and a double silk standard of brilliant solid red with the embroidered words, "Toujours Pret"—Always Ready. It

(left) Michael O'Brien, member of the Volunteer Firemens Association, photographed in 1895. (right) Ninth NY reunion membership badge belonging to Michael O'Brien. Author's collection.

was later written in a regimental history that the spirited ovation the soldiers received "caused each man to mentally resolve that he would never bring disgrace on the beautiful standards or on the city which gave him so proud a farewell."[192] The scene must have made a profound impression on young Michael O'Brien, because when he turned 18 later that summer, he mustered into his brother's unit—Company G of the Ninth New York.

The story goes that when Michael finally caught up with his brother and Company G two months later at Newport News, Virginia, the greeting of Michael by his brother was not so warm as might have been expected. Timothy was furious that Michael had enrolled in the regiment, effectively abandoning their mother. A fistfight quickly ensued to settle the disagreement, and the two Irish brothers spent their first night of the war together in the regiment's brig. None of their later encounters with Rebel soldiers left the two men more bloodied.

Further research of Civil War records informed me that Private Michael O'Brien endured nearly five months of deprivation at Hatteras. He was in the front ranks of the famous charge of the Confederate battery on Roanoke Island. He survived unscathed a hotly contested skirmish at Camden, North Carolina, and was slightly wounded by an exploding shell in the flood of death at Antietam. But the most important fact about the original owner of the medallion, I learned from my father—he told me that the medallion had been given to me by my grandmother when I was a young boy. The medallion was her grandfather's. Michael O'Brien was my great-great-grandfather.

It took some time for the implications of this revelation to be fully comprehended. Not only had my ancestor been among the first Federal soldiers to occupy North Carolina in the opening months of the Civil War, but he quite likely had been among those who first ventured to the Cape Hatteras Lighthouse to discover its Fresnel lens missing. Michael O'Brien had conceivably gazed upon the Henry-Lepaute pedestal with curiosity, amazed by its massive, intricate gears and brightly polished chariot wheels. Perhaps, standing in the panoramic emptiness of the lantern room in 1861, he wondered where the lighting apparatus had been taken.

Truthfully, although Col. Hawkins had sufficient confidence in Company G's ability to assault Fort Clark by land, I have not yet found proof that O'Brien's unit was assigned the less-courageous task of reconnoitering the darkened lighthouse. It is just my intuition. But this I know—the blue-gray blocks of granite I stood upon during my first visit to the Cape Hatteras Lighthouse in 1971, and where I experienced a sensation of déjà vu, were the remains of the first lighthouse, the lighthouse my great-great-grandfather almost certainly visited sometime during the Hawkins' Zouaves posting on Hatteras Island in 1861.

The phenomenon of déjà vu, or paramnesia, has no scientific explanation, despite countless reported occurrences throughout the human experience. In fact, science dismisses it as an anomaly of memory, or the overlapping of short-term and long-term recollections. I am not so certain. Often, I am astonished by the eternal mysteries of Time: destiny, inevitability and the interconnectivity of generations, just as I am now holding Michael O'Brien's reunion membership badge in my hand.

I have no other answer for why I was so inspired to solve the mystery of "the lost light."

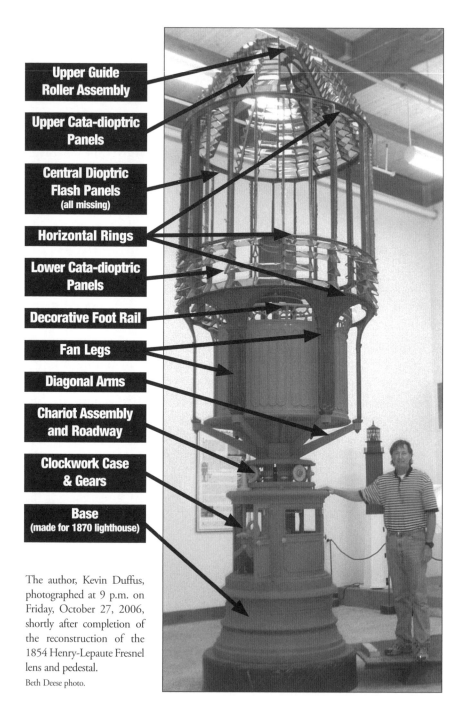

Upper Guide
Roller Assembly

Upper Cata-dioptric
Panels

Central Dioptric
Flash Panels
(all missing)

Horizontal Rings

Lower Cata-dioptric
Panels

Decorative Foot Rail

Fan Legs

Diagonal Arms

Chariot Assembly
and Roadway

Clockwork Case
& Gears

Base
(made for 1870 lighthouse)

The author, Kevin Duffus, photographed at 9 p.m. on Friday, October 27, 2006, shortly after completion of the reconstruction of the 1854 Henry-Lepaute Fresnel lens and pedestal.

Beth Deese photo.

First Hatteras light lens found

■ How the lens wound up in a climate-controlled storage facility in Manteo has been answered after months of detective work by videographer and author Kevin Duffus of Raleigh.

The Associated Press

MANTEO — The original lens for the Cape Hatteras Lighthouse, long thought lost to war or thieves, has been found in a climate-controlled storage building on Roanoke Island.

The 6,000-pound Fresnel lens is made up of 1,000 pieces of precision glass prisms. Lighthouse lantern rooms using Fresnel lenses captured and concentrated light from the prisms and bounced it through a panel, making the beam blink.

"It's a tremendous find," said Jim Woodward, a Cleveland, Ohio, lighthouse lamp expert. "It's like a lost shipwreck."

How it wound up in Manteo also has been answered after months of detective work by videographer and author Kevin Duffus of Raleigh, who last month found a document in a dim room of the National Archives in Washington, D.C., that pulled the story together.

Duffus found a letter written May 27, 1870, to an inspector in New York by the chairman of the federal Lighthouse Board. The letter ordered the return of the lens — which had been sent to Paris in 1868 for repairs and was being stored in New York — to Buxton for service in the new Cape Hatteras Lighthouse under construction.

"I was extremely excited — you don't get an opportunity to discover things anymore," he said.

Each prism, ranging between 3 and 12 inches, was made to an exacting size and shape. Each prism was fixed in frames covered in a green patina, each stamped with a name and number.

"When you put it in the frame, it had to be just right. It's pretty amazing," said Steve Harrison, chief resource manager for the National Park Service Outer Banks Group.

As the decades passed, it became widely assumed that the lens sent back to Hatteras wasn't the original Fresnel.

The Fresnel, a breakthrough in technology at the time, was installed in the 1803 Cape Hatteras tower in 1854 as part of a general upgrade of all U.S. lighthouses, which were built to alert ship captains approaching challenging coastal areas.

The Cape Hatteras Lighthouse is situated by the treacherous Diamond Shoals. It was considered strategically important to both the Confederacy and the Union during the Civil War.

The Confederacy took control of the lighthouse in 1861 and ordered it turned off a year later. The lens was then carefully removed to keep it out of the hands of Union troops.

The lens was taken to Washington, N.C. When Union troops approached Washington, it was put on a steamboat with townspeople evacuating to Tarboro. From there, a Washington doctor shipped it by rail to Townsville in Granville County, where it was hidden.

In 1865, a Union garrison found the lens in Henderson, dismantled and stored in 44 pine boxes. Duffus was not able to trace exactly how it got there.

The Union sent the lens to Norfolk, then Staten Island, N.Y., where it was stored until 1867.

It underwent repairs in Paris along with many other lighthouse lenses that had been removed across the South during the war. It was returned to New York and stored until the Lighthouse Board ordered it sent to Baltimore, the depot for materials used to build the new Cape Hatteras beacon.

After the Civil War, a different lens had been installed in the old Cape Hatteras light, which was later torn down. Engineers decided against using that lens when the existing tower was built in 1870.

The Fresnel lens performed its duties in the second lighthouse until 1936, when severe erosion forced the Coast Guard to abandon it. During World War II, the lighthouse was used as a lookout post for German U-boats.

After the war, and before the National Park Service acquired the lighthouse in 1949, the lens was vandalized, with many of its prisms taken as souvenirs. It was eventually replaced by a rotating airport beacon and put into storage.

Thieves broke into the storage site and stole prisms from the lens at least twice in the 1980s, leaving only about half of the prisms, many chipped and scarred.

A section of the lens and its frame will be displayed at the Graveyard of the Atlantic Museum, which is expected to be completed in Hatteras by 2004.

Joseph Schwarzer, the museum's executive director, said the display will show the lens portion as it looks today, a victim of the ravages of time in a salty, humid coastal climate.

This Associated Press report was published in numerous east coast newspapers soon after the discovery of the location of "the lost light" was announced by the author in September 2002.

Notes

CHAPTER ONE

1. Fulcher family genealogy by Ruth Fulcher Rickert, courtesy Hatteras Island Genealogical and Historical Society.

2. David Stick, *Dare County: A History* (Raleigh:NC Division of Archives and History, 1970), p.20.

3. Also, there was one yaupon manufacturer, one herdsman and one canoe builder. Fred M. Mallison, *The Civil War on the Outer Banks* (Jefferson, NC, McFarland & Company, Inc., 1998), p.18.

4. Ibid.

5. Keeper Benjamin Fulcher's immediate supervisors were the Collector of Customs in Washington, NC (who also served as the Superintendent of Lights at Pamlico Point and Royal Shoal in Pamlico Sound) and the U.S. Light House Board's 5th District Inspector (based at various times in Baltimore or Norfolk).

6. None of the orders to darken the lights are known to exist, but it is not likely the keepers tossed telegrams to the wind for concern that eventually a Federal authority might question them about their actions.

7. It is interesting to note that the beacon was the first lighthouse relocated at Cape Hatteras as a result of erosion in 1857, just one year after it was built. One hundred forty-two years later, the 198-foot tall modern Cape Hatteras Lighthouse was also relocated away from the encroaching sea.

8. R.N.Scott and others, Editors, *The War of the Rebellion: A Compilation of the Official Records of the Union and Confederate Armies* (Washington, D.C.:Government Printing Office, 1894-1901), hereinafter cited as OR.

9. Papers of Governor John Ellis, North Carolina Division of Archives and History.

10. Ibid.

11. William R. Trotter, *Ironclads and Columbiads, The Civil War in North Carolina-The Coast* (Winston-Salem:John F. Blair, Publisher. 1989), p.16.

12. John G. Barrett, *The Civil War in North Carolina* (Chapel Hill: The University of North Carolina Press 1963), p.14; and H.C. Graham, "How North Carolina Went Into the War," *Blue and Gray*, III (Nov. 1894) 283-84.

13. "Events of the Day," *Washington Daily News*, Aug. 17, 1951, describing an 1861 newspaper.

14. Before and after the war known as Federal Point.

15. Those navigational aids included Wade's Point, Croatan Sound, North West Point Royal Shoal, Roanoke Marshes, *Arctic* Lightship, Campbell Island, Cape Fear, Frying Pan Lightship, Oak Island, Orton Point, Price's Creek, and the Upper Jettee light on the Cape Fear River. At various times throughout the war even these vital navigational lights were doused along North Carolina's 375-mile coastline.

16. Archie K. Davis, *Boy Colonel of the Confederacy—The Life and Times of Henry King Burgwyn* (Chapel Hill: The University of North Carolina Press, 1985), pp.76-77.

17. *Frank Leslie's Illustrated Newspaper*, Nov. 2, 1861, (no. 310, v. XIII), p.375. Curiously, the critics in the North must have already forgotten that the War of Rebellion was not the first war during which North Carolina lighthouses were darkened to prevent them from aiding the enemy. The 63-foot tall Shell Castle Lighthouse at Ocracoke Inlet was initially damaged by the British during the War of 1812 but was later kept inoperative by the Ocracoke Customs Collector to prevent the

beacon from further aiding the enemy's Navy (although it would seem that since the Royal Navy were the first to knock it out of service they did not consider the Shell Castle light very helpful to begin with). Samuel Tredwell to Samuel Smith, Edenton, July 16, 1814, Letters from Lighthouse Superintendents, Record Group 26, National Archives and Records Administration, hereinafter cited as RG 26 NARA.; and, Francis Ross Holland, Jr., *A History of the Cape Hatteras Light Station*, Division of History, Office of Archeology and Historic Preservation, National Park Service, Sep. 30, 1968, pp.16-17, FN15.

18. Lavrentiy Alekseyvich Zagoskin, *Lt. Zagoskin's Travels in Russian America*, edited by Henry N. Michael (Canada: University of Toronto Press, 1967); and Francis Ross Holland, Jr., *America's Lighthouses—An Illustrated History* (New York: Dover Publications, 1988), p.56.

CHAPTER TWO

19.1. Holland, *A History of the Cape Hatteras Light Station*, p.4; Lighthouse Letters, 1792-1798, v.1, pp.460-462, RG 26 NARA.

19.2. An urban legend has been perpetuated for more than 50 years that the first lighthouse on Cape Hatteras had been the idea of Treasury Secretary Alexander Hamilton, ever since he had been a teenager. The story goes that Hamilton conceived the lighthouse following a near-death experience when his ship, *Thunderbolt*, caught fire and nearly foundered off Hatteras. Hamilton scholars today, including Yale historian, Joanne Freeman, author of *Hamilton Writings*, have found no evidence of the Hatteras accident. The myth was fabricated by a popular writer who began his book by admitting that he was not a historian and his book was not a history, yet successive writers accepted his fantasy as fact. Hamilton did not initiate the idea for a lighthouse at the Cape, but without question, he paid for it.

20. American State Papers, Class IV, Commerce and Navigation, Vol. VII (Washington: Gales & Seaton, 1832), (Serial #014), pp.639, 690-691; and Holland, *A History of the Cape Hatteras Light Station*, p.29.

21. A pole is sixteen and a half feet.

22. Sessions to the United States pp.177-178.

23. Holland, *A History of the Cape Hatteras Light Station*, p.23.

24. R. H. J. Blount to Thomas Corwin, Washington, N.C., January 7, 1851, Lighthouse Letters, Treasury Department, 1851-1852, Series P, pp.2-7.

25. Today, the name, Saint-Gobain, survives as a multi-national corporation specializing in diversified glass and silica products and still is known for exceptional quality, having produced the glass for the Lourve Pyramid.

CHAPTER THREE

26. David Schenck Journal, May 20, 1861, Southern Historical Collection, University of North Carolina, Chapel Hill. Schenck was a Lincolnton, NC, lawyer.

27. Col. L.D. Starke, former Superintendent of Lights, Elizabeth City District to Thos.E. Martin, Richmond, VA, Nov. 22, 1861, Records of the Lighthouse Bureau, Treasury Dept. Collection of Confederate Records, RG 365 NARA II, College Park, MD.

28. The Confederate lighthouse establishment even recycled the remaining forms and letterhead of its Federal counterpart, now its enemy, by simply marking out the "U" of U.S. and adding a "C." "Memminger was a native of Germany, but he had a summer home in the mountains of [North Carolina] and is buried there." William S. Powell, *North Carolina—A History* (Chapel Hill:The University of North Carolina Press, 1977), pp.137-137.

29. J.T. Miller, Wilmington, NC, to Thos. E. Martin, Richmond, VA, Nov. 23, 1961, Records of the Lighthouse Bureau, Treasury Dept. Collection of Confederate Records, RG 365 NARA II, College Park, MD.

30. Thomas E. Martin Circular to Superintendents, November 9, 1861, from the archives of the

Virginia Historical Society.

31. The 30-foot range light (sixth-order lens) is indicated on a 1858 nautical chart, "Cape Hatteras to Cape Lookout," and was apparently positioned on the east side of Fort Macon while the 50-foot Bogue Banks light (fourth-order lens) was located on the west side of the fort. Neither lighthouse stands today.

32. Records and books of Josiah Bell, Collector and Superintendent of Lights Beaufort District, July 19, 1861 and Josiah Bell to Thomas E. Martin, Acting Chief of Light-House Bureau, Richmond, VA, Nov. 14, 1861, Records of the Lighthouse Bureau, Treasury Dept. Collection of Confederate Records, RG 365 NARA II, College Park, MD.

33. It is believed that the machinist from Washington brought an extra hand because they were also to remove the lenses at the water-bound screwpile light at Pamlico Point and the North West Point of Royal Shoal light vessel out in the sound. Lighthouse lenses were unfamiliar to the machinist because in peacetime the U.S. Light House Board used its own engineers for the installation and removal of lanterns and lenses.

34. Myers also owned the *Governor Morehead*, and Superintendent Hancock recorded no expenses for the transportation of the lenses to Washington.

35. Because of Fulcher's age and relative wealth it is more likely that Assistant Keeper Bateman A. Williams stayed on the job (with or without pay until the Union recaptured the island in August, 1861) since records indicate he did not vacate the position until 1865.

CHAPTER FOUR

36. "Thatch's Hole" is a reference to the place where the notorious pirate Blackbeard, also known as Teach, was ambushed and killed by a posse of Royal Navy sailors commissioned by the pirate-pestered Governor of Virginia on November 22, 1718. Thatch's Hole is today called Teaches Hole. Moseley's 1733 map is held in the H.P. Kendall Collection, South Caroliniana Library, University of South Carolina.

37. Edward Warren, *A Doctor's Experiences in Three Continents* (Baltimore:Cushings & Bailey, 1885).

38. Mallison, *The Civil War on the Outer Banks*, p.27; and The Windsor Story 1768-1968, p.53.

39. William Henry von Eberstein Papers, East Carolina Manuscript Collection, East Carolina University.

40. A reverse of sorts of the privateering Mosquito Fleet would take place on the same waters during World War I and then more successfully during World War II when German U-boats conducted a "tonnage war" against the United States and her Allies, sinking 397 ships in six months. Kevin P. Duffus, producer, *War Zone-World War II on North Carolina's Outer Banks*, DVD, 2 volumes, 2005.

41. *Frank Leslie's Illustrated Newspaper*, Sept. 7, 1861, p.263.

42. Ironically, the U.S. Navy described the same coastline in April, 1942, as "the most dangerous area for merchant shipping in the entire world." Duffus, *War Zone*.

43. Union Lt. Thomas Selfridge to Gideon Welles, Sec. of Navy, August, 1861, *Official Records of the Union and Confederate Navies in the War of the Rebellion* (hereinafter ORN), Series I, Vol. 6, p.42.

44. Mallison, *The Civil War on the Outer Banks*, p.30.

45. Trotter, *Ironclads and Columbiads*, pp.22-23.

46. William Morrison Robinson, Jr., "The Rendezvous at Hatteras," from *The Confederate Privateers* (New Haven:Yale University Press, 1928); and, David Stick, ed., *An Outer Banks Reader* (Chapel Hill: The University of North Carolina Press, 1998), pp.132-134.

CHAPTER FIVE

47. J.A. Marshall, ed., *Private and Official Correspondence of General Benjamin F. Butler During the Period of the Civil War* (Norwood, Mass.: Plempton Press, 1917), Vol. I, pp.227-228.

48. OR, Series I, Vol. IV, p.589.

49. David Stick, *The Outer Banks of North Carolina* (Chapel Hill: The University of North Carolina Press, 1958), pp. 122 & 124.

50. *Frank Leslie's Illustrated Newspaper*, Sept. 14, 1861, p.282.

51. Ibid., p.274.

52. Ibid., p.44. And William Henry von Eberstein Papers, East Carolina Manuscript Collection, East Carolina University, Greenville, NC, p.128.

53. Mallison, *The Civil War on the Outer Banks*, pp.43-44.

54. William S. Gaskill to Governor Clark, September, 1861, Records of the Lighthouse Bureau, Treasury Dept. Collection of Confederate Records, RG 365 NARA II, College Park, MD.

55. Hanson R. Ruark, keeper of Price's Creek Lights, to Mr. Edward Savage, Collector of Customs, Wilmington, N.C., Feb. 2, 1863, re. effort to be paid for service Nov. 27, 1861, Records of the Lighthouse Bureau, Treasury Dept. Collection of Confederate Records, RG 365 NARA II, College Park, MD; and Letters from the LH Board RG 26 Entry 20, Vol. 16, Entry 20, page 59, Nov. 10, 1869 to E. Legg, Esq., Smithville, NC.

CHAPTER SIX

56a. ORN, Series I, Vol. 6, p.270.

56b. ORN, Series I, Vol. 6, pp.220-221.

57. On September 10, 1861, the USS *Pawnee*, captured the Southern schooner *Susan Jane* that was returning to Hatteras Inlet. Other blockade-runners, unaware that the Union Navy controlled the inlet, were also taken as prizes. *Civil War Naval Chronology* (Washington: Naval History Division, Navy Department, 1971), p. I-26.

58. ORN, Series I, Vol. 6, p.429.

59. After the war, Captain Williams returned to the *Paragon*, refloated her and put her back in service. Williams' son, Horatio Jr., said, "She was just about as good as ever." Mallison, *The Civil War on the Outer Banks*, pp.22, 179-180.

60. *Frank Leslie's Illustrated Newspaper*, Nov. 9, 1861, p.389.

61. J. Thomas Scharf, *History of the Confederate Navy* (New York: Rogers & Sherwood, 1887), p.379.

62. For the complete text of the account, see Stick, *An Outer Banks Reader*, pp.132-134, "The Chicamacomico Races," Edward A. Duyckinck, 1861.

63. "Bodie Island" was spelled, "Body's Island" in 1861.

64. Ebenezer Farrand, Commander CSN, "ordered Officers and crew of CSS *Virginia* [scuttled by same on May 11, 1862 off Craney Island, VA, to avoid capture] to report to his office, to establish a battery below Drewry's Bluff on the [James] River." *Civil War Naval Chronology* p.II-63. On September 16, 1862, the "Confederate Congress passed a resolution expressing thanks to [Farrand, who, as] senior officer in command of the combined naval and military forces at Drewry's Bluff on 15 May, 'for the great and signal victory achieved over the naval forces of the United States in the engagement…at Drewry's Bluff.' Farrand was praised for his 'gallantry, courage, and endurance in that protracted fight…' which Confederate statesmen knew could have been so disastrous to their cause." *Civil War Naval Chronology* p.II-97. Except for the failure of Union troops to attack the bluff from the rear, the James River Flotilla would have likely been able to steam all the way to Richmond, possibly shortening the war considerably. The USS *Monitor* also took part. Commodore Farrand, on May 4, 1865 surrendered "all confederate naval forces, officers, men and

public property yet afloat under his command and now blockaded by a portion of our naval forces in the Tombigee River," Alabama.

65. Thos. E. Martin to District Superintendents, Nov. 9, 1861, Virginia Historical Society.

66. The *Arctic* was refloated after the war and, repaired and refitted, returned to service as a light-ship until, "old and worn out," she was sold at public auction, presumably as scrap. Holland, *America's Lighthouses*, p.56.

67. "Burning Of A Lightship Captured By The Rebels, By the U.S. Steamer *Mount Vernon*," *Frank Leslie's Illustrated Newspaper*, Feb. 8, 1862, p.182. The Northern correspondent must have been unaware of the occasion when the Union Navy burned and sank the operational Ocracoke Inlet Lightship three months earlier.

68. Ibid.

CHAPTER SEVEN

69. A.E. Burnside, "The Burnside Expedition," *Battles and Leaders of the Civil War* (New York: Century Co., 1887), Vol. I, pp.660-661.

70. Stick, *The Outer Banks of North Carolina*, p.139.

71. Drew Pullen, *Portrait of the Past—The Civil War on Hatteras Island* (Mount Holly, New Jersey: Robert V. Drapala Publishing, 2001), p.110; and 25th Regiment of Massachusetts, p.50.

72. D.L.Day, *My Diary of Rambles with the Twenty-fifth Volunteer Infantry with Burnside's Coast Division* (Milford:King and Billings, 1884) p.23.

73. Ibid.

74. The New Bern *Daily Progress*, and Mallison, *The Civil War on the Outer Banks*, p.68.

75. Elizabeth Collier Diary, Aug. 28, 1861, Southern Historical Collection, University of North Carolina, Chapel Hill.

76. R.B. Creecy to Daughter, February, 1862, R.B. Creecy Papers, Southern Historical Collection; "Old Times in Betsy," *Elizabeth City Economist*, Aug. 10, 1900.

77. T.C. Parramore, "The Roanoke-Chowan Story," Chapter 7, "The Burning of Winton," Ahoskie *Daily Roanoke-Chowan News*, Civil War Supplement, 1960. And: Barrett, *The Civil War in North Carolina*, p.94

78. OR, Series I, Vol. IV, pp.658-659.

79. David S. Cecelski, *The Waterman's Song—Slavery and Freedom in Maritime North Carolina* (Chapel Hill: The University of North Carolina Press, 2001), p.180.

80. Stick, *The Outer Banks of North Carolina*, p.84.

81. Part of Granville County was annexed in 1872 to form Vance County, named for the Civil War Governor, Zebulon B. Vance, and Townsville and Hibernia were included in the new county.

82. Author's interview with Olivia Taylor Feduccia, great-granddaughter of John Hargrove.

CHAPTER EIGHT

83. Letters from the LH Board, Entry 20, page 66, Vol. 7 of 31, Chairman of the L.H. Board, Rear Admiral W.B. Shubrick, US Navy, to Brig. Gen. A.J. Williams, U.S.A., Hatteras Inlet. RG 26 NARA.

84. Barrett, *The Civil War in North Carolina*, p.106.

85. For an excellent description of African-American spies, scouts and guides after the fall of New Bern see Cecelski, *The Waterman's Song*, p.186.

86. Treasury Department, Lighthouse Letters, 1860-1861, P Series, pp.188-189; and Holland, *A History of the Cape Hatteras Light Station*, pp.68-69.

87. The hull of the Confederate gunboat, one of 100 "of identical pattern," commissioned by the Richmond government in the Fall of 1861, was towed up Chicod Creek, a tributary of the

Tar River, halfway between Washington and Greenville. The night of the Federal capture of Washington, the vessel was holed, sunk and its exposed bow coated with turpentine and burned. In 1971, the author dove on the gunboat and also interviewed Mr. John Wilson, 86, whose grandfather owned property adjacent to where the gunboat was scuttled and was an eyewitness of the event.

88. ORN, Series I, pp. 150-153.

89. Ibid.

CHAPTER NINE

90. Unbeknownst to Capt. Brown, Farrand had long since departed the Lighthouse Bureau for service in the Confederate Navy and was at the time busy preparing to defend against McClellan's long awaited Peninsular Campaign.

91. C.L. Price, "North Carolina's Railroads in the Civil War," *Civil War History*, Vol. VII, September 1961, p.302.

92. James Sprunt, *Chronicles to the Cape Fear River*, 1860-1916 (Raleigh 1916) p.289; and Price, "North Carolina's Railroads in the Civil War," *Civil War History* p.300.

CHAPTER TEN

93. D.R. Larned to Mrs. A.E. Burnside, Apr. 25, 1862, D.R. Larned Papers, Library of Congress; and Barrett, p.116.

94. OR, Series I, Vol. IX, p. 284.

95. Letters from the LH Board RG 26 Entry 20, Vol. 7 of 31, Chairman of the L.H. Board, Rear Admiral W.B. Shubrick, US Navy, to Gen. J.G. Parke, USA.

96. G.B. McClellan, *McClellan's Own Story* (New York: Charles L. Webster and Co., 1887), pp. 206-207.

97. Jos. Ramsey, Custom House, Plymouth, NC, to Ebenezer Farrand, Esq., Chief of Light House Bureau, Richmond, VA, May 18, 1862, Records of the Lighthouse Bureau, Treasury Dept. Collection of Confederate Records, RG 365 NARAII, College Park, MD.

98. Ibid, May 31, 1862.

99. Joseph Ramsey, Custom House, Plymouth, N.C. to Ebenezer Farrand, Esq., Chief of Light House Bureau, Richmond, VA, May 29, 1862, Records of the Lighthouse Bureau, Treasury Dept. Collection of Confederate Records, RG 365 NARA II, College Park, MD. Ramsey, like Tarboro's Capt. Brown before him, must not have been aware that Farrand was long gone from the Light House Bureau and had, in May, valiantly defended McClellan's incursion up the James River, in effect, bogging down the Peninsular Campaign.

100. Jos. Ramsey, District of Plymouth, NC, from Hamilton, to Ebenezer Farrand, Esq., Chief of Light House Bureau [former], Richmond, VA, July 1, 1862, Records of the Lighthouse Bureau, Treasury Dept. Collection of Confederate Records, RG 365 NARA II, College Park, MD.

CHAPTER ELEVEN

101. Letters to the Light House Board, Index to General Correspondence 1791-1900, RG 26, NARA, Washington, D.C.

102. Letters sent by the LH Board Entry 20, Vol. 4 of 31, May 10, 1862 to August 13, 1869, Page 1, Shubrick to Messrs. Blatchford, Seward & Griswold, New York City, May 12, 1862. RG 26, NARA.

103. Treasury Department, Lighthouse Letters, 1862-1864, P Series, pp.4-5; and Holland, A *History of the Cape Hatteras Light Station*, p.71.

104. Letters sent to District Inspectors and Engineers, Entry 23, Vol. 43 of 107, p.78, RG 26 NARA.

105. The letterbooks of the Board to the 5th District Engineer and Inspectors reflect an abrupt gap

between these dates, and the gap itself speaks volumes.

106. Letters sent by the LH Board, Entry 20, Vol. 7 of 31, page 148, RG 26 NARA.

107. Bruce Roberts, "In Memory of Croatan Light," *Our State-Down Home in North Carolina*, June 2002, Greensboro:Mann Media, pp.90-92.

108. Letters sent by the Light House Board, Entry 20, Vol.7 of 31, RG 26 NARA.

109. OR, Series I, Vol. VI, p. 193; and Barrett, *The Civil War in North Carolina*, Footnote, p.138.

110. Tayloe was further described as "tenderly nursing the sick; cooling the fevered brow of the wounded or ministering to the dying wants of a fallen comrade, his kind heart and genial presence gave comfort to the weak and dispelled the gloom of the gathering shadows, nobly exemplifying those beautiful lines, 'the tender are the brave: the loving are the daring.'" *The Confederate Reveille* (a collection of biographies of Beaufort County soldiers).

111. David Stick, *The Graveyard of the Atlantic* (Chapel Hill: The University of North Carolina Press, 1952), p.54.

112. "The Foundering of the USS *Monitor*," by William F. Keeler, from Robert W. Daly, ed., Aboard the USS *Monitor*: 1862: The Letters of Acting Paymaster William Frederick Keeler, U.S. Navy, to His Wife, Anna (Annapolis: U.S. Naval Institute, 1964), pp.253-260. For the complete text of "The Foundering of the USS *Monitor*," see, *An Outer Banks Reader*, David Stick, ed., pp.79-85.

113. Ibid.

CHAPTER TWELVE

114. The Cape Lookout Lighthouse was re-lit on February 24, 1863, and G. Chadwick was appointed keeper, according to Harriet Lawrence Stapleton in "Lighthouse Keepers," from *Carteret County Heritage*, p.420-421.

115. Barrett, *The Civil War in North Carolina*, p.71.

116. OR, Series I, Vol. IV, p.613.

117. Ben Dixon MacNeil, *The Hatterasman* (Winston-Salem:John F. Blair, 1958), pp.178-179.

118. From the diary of Edwin Graves Champney, drawings and diary permanently housed at the Outer Banks History Center, Manteo, NC, and donated to the state of NC by the North Carolina Maritime History Council through a significant contribution from the Frank Stick Trust.

119. Letters to the Light House Board, Entry 24, various dates and volumes. RG 26, NARA, Washington, D.C.

120. Dr. Tayloe resigned his commission prior to Gen. Foster's December, 1862, raid on Kinston, because of "a sense of duty to his aged mother & as the only male relation & his mother and family [had] been driven from their home by the enemy." His resignation was accepted and Tayloe served the remainder of the war as a state health inspector. Information provided by Dr. John Cotton Tayloe.

121. D.M. Carter to Z.B. Vance, Oct. 5, 1864, D.M. Carter Papers, Southern Historical Collection, UNC; and Barrett *The Civil War in North Carolina*, p.221.

122. Clint Johnson, *Touring the Carolinas' Civil War Sites* (Winston-Salem:John F. Blair, 1996), p.85.

123. James Evans to Father, May 10, 1864, James Evans Papers, Southern Historical Collection, University of North Carolina, Chapel Hill. Among the townspeople who lost their homes was a young boy, Josephus Daniels, Jr., who later became the editor of the *Raleigh News & Observer* and Secretary of the Navy under President Woodrow Wilson. Mallison, *The Civil War on the Outer Banks*, p.146. The doctor who delivered Josephus Daniels was David T. Tayloe.

CHAPTER THIRTEEN

124. Confederate cavalry officer J.P. Austin, quoted by Kenneth C. Davis, *Don't Know Much About the Civil War*, (New York:William Morrow & Company, 1996), pp.393-394.

125. It was William Whiting, in 1861 a major dispatched to North Carolina by Jefferson Davis, who implemented Governor Ellis' orders to extinguish the state's lighthouses. Whiting died of his wounds suffered during hand-to-hand combat within the fort. "'Surrender!' yelled the men in blue. 'Go to hell, you Yankee bastards!' shouted General Whiting in reply." Barrett, *The Civil War in North Carolina*, p.277.

126. D.A. Buie to "Kate," Jan. 21, 1865, Catherine Buie Papers, Duke University.

127. OR, Series I, Vol. XLVII, Part 2, p.719.

128. Barrett, *The Civil War in North Carolina*, p.293.

129. John G. Barrett, *Sherman's March Through the Carolinas* (Chapel Hill: The University of North Carolina Press 1956), pp.183-184.

130. Ibid, p.346; from H. Reid to sister, April 7, 1865, State Historical Society of Wisconsin.

131. Ibid, p.344.

132. William Tecumseh Sherman, *Memoirs of General W.T. Sherman* (New York:D. Appleton and Company), Vol. 2, pp.324-328.

133. Ibid.

134. C. Manly to D.L. Swain, March 29 and April 8, 1865, D.L. Swain Papers, Southern Historical Collection, UNC.

135. OR, Series I, Part III, Vol. XLVII, p.178.

136. Devereux, Margaret, *Plantation Sketches* (Cambridge:The Riverside Press, 1906), p.150.

137. *From the Manuscript Prepared by the Late Chaplain John J. Hight During His Service with the Regiment in the Field* (Princeton:Press of the Clarion, 1895), p.514. And Barrett, *The Civil War in North Carolina*, p.370.

138. H.J. Aten, *History of the Eighty-fifth Regiment*, Illinois Volunteer Infantry (Hiwawatha, Kansas: Regimental Association, 1901), p.303.

139. OR, Series I, Part III, Vol. XLVII, p.178.

140. Cornelia Phillips Spencer, *The Last Ninety Days of the War in North Carolina* (New York: Watchman Publishing Company, 1866), p.157-160.

CHAPTER FOURTEEN

141. George C. Round, "A Yankee on the Dome," *The News & Observer's, Raleigh—A Living History of North Carolina's Capital*, edited by David Perkins (Winston-Salem:John F. Blair, 1994) pp.60-66. Reprint of Lt. George C. Round from 1902 publication of the United States Veteran Signal Corps Association.

142. Captain Thomas and Lieutenant Round may not have been the first Federal officers to see the lighthouse lenses in the rotunda. Earlier in the day, soldiers raised the U.S. flag over the capitol dome.

143. The opinion of Major John Chipman Gray, Judge Advocate on the staff of Major General Quincy Adams Gillmore, commander of the Department of the South. Barrett, *Sherman's March Through the Carolinas*, p.33.

144. Stephen R. Mallory, "Reminiscences," S.R. Mallory Papers, Southern Historical Collection, UNC.

145. R.S. Naroll, "Lincoln and the Sherman Peace Fiasco—Another Fable?" Journal of Southern History, Vol. XX, Nov. 1954, p.478.

146. OR, Series I, Part III, Vol. XLVII, pp.243-244.

147. *Raleigh Daily Standard*, April 28, 1865.

148. George Whitefield Pepper, *Personal Recollections of Sherman's Campaigns in Georgia and the Carolinas* (Zanesville:Hugh Dunne, 1866), pp.387-389.

149. Author Kenneth C. Davis wrote that Meigs was "one of the obscure and unsung heroes of the

Union effort." Davis, *Don't Know Much About the Civil War*, p.220.

150. Microfilm M745, Letters sent by the QM Gen, roll 50 (April 3-Aug 5), 080-07, page 242. Gen. Meigs to Adm. Shubrick, Apr. 26, '65. NARA, Washington, D.C.

151-1. Walter Clark Papers, North Carolina Division of Archives and History (NCDAH); Governor's Papers—Glenn, February-March, 1906 (G.P. 313), NCDAH; Congressional Record: The Proceedings and Debates of the Fifty-Ninth Congress, X403, Vol. XL. (Washington:G.P.O., 1906), pp.1739-1741.

151-2. North Carolina's copy of the Bill of Rights was officially returned to the state's possession on Aug. 4, 2005, after the historic document was recovered in an FBI sting operation in Philadelphia on March 18, 2003. One of the fourteen original copies of the Bill of Rights commissioned by George Washington for the thirteen colonies and the federal government, the stolen document resurfaced several times, most notably in 1925 and 1995 when offers to sell the document back to the State of North Carolina were rejected by state officials. The document's value has been estimated at between $30 million and $40 million. (Source: NC State Archives.)

CHAPTER FIFTEEN

152. Letters sent by the Light House Board Entry 20, RG 26 NARA, Washington, D.C.

153. Ibid.

154. Tayloe was listed as executor and Hargrove as witness on a Beaufort County will extract dated September 13, 1865. Beaufort Co. Will Extracts 1720-1868 (RNC 929.37 B p.308).

155. "Kitrell" is spelled "Kittrell" today.

156. Light House Board, Letters Sent to the 5th District Inspector, 1860-1871, Entry 23, Vol. 43 of 107, p.233, Sep. 25, 1865, RG 26 NARA, Washington, D.C.

CHAPTER SIXTEEN

157. Reference made to the Special Committee in Entry 23, Vol. 15 of 107, p. 15, Letters to the 3rd Dist. Inspector from Shubrick, Nov. 27, 1865, RG 26 NARA, Washington, D.C.

158. Letters sent by the Light House Board, Entry 20, RG 26 NARA, Washington, D.C.

159. Federal Point was relighted on April 30, 1866. Letters to the Light House Board, Entry 24, RG 26 NARA, Washington, D.C.

160. The lighthouses were: Southwest Point Royal Shoal, Long Shoal, Croatan Sound, North River and Wade's Point.

161. Letters to the 3rd Dist. Inspector, Entry 23, Vol. 15 of 107, p. 127, March 19, 1867. RG 26 NARA, Washington, D.C.

162. *Light House Board, Annual Report*, 1869, p.47 (Washington:G.P.O.).

163. A couple of years later, Newman applied to the board for work and was curtly denied even the slightest consideration, suggesting maybe that the board was aware of the terrible mistake of the Hatteras light's location and conveniently held Newman responsible.

CHAPTER SEVENTEEN

164. Holland, A *History of the Cape Hatteras Light Station*, pp.91-92.

165. "Let Us Have Light," *Daily Alta California*, November 30, 1868, p.3; and Frank Perry, *The History of Pigeon Point Lighthouse* (Santa Cruz:Otter B Books, 1986), p.25.

166. Miscellaneous Letters from the L.H. Board, Aug. 13, 1869 to Sep. 14, 1871, From Naval Secretary Rear Admiral T.A. Jenkins, USN, to Mssrs. Henry-Lepaute, Entry 20, Vol. 16 of 31, p. 190-191, RG 26 NARA, Washington, D.C.

167. *Illustrated History of San Mateo County*, California (Oakland:Moore and DePue, 1878), p.25.

168. *California: A Guide to the Golden State*, WPA guidebook published in 1939; and Perry, *The History of Pigeon Point Lighthouse*, p.37.

CHAPTER EIGHTEEN

169. *Annual Report of the Operations of the United States Life-Saving Service for the Fiscal Year Ending June 30, 1885* (Washington:Government Printing Office, 1886), p.162.

170. C.F. Shoemaker to Sumner I. Kimball, General Superintendent, U.S. Life-Saving Service, Feb. 7, 1885. Outer Banks History Center.

171. Charles Stowe of Hatteras, interviewed by the author in 1996.

172. The land for the steel tower was sold to the government by Unaka Jennette for $266.88.

173. *Light House Board-Annual Report, 1886* (Washington:Government Printing Office, 1886), p.139.

174. Ibid.

175. From an interview with Ormond Fuller, featured in the documentary film, *War Zone—World War Two Off North Carolina's Outer Banks*, produced by the author in 2001.

176. Stick, *The Outer Banks of North Carolina*, pp.242-243.

177. Ibid.

178. Thomas Yocum, Bruce Roberts, Cheryl Shelton-Roberts, *Cape Hatteras—America's Lighthouse, Guardian of the Graveyard of the Atlantic*, (Nashville:Cumberland House, 1999), pp.81-86.

179. Ibid.

CHAPTER NINETEEN

180. This was the document that indicated what happened to the original Hatteras lens, the revelation that solved the mystery of the "lost light." Letters to the 3rd District Inspector, Entry 23, Vol. 16 of 107, p.33, from Chairman of the L.H. Board, Rear Admiral W.B. Shubrick, US Navy, May 27, 1870, RG 26 NARA, Washington, D.C.

CHAPTER TWENTY

181. Elizabeth Abbott, "Lighthouse Controversy Angers North Carolina Residents," *Providence Journal-Bulletin*, Nov. 23, 1995.

182. Ibid.

183. Couch, Daniel C., "Islanders Share Their Lighthouse Memories," *The Island Breeze*, Summer 1999.

EPILOGUE

184. James S. Woodward, "Report of Findings and Recommendations Concerning the Cape Hatteras 1st Order Classical Fresnel Lens," July 2003, private report on file at NPS Cape Hatteras National Seashore, Roanoke Island, NC, and Graveyard of the Atlantic Museum, Hatteras, NC.

185. Private interviews with the author, 2006.

186. http://waldo.jaquith.org/blog/2006/10/cape-hatteras-lighthouse/

187. http://www.schundler.net/10-10bsss.htm

188. Catherine Kozak, "Lighthouse Lens, Pedestal Reunited at Hatteras Museum," *The Virginian-Pilot*, November 6, 2006.

189. Interview with the author, 2006.

190. USCG 5th District Memorandum from Lt. Cmdr. F.I. Phippany to Chief, Civil Engineering Division, September 2, 1943.

191. USCG 5th District Memorandum from Lt. Cmdr. F.I. Phippany to Chief, Civil Engineering Division, October 27, 1944.

POSTSCRIPT

192. Lt. Matthew J. Graham, *The Ninth Regiment New York Volunteers*, (Lancaster, Ohio: Vanberg Publishing, 1998), p.53.

Much of the research for this story of "the lost light" of Cape Hatteras was found at the National Archives facilities on Pennsylvania Avenue in Washington, D.C., and at College Park, Maryland. All of the Confederate Light House Bureau records are contained in Record Group 365, Records of the Light House Bureau, Treasury Department, at College Park (or NARA II). The Washington, D.C. facility contains Record Group 26, which includes the vast holdings of the U.S. Coast Guard and the consolidated organizations that preceded it, including the Lifesaving Service, the Lighthouse Service (also, U.S. Light House Board) and the Revenue Cutter Service. Researchers may be discouraged by the fact that some of the old U.S. lighthouse records were lost in a Commerce Department fire in the 1920s, but the fact is that many more survived and there are multiple paths to follow to find key facts. The essential finding aid for RG 26 is titled, "Preliminary Inventory of the Records of the United States Coast Guard," and was complied in 1963 by Forrest Holdcamper. The records comprise 10,194 cubic feet of material and include papers, ledgers, journals, letter books, and correspondence. The records are organized under "entries," 1 through 278. By far, the most useful sources for this work were found in entry 20, Letters Sent by the Light House Board; entry 23, Letters Sent to District Engineers and Inspectors; and entry 24, Letters Received from District Engineers and Inspectors. All of the extant Confederate Treasury records comprise less than a cubic foot of material and lighthouse papers fill two small storage boxes. The Confederate lighthouse records are organized according to locations.

PRIMARY SOURCES

Manuscripts

Records of the Lighthouse Bureau, Treasury Dept. Collection of Confederate Records, RG 365 NARA II, College Park, MD.

Appendix IV, Confed. Lighthouse Establishments for which there are records, NC:

Beaufort District: Bogue Banks and Cape Lookout.

Camden District (also Elizabeth City): Bodie Island, Croatan, Roanoke Marshes, Wades Point.

Ocracoke District: Ocracoke.

Plymouth District: Roanoke River Lightship.

Washington District: Cape Hatteras, Cape Hatteras Beacon, Pamlico Point, Royal Shoal.

Wilmington District: *Arctic* Lightship, Campbell I., Cape Fear, Confed. Point, Frying Pan Lightship, Oak Island, Orton Point, Price's Creek, Upper Jettee.

Thomas E. Martin Circular to Superintendents, November 9, 1861, from the archives of the Virginia Historical Society.

John W. Ellis Letter Book, 1861, Manuscript Division, North Carolina Department of Archives and History.

Papers of Governor John Ellis, North Carolina Division of Archives and History.

Zebulon Baird Vance Letter Book, 1863-1865, Manuscript Division, North Carolina Department of Archives and History.

Letters sent by the Quartermaster General, Gen. Meigs to Adm. Shubrick, Apr. 26, 1865. National Archives and Records Administration, Washington, D.C.

American State Papers, Class IV, Commerce and Navigation, Vol. VII. Washington: Gales & Seaton, 1832, Serial #014.

Walter Clark Papers, North Carolina Division of Archives and History.

Governor's Papers—Glenn, Feb.-Mar., 1906 (G.P. 313), North Carolina Division of Archives and History.

D.M. Carter to Z.B. Vance, Oct. 5, 1864, D.M. Carter Papers, Southern Historical Collection, University of North Carolina, Chapel Hill.

James Evans to Father, May 10, 1864, James Evans Papers, Southern Historical Collection, University of North Carolina, Chapel Hill.

D.A. Buie to "Kate," Jan. 21, 1865, Catherine Buie Papers, Duke University.

H. Reid to sister, April 7, 1865, State Historical Society of Wisconsin.

D.L. Swain Papers, Southern Historical Collection, University of North Carolina, Chapel Hill.

R. H. J. Blount to Thomas Corwin, Washington, N.C., January 7, 1851, Lighthouse Letters, Treasury Department, 1851-1852, Series P.

Official Documents

Scott, R.N. and others, editors. *The War of the Rebellion: A Compilation of the Official Records of the Union and Confederate Armies.* 128 Vols. Washington, D.C.: Government Printing Office, 1894-1901.

Rush, Richard, and others, Eds. *Official Records of the Union and Confederate Navies in the War of the Rebellion.* 31 Vols. Washington, D.C.: Government Printing Office, 1894-1924.

Morgan, Dr. William J. and others, editors, *Civil War Naval Chronology.* Washington: Naval History Division, Navy Department, 1971.

United States Census Records for North Carolina on microfilm.

Annual Report of the Operations of the United States Life-Saving Service for the Fiscal Year Ending June 30, 1885, Washington: Government Printing Office, 1886.

Congressional Record: The Proceedings and Debates of the Fifty-ninth Congress. X403, Vol. XL. Washington: Government Printing Office, 1906.

Beaufort County Will Extracts 1720-1868. RNC 929.37 B.

Light House Board, Annual Report, 1869. Washington: Government Printing Office, 1870.

Memoirs

Devereux, Margaret. *Plantation Sketches.* Cambridge: The Riverside Press, 1906.

Grant, Ulysses Simpson. *Personal Memoirs of U.S. Grant.* 2 vols. New York: Charles L. Webster, 1886.

Sherman, William Tecumseh. *Memoirs of General W.T. Sherman*. 2 vols. New York: D. Appleton and Company, 1875.

Interviews, Correspondence (all notes are in possession of the author)

Couch, Daniel, of Buxton, NC. Interviewed by the author in 1996, 1998.

Dolan, Dr. Robert, Professor of Environmental Sciences, University of Virginia. Interviewed by the author in 1998

Feduccia, Olivia Taylor. Interviewed by the author in 2001 and 2002.

Fuller, Ormond, Buxton, NC. Interviewed by the author in 2000.

McArthur, Beatrice (Miss Beatie). Interviewed by the author in 1999. Miss Beatie was a descendent of William Jennett, one of the four children who sold the U.S. government the original four acres for the first Hatteras lighthouse in 1797. Miss Beatie was also a great-great granddaughter of Benjamin T. Fulcher.

Robinson, Joan, of Nevis Historical & Conservation Society, Nevis, West Indies. Correspondence in 2002. The Nevis Historical & Conservation Society has an extensive Alexander Hamilton collection.

Schliff, Michal. Interviewed by the author in 1999.

Stick, David, Kitty Hawk, NC. Interviewed by the author in 1979, 1996, 1998.

Stowe, Charles, of Hatteras. Interviewed by the author in 1996.

Tayloe, David T. IV, MD, and Tayloe, John Cotton, MD. Interviewed by the author in 2002.

Wilson, John, of Grimesland, NC. Interviewed by the author in 1971. Wilson's grandfather witnessed the scuttling of the Confederate gunboat in Chicod Creek.

Woodward, James, The Lighthouse Consultant, LLC, of Cleveland, Ohio. Interviewed by the author on numerous occasions in 2002.

Unpublished Works

Francis Ross Holland, Jr., *A History of the Cape Hatteras Light Station*, Division of History, Office of Archeology and Historic Preservation, National Park Service, Sep. 30, 1968

SECONDARY SOURCES

Books

Barrett, John G. *Sherman's March Through the Carolinas*. Chapel Hill: The University of North Carolina Press 1956.

_____. *The Civil War in North Carolina*. Chapel Hill: The University of North Carolina Press 1963.

Carr, Dawson. *The Cape Hatteras Lighthouse-Sentinel of the Shoals*. Chapel Hill: The University of North Carolina Press, 1991.

Cecelski, David S. *The Waterman's Song—Slavery and Freedom in Maritime North Carolina*. Chapel Hill: The University of North Carolina Press, 2001.

Cloud, Ellen Fulcher. *Ocracoke Lighthouse*. Ocracoke, NC: Live Oak Productions, 1993.

Daly, Robert W., editor. *Aboard the USS Monitor: 1862: The Letters of Acting Paymaster William Frederick Keeler, U.S. Navy, to His Wife, Anna*. Annapolis: U.S. Naval Institute, 1964.

Davis, Archie K. *Boy Colonel of the Confederacy—The Life and Times of Henry King Burgwyn*. Chapel

Hill: The University of North Carolina Press, 1985.

Davis, Kenneth C. *Don't Know Much About the Civil War*. New York: William Morrow & Company, 1996.

Day, D.L. *My Diary of Rambles with the Twenty-fifth Volunteer Infantry with Burnside's Coast Division*. Milford: King and Billings, 1884.

Gannon, Michael. *Operation Drumbeat-The Dramatic True Story of Germany's First U-boat Attacks Along the American Coast in World War II*. New York: Harper & Row, Publishers, 1990.

Graham, Lt. Matthew J., *The Ninth Regiment New York Volunteers*, Lancaster, Ohio: Vanberg Publishing, 1998.

Holland, Francis Ross Jr. *America's Lighthouses—An Illustrated History*. New York: Dover Publications, 1988.

Illustrated History of San Mateo County, California. Oakland: Moore and DePue, 1878.

Johnson, Clint. *Touring the Carolinas' Civil War Sites*. Winston-Salem: John F. Blair, 1996.

Johnson, Robert U., and Clarence C. Buell, editors. *Battles and Leaders of the Civil War*. New York: Century Co., 1887.

MacNeil, Ben Dixon. *The Hatterasman*. Winston-Salem: John F. Blair, 1958.

Mallison, Fred M. *The Civil War on the Outer Banks*. Jefferson, NC: McFarland & Company, Inc., 1998.

Marshall, J.A. editor. *Private and Official Correspondence of General Benjamin F. Butler during the Period of the Civil War*. Norwood, Mass.: Plempton Press, 1917.

McClellan, G.B. *McClellan's Own Story*. New York: Charles L. Webster and Co., 1887.

Pepper, George Whitefield. *Personal Recollections of Sherman's Campaigns in Georgia and the Carolinas*. Zanesville: Hugh Dunne, 1866.

Perry, Frank. *The History of Pigeon Point Lighthouse*. Santa Cruz: Otter B Books, 1986.

Powell, William S. *North Carolina—A History*, Chapel Hill: The University of North Carolina Press, 1977.

Pullen, Drew. *Portrait of the Past—The Civil War on Hatteras Island*. Mount Holly, New Jersey: Robert V. Drapala Publishing, 2001.

Robinson, William Morrison Jr. *"The Rendezvous at Hatteras," from The Confederate Privateers*. New Haven: Yale University Press, 1928.

Round, George C. "A Yankee on the Dome," *The News & Observer's, Raleigh—A Living History of North Carolina's Capital,* David Perkins, editor. Winston-Salem: John F. Blair, 1994. Reprint of Lt. George C. Round from 1902 publication of the United States Veteran Signal Corps Association.

Shelton-Roberts, Cheryl, editor. *Hatteras Keepers-Oral and Family Histories*. Morehead City: Outer Banks Lighthouse Society, 2001.

Spencer, Cornelia Phillips. *The Last Ninety Days of the War in North Carolina*. New York: Watchman Publishing Company, 1866.

Stick, David. *The Graveyard of the Atlantic*, Chapel Hill: The University of North Carolina Press, 1952.

_____. *An Outer Banks Reader*. Chapel Hill: The University of North Carolina Press, 1998.

_____. *Dare County: A History*. Raleigh: NC Division of Archives and History, 1970.

_____. *North Carolina Lighthouses*. Raleigh: North Carolina Department of Cultural Resources, Division of Archives and History, 1980.

_____. *The Outer Banks of North Carolina*. Chapel Hill: The University of North Carolina Press, 1958.

Trotter, William R. *Ironclads and Columbiads-The Civil War in North Carolina*, The Coast. Winston-Salem: John F. Blair, Publisher, 1989.

Warren, Edward. *A Doctor's Experiences in Three Continents*. Baltimore: Cushings & Bailey, 1885.

Yocum, Thomas and Bruce Roberts, Cheryl Shelton-Roberts, *Cape Hatteras—America's Lighthouse, Guardian of the Graveyard of the Atlantic*. Nashville: Cumberland House, 1999.

Zagoskin, Lavrentiy Alekseyvich. *Lt. Zagoskin's Travels in Russian America*. Edited by Henry N. Michael. Canada: University of Toronto Press, 1967.

Journals, Newspapers and Periodicals

Graham, H.C. "How North Carolina Went Into the War," *Blue and Gray*, Vol. III, Nov. 1894.

"Events of the Day," *Washington Daily News*, Aug. 17, 1951.

"Hatteras Island and Its Lighthouse," *Frank Leslie's Illustrated Newspaper*, Nov. 2, 1861.

"Hatteras Inlet, N.C.," *Frank Leslie's Illustrated Newspaper*, Nov. 9, 1861.

"Burning Of A Lightship Captured By The Rebels, By the U.S. Steamer *Mount Vernon*." *Frank Leslie's Illustrated Newspaper*, Feb. 8, 1862.

"Brilliant Achievement in North Carolina," *Frank Leslie's Illustrated Newspaper*, Sept. 7, 1861.

"Destruction of Fort Ocracoke, On Beacon Island, North Carolina," *The Illustrated London News*, October 19, 1861.

"The Capture of Fort Hatteras," *Frank Leslie's Illustrated Newspaper*, Sept. 14, 1861.

Abbott, Elizabeth "Lighthouse Controversy Angers North Carolina Residents," *Providence Journal-Bulletin*, Nov. 23, 1995.

Couch, Daniel C., "Islanders Share Their Lighthouse Memories," *The Island Breeze*, Special Edition, 1999.

Wheeler, Wayne, "Cape Hatteras!" *The Keeper's Log*, Vol. XIV No. Four, July, August, September, 1998, U.S. Lighthouse Society.

C.L. Price, "North Carolina's Railroads in the Civil War," *Civil War History*, Vol. VII, September 1961.

Roberts, Bruce. "In Memory of Croatan Light," *Our State-Down Home in North Carolina*, June 2002, Greensboro: Mann Media.

Naroll, R.S. "Lincoln and the Sherman Peace Fiasco—Another Fable?" *Journal of Southern History*, Vol. XX, November 1954.

"Let Us Have Light," *Daily Alta California*, November 30, 1868.

California: A Guide to the Golden State, WPA guidebook published in 1939.

Raleigh Daily Standard, April 28, 1865.

"Old Times in Betsy," *Elizabeth City Economist*, Aug. 10, 1900.

Parramore, T.C. "The Roanoke-Chowan Story," Chapter 7, "The Burning of Winton," *Ahoskie Daily Roanoke-Chowan News*, Civil War Supplement, 1960

Acknowledgements

This endeavor has been a leap of faith. It began with a naive curiosity and a desire to solve a mystery but the journey unexpectedly led me to write this book. While I was accumulating clues to the mystery, I didn't have my own clue as to how challenging it would be to tell the story in words. For months I toiled, never looking up to see how far I was from the finished product. When I finally reached this moment to write the acknowledgements, I was struck by how many people had helped me along the way and how many new, engaging friends I have made in the process. The people who have helped me are, as author Martin Cruz Smith has eloquently written, "the bridge that mysteriously appears as [the writer] crosses an abyss." I apologize if I have somehow not included everyone who helped me.

I begin by remembering my late parents. I feel their loving presence over my shoulder every minute. I am thankful for my friendship with David Stick, a remarkable North Carolinian and Outer Banker. Many writers follow David's footsteps in the sand, but few share his broad vision of the past, present, and future of the Outer Banks. Irene Nolan, publisher of *The Island Free Press*, has been my editor, my teacher, and my friend. I have long been an admirer of Irene's wisdom and experience. I am also indebted to Joseph Schwarzer of the Graveyard of the Atlantic Museum. I am grateful for the contributions of Jim Woodward, lighthouse consultant and Fresnel lens expert. Another new friend I found is Doug Ellington, geologist, "detective," conversationalist, and all-around good guy. I am appreciative of the creativity of Hatteras Island artist, Stephanie Kiker. I am also grateful to Debra Rezeli and her husband, Jeff. Debra designed the first edition of this book and her commitment to perfection is more than I could ask. Linda Turner proofread the manuscript with a sharp eye, and I thank her for her diligence and professionalism.

Had it not been for Raymond Beck, former North Carolina State Capitol historian, half of the story of "the lost light" might never have been told. And few books concerning the history of North Carolina are published without the name of archivist George Stevenson listed among the acknowledgements. Other dedicated state archivists who helped me were Steve Massengill, Chris Meekins, and Earl Ijames. I also appreciate the assistance of Brian Edwards and Sarah Downing at the Outer Banks History Center on Roanoke Island. Mike Murray, Doug Stover, Mary Doll, Steve Harrison, and Warren Wrenn, National Park Service resource managers of the Cape Hatteras National Seashore, provided guidance and support. I am also thankful for the assistance of Fann Montague, Granville County Library; Michael Southern, NC Historic Preservation; Monika Fleming, volunteer historian at Tarboro's Blount-Bridgers House; Mark Bradley, Raleigh historian; Jane Oakley, Executive Director, Bald Head Island Museum; Cullen Chambers of Tybee Island Lighthouse; Thomas Tag, Great Lakes Lighthouse Research, Dayton, Ohio; Toni M. Carter of the Virginia Historical Society; Lindley Butler, historian and author; Matthew Lawrence, ECU graduate student; and the folks at Preservation North Carolina. At the National Archives in Washington, D.C., Becky Livingston, Charles Johnson, David Wallace, Mike Musik, and Milton Gustafson, were courteous, helpful, and generous with their time.

Hatteras Island writer Danny Couch has helped me open doors and be welcomed by some of the island's original families. I have also benefited from the assistance of the Hatteras Island Genealogical and Historical Society, especially Ormond Fuller and the late Beatrice McArthur. I also want to recognize Bruce Roberts, Cheryl Shelton-Roberts, Bett Padgett and the Outer Banks Lighthouse Society. I am appreciative of the words and support of Timothy Harrison, founder of the American Lighthouse Foundation. I am grateful for the assistance and generosity of Nelson Morosini, Interpretive Specialist at Pigeon Point Lighthouse State Historic Park, Mariam Hegel of the National Lighthouse Museum, Wayne Wheeler, past-president of the United States Lighthouse Society. I also thank my niece Rachel who accompanied me on a research visit to North Carolina Archives.

Additional information for this second edition has been made possible by the kind assistance of Kirk Bradley, Michael Zatarga, Mary Elizabeth Gray, Eric Wittenberg, and John Walters of USCG 5th Disctrict Headquarters. I also wish to remember the late Ed Chaisson of Sealites, whose craftmanship and attention to detail was second to none.

Among my greatest pleasures throughout the long journey of writing this book was meeting Dr. David T. Tayloe IV and his cousin, Dr. John Cotton Tayloe, Jr. We spent a couple of hours discussing the adventures of the first "Doctor Dave" on a sunny, late summer day along the banks of the Tar River. I am also most grateful for the kind assistance and counsel of Olivia Taylor Feduccia, great-granddaughter of Colonel John Hargrove.

Discovering "the lost light" of the Cape Hatteras Lighthouse has been my good fortune and a satisfying accomplishment, to be sure. But I consider my greatest lifetime achievement to be finding my friend, my wife, and my research assistant, Susan Kavanaugh.

Finally, I want to thank you, the reader, for without readers, there would be no reason to write. I have not been trained as a writer or a historian, but I have an intense passion for history, for North Carolina, and for its maritime heritage. I hope my earnestness makes up for my writing skills. I appreciate your time and interest in reading this, my first book.

Index

About the Author

Kevin P. Duffus is an award-winning filmmaker, researcher, author, and investigative journalist of historical events. During his first career as a television executive at WRAL-TV, Duffus produced pioneering satellite news broadcasts from Plymouth, Portsmouth and London, England, for North Carolina's 400th anniversary. In 1985, he produced a documentary about drought and famine in east Africa, which was honored by the World Hunger Media Judges Award at the United Nations. He is also a co-recipient of the George F. Peabody award for excellence in journalism.

In a recent 10 year span, Duffus has published three books and produced four films on various maritime topics, including shipwrecks, lighthouses and the devastating German U-boat attacks off our coast in 1942. Most recently, after researching original, handwritten records in England, Kevin Duffus published a groundbreaking analysis of the pirate Black Beard's final six months in North Carolina. The controversial book presents stunning contradictions to traditional historical accounts about the seafaring rogue's origins, his travels and motivations as a pirate, his death, and the identity and fate of his most trusted crew members.

He is the author of *The Lost Light—A Civil War Mystery*; *Shipwrecks of the Outer Banks—An Illustrated Guide*; and *The Last Days of Black Beard the Pirate*.

Kevin Duffus is available to speak to groups of 50 people or more on "Shipwrecks of the Outer Banks," "World War II Off North Carolina's Outer Banks," "The Mystery of the Lost Hatteras Fresnel Lens," and "The Last Days of Black Beard." Send E-mail requests to: looking_glass@earthlink.net.

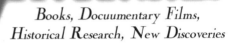

Looking Glass Productions

*Books, Docuumentary Films,
Historical Research, New Discoveries*

Book

Book

Book

DVD

DVD   DVD   DVD   DVD